Golden Images

Golden Images

41 Essays on Silent Film Stars

by EVE GOLDEN

foreword by BOB KING

McFarland & Company, Inc., Publishers
Jefferson, North Carolina, and London

Library of Congress Cataloguing-in-Publication Data

Golden Eve.
Golden images : 41 essays on silent film stars / by Eve Golden ;
foreword by Bob King.
p. cm.
Originally published in Classic images.
Includes bibliographical references and index.
Contents: Clara Bow—Gladys Brockwell—Vernon and Irene Castle—
Bebe Daniels—Marion Davies—Jeanne Eagels—Harrison Ford—
Dorothy Gish—William Haines—Robert Harron—May Irwin—
Arthur Johnson—Alice Joyce—Florence LaBadie—Max Linder—
Ormer Locklear—Douglas MacLean—Martha Mansfield—Mae Marsh—
Colleen Moore—Antonio Moreno—Nita Naldi—Alla Nazimova—
Pola Negri—Mary Nolan—Anita Page—Marie Prevost—Esther Ralston—
Wallace Reid—Alma Rubens—Clarine Seymour—Milton Sills—
Constance Talmadge—Norma Talmadge—Lilyan Tashman—
Olive Thomas—Rudolph Valentino—Fannie Ward—Pearl White—
Kathlyn Williams—Clara Kimball Young.
ISBN 0-7864-0834-0 (softcover : 50# alkaline paper) ♾
1. Motion picture actors and actresses—United States—Biography.
I. Title.
PN1998.2.G65 2001 791.43'028'092273—dc21 [B] 00-66236

British Library cataloguing data are available

Cover image: Lilyan Tashman (the Metaluna Collection).

Manufactured in the United States of America

McFarland & Company, Inc., Publishers
Box 611, Jefferson, North Carolina 28640
www.mcfarlandpub.com

Dedicated to Bob King
and all the *Classic Images* and *Films of the Golden Age* staff

and to

Randye Cohen (1952–1995)
who first introduced me to *Classic Images*

Acknowledgments

I must sound like a fund-raiser, but once again I emphasize how much of my work has its foundation in the Billy Rose Theater Collection at The New York Public Library for the Performing Arts at Lincoln Center. The overwhelming majority of information in these essays comes from the scrapbooks and clippings files in this invaluable library. From big names like Clara Bow and Rudolph Valentino to obscure figures like May Irwin and Douglas MacLean, I was able to find newspaper and magazine articles, interviews, press releases, studio memos, correspondence, and book references for each. I can't begin to name all the newspapers (from all over the world) which were contained therein, but some of the magazines which cropped up time and again are *Films in Review*, *Photoplay*, *Motion Picture* and *Motion Picture Classic*, *Moving Picture Stories*, *Variety*, *Photo-Play Journal*, *The American Magazine*, and *Pictorial Review*.

* * *

I would also like to thank the following people, who provided invaluable information for these articles:

Michael Ankerich, Victor A. Beroh, the late Dewitt Bodeen, Q. David Bowers, the late Alan Brock, Kevin Brownlow, the late Randye Cohen, Glen Distefano, Billy H. Doyle, William Drew, Allen Ellenberger, James Frasher, the late Lillian Gish, Marlene Hanifan, the late George Katchmer, Bob King, the late Robert K. Klepper, Dana Lauren, Eileen Lazar, Maud Linder, Dorothy Sills Lindsley, Bruce Long (*Taylorology*), Randal Malone, Leonard Maltin, Stephen O'Brien, Anita Page, Philip Paul, Jonathan Pettit, Michael Powazinik, the late Esther Ralston, Art Ronnie, Bryan Smith, and Roi Uselton.

Contents

Foreword

by Bob King
Editor, *Classic Images* and *Films of the Golden Age*

As the editor of *Classic Images*, I feel especially grateful to Eve Golden, even though we have been blessed with many good writers over the last thirty years. The likes of Leonard Maltin, Michael Ankerich, Billy Doyle, Anthony Slide, and Herman G. Weinberg have made contributions to our pages, but few have been more popular than Eve Golden.

Our readers aren't easy to satisfy, either. A typical *Classic Images* reader has a profound knowledge of film history. When a great scholarly work like an AFI catalog of feature films is printed, you can count on *CI* readers to spot any and all errors the book may contain.

Our readers don't simply skim the surface of film history. Clara Bow, Rudolph Valentino, and Norma Talmadge interest them, of course, but they also want to read about Gladys Brockwell, Ormer Locklear, and Martha Mansfield. They won't accept a simplified or distorted picture of film history. They want the truth, the whole truth, and nothing but the truth.

Do they sound like a tough audience? They are. Eve's popularity with *CI* readers is proof of the quality of her work. But what explains the special loyalty readers have for her? I think that Eve's style has a lot to do with it. Her writing is clear and colorful at the same time. That's a very difficult tightrope for a writer to walk. Our readers appreciate that. They hate hype and despise writers with bubble reputations. They want substance and style; Eve gives them both.

As an editor, I especially value Eve's writing. No bombast, no pompous phrasing. She is lucid, accurate and fair. In other words, she is a breath of fresh air in an industry that is often driven by downright dishonesty. She is also fun to read. Other writers can be boring, because they are interested only in themselves. Eve never stands between the audience and the screen.

Those of us who love film know that Eve Golden is one of us. She writes about film not because she thinks it will land her a guest spot on network television. She writes about film because she loves it. She loves the people, the history, the films. It shows in everything she writes.

Bob King, Editor
Classic Images and
Films of the Golden Age

Preface

The first time I wrote for *Classic Images* was when my Jean Harlow biography, *Platinum Girl,* came out in 1991. Bob King, the new editor at *CI*, asked me to submit a short article about Harlow, three or four pages. When that was published, he suggested that perhaps I write about other stars.

I was delighted, and somewhat stunned; in the magazine business, you rarely get to pick and choose your subjects. I had been interviewing new stars like Nicolas Cage, Ashley Judd, Adam Sandler, and this had been both fun and (somewhat) profitable, but my heart was still in pre–1950 movies. Here was a publication actually asking me for articles on the Talmadge Sisters, Rudolph Valentino and Betty Grable! I set to work, and now—cut to ten years later—have written nearly 100 articles for *Classic Images* and its newer sister publication, *Films of the Golden Age.* The subjects have ranged from the very earliest film stars (Florence Lawrence, Arthur Johnson) through the stars of the 1950s and even '60s (Jayne Mansfield, Sharon Tate).

This collection consists of most of my silent-screen era profiles. It should by no means be considered an overview of the silent screen's biggest stars. Think of it as a grab-bag. Herein are, indeed, some of the era's most popular performers: Valentino, Norma Talmadge, Max Linder, Pearl White. Some—like Florence Lawrence, Alla Nazimova, William Haines—have been the subjects of recent biographies. But there are also the hard-working, largely forgotten reliables such as Harrison Ford, Gladys Brockwell, Douglas MacLean, Esther Ralston, who were well-known stars in their day but have been utterly forgotten in the years since. No full-length studies have been done of some of these people in the past 30 or 40 years (since Dewitt Bodeen, the late, great *Films in Review* writer, retired).

Everyone here has a story of his or her own to tell, and some of them have been utterly neglected. Florence LaBadie, for instance, was one of the biggest stars of the mid–1910s. But, after her death in a 1917 auto accident, she was completely forgotten. Arthur

Johnson was a triple-threat—actor, writer, director—before he virtually worked himself to death while still in his forties. And the delightful Max Linder was the screen's king of comedy long before Chaplin, Keaton or Lloyd had ever stepped in front of a camera.

One thing in particular struck me as I did the research for these pieces, as I leafed through crumbling scrapbooks and newspaper files in the Lincoln Center research library. The color of personality in all cases shone through, and the people behind the celebrity seemed nearer, more vital for it: Pearl White's zany humor; Nita Naldi's clear-eyed bitterness; Arthur Johnson's weary brush-off to a reporter; the enthusiastic feminism of Gladys Brockwell; the good-natured pragmatism of May Irwin. I'd seen most of them in scratchy, black-and-white images, but suddenly they were real people. I hope I have brought some of that to these pages.

The stories vary more than you might expect; not all silent stars ended like Norma Desmond. Yes, there were too many early deaths through drugs and alcohol: Jeanne Eagels, Mary Nolan, Marie Prevost, Wallace Reid, Alma Rubens. And there were enough horrific demises to keep the documentarians of cable TV busy for years: car accidents (Gladys Brockwell, Florence LaBadie), plane crashes (Vernon Castle, Ormer Locklear), suicide (Olive Thomas, Max Linder), fire (Martha Mansfield), deathly illness (Rudolph Valentino, Clarine Seymour). But there were also a good many happy endings—people who lived long, happy lives, hanging onto their money and their sanity well into old age. Certainly Colleen Moore, William Haines, Bebe Daniels and Mae Marsh leave one with a smile. And Clara Kimball Young, for all her career and money troubles, was one of the most well-adjusted and cheerful people I have ever profiled.

Some of your favorite stars may be missing; there are several reasons for this. I simply had nothing more to add about Gloria Swanson, Charles Chaplin, Mary Pickford, that others haven't said before. Some of my personal favorites—Ramon Novarro, Mabel Normand—had already been profiled by other *CI* writers before I got a crack at them. And I was simply unable to find enough material on some people (Virginia Rappe, Flora Finch) to do the kind of article I wanted to.

I hope you enjoy meeting these people as much as I did, and that you can enjoy their performances, as well. With the video and cable revolution of the past 20 years, more people can see the few remaining silent films, and the talents of these performers will live on well into the new century.

Eve Golden
New York, fall 2000

Clara Bow

For nearly half a century after her 1933 retirement, Clara Bow was looked down upon as a quaint relic of the Roaring Twenties: a cute, bubble-headed flapper, Betty Boop come to life. But with the resurgence of interest in silent films and the availability of her work on cable and video, Clara Bow is recognized as one of the greatest actresses of her generation. A 1988 New York showing of her films played to standing-room-only crowds. She's even been mentioned in the same breath as Garbo and Gish. But with recognition of her talent comes sadness at her private life, which was more tumultuous than any of her film roles.

Clara Gordon Bow was born into Dickensian squalor on July 29, 1905, in Brooklyn, New York. Her father, Robert, was an abusive alcoholic; her mother, Sarah, was mentally unstable (Sarah was finally committed to an institution after allegedly trying to kill her daughter). Clara was, by her own admission, "the worst-looking kid on the block ... I became a regular tomboy—played baseball, football and learned to box." She also became prey to an inferiority complex that belonged in a museum under glass.

Movie-mad Clara entered a fan magazine contest in 1921. The January 1922 issue of *Motion Picture Magazine* featured her softly lit photo under the prophetic headline, "The New Star." "Miss Clara Bow, 857 73rd Street, Brooklyn ... is full of confidence, determination and ambition," the article read. "She screens perfectly." None of the runners-up (Eileen Eliott, Laura Lyle, Maurice Kaines) amounted to much in films, but they probably led happier lives. "I hope that with the proper training I will grow into a good actress," wrote Clara in her very first interview. "I intend to work very hard and try and perform the smallest role that is given me to the best of my ability." Her prize, a role in *Beyond the Rainbow* (1922), landed on the cutting-room floor, but Clara wasn't discouraged.

She landed a supporting part as a tomboyish stowaway in the whaling epic *Down to the Sea in Ships* (1923), and proved a great hit, natural and unaffected.

Clara Bow in her biggest hit, *It* (1927).

She made another four unremarkable films before being signed on by Preferred Pictures' B. P. Schulberg and sent to the West Coast. In 1924 and 1925, Clara Bow was to work her tail off, appearing in an amazing twenty-one films.

Only six of these were for Preferred; Schulberg loaned the budding starlet out to large studios such as Warner's (*Kiss Me Again*, with Marie Prevost), Universal (*Wine*), and First National (*The Scarlet West*). Clara also turned up at cut-rate Poverty Row companies like Banner (*Empty Hearts*), Gotham (costarring with dog star Thunder in *Black Lightning*), and Arrow (*The Primrose Path*). Many have blamed Schulberg for overworking and financially cheating Clara during these years, and they have a point. But Clara also got invaluable training. In these cheap, mostly ridiculous films, the untrained actress learned her craft and was exposed to a wide, appreciative audience. Clara Bow was slowly—inch by inch—becoming a star.

Late in 1925 Clara and Schulberg moved to Paramount. The twenty-year-old actress was finally in the big leagues, and things looked up immediately. Her first Paramount film was the modern, feminist tale, *Dancing Mothers* (1926). Clara—as Alice Joyce's spoiled, jazzy daughter—was an enormous success. With her severely bobbed hair, she bounced about the screen, smoking, drinking, flirting—the very emblem of the jaunty postwar modern girl. Her character was selfish and shallow, but Clara made her adorable, as well.

In the waning years of the 1920s, Clara Bow starred in another sixteen silent films for Paramount. Many, of course, were run-of-the-mill programmers. But a surprising number were gems, containing flashes of sheer brilliance on Clara's part. With her heart-shaped face, perfect features, and mop of brown hair (eventually lightened to red), she was also one of the most beautiful actresses of the day.

Arguably her best, most delicate performance was in *Mantrap* (another protofeminist film of 1926) as a frontier bride who abandons her husband. She costarred with Eddie Cantor in his film debut, *Kid Boots*, that same year. Her most famous film, *It*, came next. *It* was a delightful comedy about a shopgirl in love with boss Antonio Moreno, and Clara was nothing less than perfect, combining outrageousness with vulnerability in a way later associated with Judy Garland and Marilyn Monroe. It was at this time that authoress Elinor Glyn (the Jackie Collins of her day) dubbed Clara "The It Girl," a title that stuck for eternity.

Clara also turned in intelligent,

powerful dramatic performances in *Children of Divorce* (1927, with Gary Cooper), *Wings* (the Oscar-winning war film with Richard Arlen and Charles "Buddy" Rogers), and *Ladies of the Mob* (a 1928 gangster film, again with Arlen). They weren't all like that, of course. *Rough House Rosie*, *Get Your Man* (both 1927), *Red Hair*, *The Fleet's In*, and *Three Weekends* (all 1928) were little more than forgettable programmers. Clara played gold diggers, manicurists, singers; she shook her shimmy, rolled her eyes, and threw off enough sparks to attract audiences. "She danced even when her feet were not moving," said Paramount's Adolph Zukor.

Clara was not only loved by her fans but by her coworkers as well. Her low opinion of herself led her to seek others' approval. She was invariably cheerful, even mischievous, on the set and friendly to stars and extras alike. "She was so filled with excitement and fun and romance," said "Buddy" Rogers. Louise Brooks said, "She *was* the Twenties." Popular as Clara may have been among the younger set, though, the Hollywood elite looked down their noses at her. Brooks added sadly, "Everyone on the Paramount lot said, 'She's the greatest actress,' but she wasn't 'acceptable,' and of course she knew that."

Then, early in 1929, Paramount went "talkie." Legend has it that Clara Bow's "thick Brooklyn accent" ruined her career and that she slunk off to go quietly insane. The truth is a lot more complex. Actually, Clara's Brooklyn accent was no more grating than those of Barbara Stanwyck or Mae West, neither of whose careers suffered. It was the changing nature of filmmaking, not her voice, that destroyed Clara's career. She was always an instinctual actress, improvising to great effect. She bounced all over the set, reacting to her directors' offscreen suggestions and unexpectedly coming up with her own ideas. Filmmaking was fun; it was a game she excelled at. Suddenly, she was faced with scripts, microphones, and hitting chalkmarks. Filming was "just no fun anymore," she sighed.

At the same time, Clara's private life was falling apart, in the glaring spotlight of less-than-sympathetic fan magazines. Her friend and secretary, Daisy De Voe, was convicted of embezzlement and dragged Clara through the courts. An addicted gambler, Clara was accused of welshing on a debt, and she was sued for alienation of affection by a doctor's wife. She was also being taken to task for her many loves. Clara had never been shy about her affairs—conquests included director Victor Fleming and actors Gilbert Roland, Gary Cooper, Bela Lugosi (in his pre–Dracula days), and Harry Richman.

All this weighed heavily on Clara, who had never been an emotionally strong woman even when things were going well. Her first few talkies were a great ordeal; she found learning lines sheer torture. And the quality of her films was simply not up to the level of her great silent hits. A few weren't bad: *Dangerous Curves* (a 1929 circus romance), and *No Limit* and *Kick In* (crime dramas, both 1931). She sang, quite creditably, in *Paramount on Parade* and *True to the Navy* (both 1930).

On December 3, 1931, Clara married for the first and only time, to minor cowboy actor Rex Bell (*Howdy Doody* fans take note that her married name thus became Clara Bell). She spent more and more time with her husband at his large Nevada ranch. Bell was a simple,

Clara Bow at the height of her career, in the late 1920s.

uncomplicated man, just the non–Hollywood sort Clara needed to stabilize her life. Leaving Paramount, she continued filming for other studios.

Possibly her most enjoyable (and certainly her most bizarre) talkie was the 1932 melodrama, *Call Her Savage* (Fox). The pre–Code cult favorite, from a torrid Tiffany Thayer novel, runs the gamut of forbidden topics: homosexuality, prostitution, illegitimacy, interracial love, rape, sadism, and child molestation. Critics and audiences were stunned, and *Call Her Savage* was not a popular success. After one more film (the circus drama *Hoopla*, 1933), a still slim and lovely Clara retired to concentrate on being Mrs. Rex Bell. "All I want is peace of mind and a long rest," she sighed. "I was so tired and discouraged ... I'd had enough."

Clara Bow did not live happily ever after. She and Bell eventually separated after having two sons (Rex Anthony, in 1934, and George Robert, in 1938). But her health—both physical and emotional—soon began to fail. Bell became Lieutenant Governor of Nevada in the 1950s, while Clara fought her private demons.

She appeared in public from time to time: on the *Truth or Consequences* radio show in 1947, *Life* magazine in 1950, and at Rex Bell's funeral in 1962. Fighting mental illness, weight gain, and insomnia, she kept busy by taking painting, typing, and foreign language lessons. She became active in right-wing politics and kept tabs on modern Hollywood. "I slip my old crown of It Girl not to Taylor or Bardot but to Monroe," she told Hedda Hopper in 1960. Before her death from a heart attack on September 26, 1965, Clara reminisced: "We had individuality. We did as we pleased. We stayed up late. We dressed the way we wanted.... Today, they're more sensible and end up with better health. But we had more fun."

Gladys Brockwell

In her time, silent screen actress Gladys Brockwell was as respected as Jeanne Eagels, Laurette Taylor, and Lenore Ulric. Successful at a remarkably young age, Gladys starred at Fox through the 1910s and 1920s in dramatic character roles, playing the kind of wrenching, difficult parts most actresses would give their eye teeth for. She was a fascinating, intelligent, very modern woman and a dedicated actress. Sadly, her death at the dawn of the talkie era robbed the screen of one of its great talents, and today Gladys Brockwell is virtually forgotten.

She was born Gladys Lindeman in Brooklyn, New York, on September 26, 1893. Not much is known of her father, H. R. Lindeman, but her mother, Lillian "Billie" Brockwell, was an actress—a very young actress. According to some accounts, Billie was only thirteen when her daughter was born. Whatever Billie's age, she and Gladys became more "pals" than mother and daughter. "I was three years old when I played my first speaking part," Gladys recalled in 1916. "Four years later I entered dramatic work permanently with the Lyceum Stock Company of Williamsburg, Long Island ... When I was eleven I was playing the female lead in stock."

In 1913, when Gladys was twenty, she made her screen debut. She acted with Romaine Fielding for Lubin, "putting on two- and three-reel western melodramas in New Mexico." Gladys worked very briefly for D. W. Griffith, but, she said in 1918, "He wasn't exactly impressed by my ability. In fact, he took great pains to tell me that as a screen actress I was about as bad as the worst."

Not everyone felt as Griffith did. After working with Mutual (*A Man and His Mate*, 1915), Majestic (*His Guiding Angel*, 1915), and Fine Arts (*The Price of Power*, 1916), Gladys was signed by William Fox in 1916. She stayed with that studio for most of her career, with the exception of several loan-outs. She was the same age as Lillian Gish, but, while Gish played dewdrops and ingenues, Gladys was cast as harridans, mothers, and fallen angels. She was striking rather than beautiful, with large, dark eyes and strong brows, a large nose, a determined chin, and auburn hair.

In 1920, Gladys told a *Photo-Play Journal* reporter how she got in the mood for her roles: "If I am feeling too hilarious and must buckle down to play a very serious or sad role," she said, "I have to make myself feel badly. This isn't so very hard to do, when you go about the matter in downright earnest ... It is ever so much more difficult to laugh when you are not in the mood for it, than to cry when you feel like laughing."

Her private life was almost as colorful as her screen roles. Sometime in the mid–1910s, Gladys had married one Robert Broadwell, whom she divorced in March 1918. On July 1 of that same year, she wed film director Harry Edwards, ex-husband of actress Louise Glaum.

Edwards promptly shipped off to war, and the marriage lasted all of three days (it was annulled the following year). It also developed that not enough time had passed between Gladys's marriages, and her second wasn't strictly legal.

Gladys's career continued its unchecked climb; William Fox believed in keeping his employees very busy. Among her 1918 films were *For Liberty*, *To Honor and Obey*, *Her One Mistake*, *The Moral Law*, *The Soul of Satan*, *A Bird of Prey*, and *Kultur*. In 1919 Gladys starred in *The Call of the Soul*, *The Forbidden Room*, *Pitfalls of a Big City*, *The Strange Woman*, *Conscience*, *Chasing Rainbows* (a rare ingenue role), and *The Devil's Wheel*.

With America's entry into World War I, Gladys proved herself both a patriot and a woman's rights advocate. As American men moved overseas, Gladys encouraged women to fill their previously unfeminine jobs. With *Motion Picture Magazine* tagging along, she trained and worked as a lineman, blacksmith, barber, water-wagon driver, electrician, farm worker, and postal carrier. "When women begin to realize that they can perform almost any kind of manual labor," Gladys told the magazine, "and in many instances do it more skillfully than the men, we will have made giant strides towards our political enfranchisement, as well as the right to expect higher wages. But first of all," she added patriotically, "we will be one of the biggest factors in winning the war."

In the 1920s Gladys Brockwell made fewer but better films. She didn't have to worry about encroaching age as she entered her thirties, as she had always played older than her years. She enjoyed character roles, telling one reporter, "One can get thought over in them, even on the screen. It isn't the make-up at all; it's because one who plays a character role must think it out ahead of time, else it will have no flavor at all." "Do you know what I'm simply dying to do?" she asked reporter Grace Kingsley. "I want to spend a term in prison in order to study the women prisoners at first hand. I mean to deliberately get myself arrested for sassing a traffic cop, some day. Then I shall be fined fifty dollars or fifty days, and I shall take the fifty days!"

She started out the new decade in films such as *White Lie*, *The Mother of His Children*, *A Sister to Salome* and *The Devil's Riddle*, all 1920. Nineteen twenty-three was a big year for Gladys, who appeared in *Penrod and Sam*, *The Drug Traffic*, *The Darling of New York*, and Lon Chaney's *The Hunchback of Notre Dame*. In that last film, on loan to Universal, Gladys played the insane old woman who lost her daughter, Esmeralda, to gypsies (in 1922, Gladys had

Gladys Brockwell in 1917 (The Metaluna Collection).

played Nancy Sykes in Chaney's *Oliver Twist*).

Gladys also cultivated outside interests. "I write a great deal," she told *Photoplay* in 1918, "articles and short stories and poetry. I'm really quite proud of my poetry. And I do a good deal of musical composition on the piano." She did regret her lack of education, a hazard for theatrical children. "I read during most of my spare time," Gladys said. "That is, the spare time I am not giving to my

Gladys Brockwell, looking dramatic even as a bride (The Metaluna Collection).

music. For years I have been hungry to read, and now I delve deep into all manner of literature. While I am in my dressing room making up or waiting to go on a scene, Billie reads to me—Shakespeare, old plays, old books, the best standards; things that will be helpful to me as an actress and as a woman." Mr. Lindeman was out of the picture by this time, but mother Billie worked as her coach and secretary, living with Gladys in their two-story Hollywood bungalow.

The 1920s continued to be kind to Gladys, who starred in a score of films and did smaller character roles in dozens more. As the decade wore on, fans saw her in *Unmarried Wives*, *The Foolish Virgin*, and *So Big* (1924), *The Ancient Mariner*, *The Reckless Sex*, *Stella Maris*, and *The Splendid Road* (1925), *Her Sacrifice*, *The Skyrocket*, *The Carnival Girl*, *Spangles*, and *Twinkletoes* (1926). In 1927 she appeared in *The Satin Woman* and *Long Pants*, as well as two of her best-remembered films: In MGM's scandalous *Man, Woman and Sin*, she costarred with John Gilbert and Jeanne Eagels, and in *Seventh Heaven* she sadistically whipped her sister Janet Gaynor through the streets.

In 1916 Gladys had predicted, "I suppose I'll be playing Juliet's nurse in my old age, and then die with the greasepaint on." It certainly looked that way as the 1920s ended. Her voice "photographed" well, and talkies held no terrors for Gladys. She signed a long-term contract with Warner Brothers; her first talkie was *Lights of New York* (1928), in which she played an embittered gangster's moll. Looking hard and glamorous in evening frocks and a short bob, Gladys seemed slightly stilted until her final emotional scene, when she came through with flying colors.

She stayed busy in late 1928 and early 1929, making four films (all released in 1929). *From Headquarters* was a dismal lost-in-the-jungle drama, but *The Hottentot* (with Edward Everett Horton) was a clever horse-racing comedy popular with both critics and fans. Gladys next appeared in an above-average detective yarn, *The Argyle Case*, with Thomas Meighan. She went right into another whodunit, *The Drake Case*.

In the summer of 1929, Gladys was dating advertising man Thomas Drennan. In early July, the two were driving near Calabasas, about twenty-five miles northwest of Hollywood, when they lost control of their car. The vehicle plunged over a seventy-five-foot cliff, critically injuring the thirty-five-year-old actress. She died of peritonitis on July 2 at the Hollywood Hospital.

Talking pictures took off, and roles which might have gone to Gladys Brockwell were played by Ruth Chatterton, Marjorie Rambeau, or Beulah Bondi. Within a few years, Gladys Brockwell's sixteen-year film career had been forgotten, and her name had faded from history.

Vernon and Irene Castle

It's hard to overestimate the impact the dancing and acting team Vernon and Irene Castle had on American society in the early 1910s. The disco craze of the 1970s was but a pale shadow of the ballroom dancing madness that overtook big cities and small towns in the years before World War I, when the strictures of the Victorian age first began to wear off. The 1939 film *The Story of Vernon and Irene Castle* took surprisingly few liberties with the truth—perhaps because Irene took her job as technical advisor very seriously.

Vernon Blythe was born in Norwich, England, on May 2, 1887, the son of a pub owner. He started out to be an engineer, graduating from Birmingham University. But his sister Coralie took to the stage, and Vernon was enchanted by her new career. He followed her to New York shortly after the turn of the century, changed his name to Castle to avoid family disapproval, and met up with actor/producer Lew Fields.

Fields—often working with his partner, Joe Weber—specialized in slapstick, knockabout humor, and witty parodies of contemporary shows. The tall, slim, and acrobatic Vernon Castle became a regular in Fields's productions, appearing in *About Town* (1906), *The Girl Behind the Counter* (1907), *The Mimic World* (1908), *Old Dutch* (1909), *The Midnight Sons* (1909), and *The Summer Widowers* (1909–10). An accomplished, self-trained dancer and enthusiastic drummer, Castle was frustrated at being typecast as a buffoon by Fields.

Irene Foote was born on April 7, 1893, in New Rochelle, New York. Her parents were a successful doctor and his vivacious wife, and she was the second of two daughters (her older sister was named, oddly, Elroy). Irene had a happy, privileged, tomboyish childhood and grew into a slim, athletic teenager. A semiprofessional swimmer, she cut her hair into a short bob around 1910, long before it became fashionable. Irene also idolized actress Bessie McCoy and imitated her singing "The Yama Yama Man" at each and every opportunity.

Vernon Castle and Irene Foote were introduced by friends on the beach in the summer of 1910. The stage-struck Irene, who already had dancing ambitions, made her move. Soon Vernon was a regular visitor at the Foote home, managing to get Irene a role in a touring company of *The Midnight Sons* and in Castle's production of *The Summer Widowers*. They were married on May 28, 1911, honeymooning in England, before they were both cast in Fields's comedy *The Hen-Pecks* (1911). The couple moved to Paris, where they met with no success whatsoever until they danced the new Grizzly Bear at the Café de Paris and became overnight stars.

Ragtime and syncopated dances like the one- and two-steps, the Grizzly Bear, and the Turkey Trot were just catching the public's fancy, and the Castles rode the crest of that wave. Tiny, slim Irene, with her corsetless tango dresses and shocking bobbed hair, became a fashion leader. Vernon looked an awful lot like Fred Astaire: tall, thin, slightly balding. But Irene had that kind of fine-boned beauty which succeeds in any age. The two looked terrific together, and their energetic, ultramodern dancing was unlike anything ever seen.

They returned to New York in 1912 and danced in supper clubs, nightclubs, cafés, and private parties. Competing ballroom dancers cropped up: Maurice and Florence Walton, Dorothy Dickson and Carl Hyson, and Genevieve Lyon and John Murray Anderson. Dance schools were packed all over the nation, and such future stars as Rudolph Valentino, Mae Murray, and Clifton Webb got their starts as Castle wannabes.

The Castles had Broadway hits in *The Sunshine Girl* (1913) and *Watch Your Step* (1914). They opened several Manhattan nightclubs, giving exhibition dances in as many as three a night. They bought a townhouse in Manhattan and a country place in Long Island, where Irene kept her scores of pets. To help pay the bills, they also toured in vaudeville. Recordings of "The Castle Walk" and "The Castle House Rag" were played endlessly on Victrolas around the world.

The Castles had their first brush with the film world in 1914, when they appeared in an instructional short, inventively titled *Mr. and Mrs. Vernon Castle Before the Camera*. It was a series of "jerky little shorts of our different dancing steps," recalled Irene, "more or less in the form of a lesson. The background and the setting were hideous." Nonetheless, Vernon convinced his wife to star with him in *The Whirl of Life*, financed independently and written by Vernon himself.

"This was a real challenge," said Irene, "and he plunged into it with all the zeal of an explorer setting foot on an uncharted continent." *The Whirl of Life* was the story of the Castles themselves: at least, till the point where Irene is kidnapped by a rival nightclub owner. Vernon rescues her in an action sequence worthy of Jean-Claude Van Damme, and the film ends with the hero and heroine whirling triumphantly around the floor of their club. "For the cast, we used all our friends and servants," said Irene of those pre-union days, those investing in the film being rewarded with juicy parts. Even Irene's pets and Vernon's horses were featured.

The riotously amateur effort was released in 1915 and did "quite well," according to its female star (when Ed

Mr. and Mrs. Castle posing for a 1915 etiquette book.

Sullivan showed clips from it on TV in 1950, Irene promptly sued him). Today, bits remain of *The Whirl of Life*, and seeing the Castles dance is amazing. Unlike Astaire and Rogers, they rarely separated on the dance floor, but rather whirled and spun each other around like a particularly graceful set of Siamese twins.

The stars took roles in Charles Dillingham's Broadway show, *Watch Your Step* (1914–15), but patriotic Britisher Vernon began taking flying lessons, hoping to enlist in the war. In 1916 he took off for England and The Royal Flying Corps, and Irene was signed by Pathé to star in a fifteen-part serial, *Patria*. It was Vernon who started their film careers, but he never appeared before the camera again after *The Whirl of Life*. Irene went on to make another seventeen films, but she never took herself seriously as an actress. Of *Patria*, she said, "Fortunately I was not called on for any acting except to look terrified occasionally, and on those occasions I didn't need to act. I was."

Patria, costarring Milton Sills and Warner Oland, was a huge hit, and Irene's reviews indicate she was a better actress than she gave herself credit for. At a loss for a dance partner, she signed with the Astra Film Corporation in 1917 and made nine films for them over a two-year period. Most of these were second-rate Pearl White stuff, giving the athletic star a chance to run, jump, fight, swim, and ride horseback while fighting off villains. Everyone—critics and audiences—hated the films, but Irene's charm and talent shone through. "Princess Irene is becoming a keener actress with each picture," said *Photoplay*, adding after another film that "Irene Castle is charming as ever..."

The films—such as *Stranded in Arcady*, *Sylvia of the Secret Service*, *The Hillcrest Mystery* and *The Girl from Bohemia*—brought in much-needed money but sank without making a mark on film history. Irene also appeared onstage in Florenz Ziegfeld's *Miss 1917*, with her idol, Bessie McCoy.

Vernon, in the meantime, was flying over German territory, taking surveillance photos and earning a Croix de Guerre. He was shot down and injured, then sent back to Canada as a flying instructor (Irene, on a visit, was smuggled up in his plane). Vernon always insisted on taking the front seat when training his pilots; after one crash he walked away from where the student in the front seat had died.

On February 15, 1918—while Irene was making one of her Astra films, probably *The Mysterious Client*—Vernon had another accident on the training field. He veered his plane to avoid hitting another just taking off, went into a spin, and crashed. The student, in the back seat, walked away; Vernon died in the field hospital twenty minutes later. Vernon Castle had a hero's funeral, a service at New York's "Actor's Church," and a burial at Woodlawn Cemetery.

His twenty-five-year-old widow threw herself into her film work, for emotional as well as financial reasons. She had a cameo appearance in *The Common Cause* (1918) for the ailing Vitagraph Studios, then signed with Paramount-Artcraft for three films, *The Firing Line*, *The Invisible Bond* (both 1919), and *The Amateur Wife* (1920). They did not receive very good advertising or promotion, and little is known of them today. Film historian Walter Stainton claims Irene also starred in a film called *The Broadway Bride* in 1921.

The widowed Irene Castle in 1920.

Only a year after Vernon's death, Irene shocked her fans by marrying soldier and businessman Robert Treman. Treman and Edwin Hollywood formed Hol-Tre Productions, shooting three films starring Irene, all released in 1922. *French Heels* featured her as a cabaret star turned lumber-camp wife, and it did not do badly at all. *No Trespassing* was a Cape Cod story, and *Slim Shoulders* was a throwback to her adventurous Pearl White days. No matter how bad the films, Irene always got good personal notices, but both her marriage and her film career were over by 1923.

Although her obituaries stated she never danced professionally after Vernon's death, Irene did in fact tour with one Billy Reardon in the mid–1920s. There was no romance there, however. Irene married businessman Frederic McLaughlin in 1924, and they had two children, Barbara (in 1925) and Bill (in 1929). By the time McLaughlin died in 1944, Vernon and Irene Castle were world famous again through the 1939 RKO bio-pic. In making this film, Irene proved herself a royal pain, insisting on a factual script, and was understandably upset with Ginger Rogers, who refused to follow Irene's costume or hairstyle suggestions.

Irene had other interests, though, opening an animal shelter and campaigning for animal rights decades before PETA was thought of. In 1954 she married old friend George Enzinger, an advertising executive, and moved to a farm in Arkansas. Her autobiography, *Castles in the Air* (ghosted by Bob and Wanda Duncan) was published by Doubleday in 1958, and Irene was widowed for the third time the following year.

At her seventy-first birthday party in 1964 at New York's Plaza Hotel, a gray-haired, still slim and lovely Irene posed for photos, reminisced about Vernon Castle, and turned her nose up at the twist ("it's so unbecoming"). When she died on January 25, 1969, the ghost of Vernon Castle was also finally laid to rest, fifty-one years after his death.

Bebe Daniels

Most performers are grateful to hold on to one career: sex symbol, comic, character actor. Bebe Daniels excelled at many. She was a child star, slapstick comedienne, glamour queen, musical-comedy star, and radio and television performer. Yet today Bebe is mostly remembered for breaking her ankle in *42nd Street*. The lasting fame of a Garbo or Crawford was not to be hers.

Phyllis Daniels (Bebe was a childhood nickname that stuck) was the child of the Scottish-born Melville Daniels and his Spanish-born wife, Phyllis Griffin. Bebe was born in Dallas on January 14, 1901, and made her first stage appearance shortly thereafter; Mr. Daniels was a theatrical manager and Mrs. Daniels his star. By the time she was seven, Bebe was a seasoned trouper. That year—1908—she made her film debut in Selig's *The Common Enemy*. For the next seven years, Bebe attended the Sacred Heart Convent School in Los Angeles, spending her vacations appearing in stage and film productions (the fact that her mother was working as Pathé's casting director certainly didn't hinder her career).

At the age of fourteen, a mature-looking Bebe Daniels appeared at Hal Roach's office, applying for the job of Harold Lloyd's leading lady. Lloyd and Roach wanted a blonde but were so impressed that they hired the small, dark Bebe. She spent the next four years costarring in (and cowriting) Lloyd's two-reel *Lonesome Luke* comedies. "We used to make a picture a week," she recalled. "If we wanted a holiday, we had to make two pictures in a week." The costars became great friends, entering dancing contests and horsing around, but no romance developed. When Bebe was offered a contract by Paramount's Cecil B. De Mille, Lloyd and Roach generously insisted she take it (Mildred Davis replaced her in Lloyd's films and eventually married her leading man).

Bebe's first De Mille film was the spectacular *Male and Female* (1919), starring Gloria Swanson and Thomas Meighan. Bebe played a small but flashy part in a Babylonian flashback. She appeared in two more De Mille/Swanson epics, as a cheap tart in *Why Change Your Wife?* (1920), and a baby vamp, deliciously named Satan Synne, in *The Affairs of Anatol* (1921). Bebe spent the 1920s at Paramount and its subsidiary, Realart (with only one loan-out, for 1924's *Daring Youth*, at Principal). She made fifty-one films for Paramount between 1919 and 1928, becoming one of the decade's most recognizable faces. Many of these films' titles are almost comically evocative of the era: *Singed Wings* (1922), *Sinners in Heaven* (1923), *Wild, Wild Susan* (1925), *The Campus Flirt* (1926), and *Stranded in Paris* (1926). Bebe was never a sex symbol like Clara Bow; her career was more analogous to Colleen Moore's at First National. Both stars were striking rather than beautiful, adept in both comedy and drama, and were tireless workhorses for their studios. Although she wasn't as idolized as Garbo or Bow, many of Bebe's films were classics of their time.

Bebe Daniels at the dawn of her career.

One was written especially for her: *The Speed Girl* (1921) was based on Bebe's own escapades as a reckless daredevil, known in the Hollywood community for her vast accumulation of unpaid traffic tickets. She was finally nabbed by a cop who wasn't impressed by film stars, and she spent ten days in the slammer. "My cell was furnished by the best decorator in town," she later bragged, "and every time anyone called to see me ... I'd say, 'Tell them I'm not in.'" Her flummoxed jailer objected, "Look, Miss Daniels, I've done everything in the world for you, but I can't say that!"

Bebe costarred with Rudolph Valentino in the costume epic *Monsieur Beaucaire* (1924); with Warner Baxter in *Miss Brewster's Millions* (a sex-changed version of the stage and film hit, 1926); and with William Powell in the Valentino parody *She's a Sheik* (she kidnaps Legionnaire Richard Arlen in this 1928 film). Among Bebe's other costars at Paramount were Wallace Beery, Anna Q. Nilsson, Conrad Nagel, Nita Naldi, Mary Astor, and Alfred Lunt, as well as the ill-fated Wallace Reid in several films, and later, the equally ill-fated James Hall. Reid and Valentino, she said, "were two of the nicest men I've ever known. I've never known a more modest man in my life than Rudy was ... he didn't know what conceit was."

Despite her enormous successes at Paramount, Bebe was let go in 1928, the dawn of the talkie era, after completing *What a Night!* with Neil Hamilton; by this time she was earning $5,000 a week. "They didn't even take tests of anyone's voice to see if they could talk," she later said incredulously. "They just wanted stage people." Bebe had never sung professionally, but RKO's William LeBaron hired her on faith for his musical *Rio Rita.* She—and the movie—were huge successes. Bebe had a whole new career before her. She also sang in *Love Comes Along* and *Dixiana* (both 1930). The films did quite well but are almost unwatchable today: stilted, stagey, and unbearably long.

Fortunately for her long-term reputation, Bebe was given other assignments as well. In one, *Alias French Gertie* (1930), she costarred with Ben Lyon, a boyishly handsome thirty-year-old actor who had been a film star since the mid–1920s. The two had first met in 1925; by 1928 they were dating, and by the time of *Alias French Gertie* they were engaged. They married in 1930 and stayed together for life. Before that, Bebe had enjoyed quite a reputation as a girl about town. Among her many reported suitors were actors Rod La Roque, Richard Arlen, Richard Dix, and Jack Pickford, boxer Jack Dempsey, and writer Michael Arlen.

Bebe Daniels in her flapper period (late 1920s).

Bebe's career continued on a generally upward swing through the early 1930s, as she hopped from studio to studio. She sang a red-hot "Doin' the Mean Low-Down" in Douglas Fairbanks's *Reaching for the Moon* (1931); played the Mary Astor role in a 1931 *Maltese Falcon*; played a Baby Doe Tabor–like character in *Silver Dollar* (1932, with Edward G. Robinson); and was terrific as John Barrymore's lovelorn secretary in the superb *Counsellor-at-Law* (1933). But her most fondly remembered role was as washed-up Broadway star Dorothy Brock in *42nd Street.* Not many actresses would agree to play a middle-aged has-been (especially at the tender age of thirty-two), but this role is Bebe's most famous moment onscreen. Bitching at doe-eyed little Ruby Keeler, singing "You're Getting to Be a Habit with Me" and getting her comeuppance in the final reel, Bebe is one of the chief delights in an altogether delightful film.

Bebe returned to the stage in the mid–1930s with *The Last of Mrs. Cheyney* and *Hollywood Holiday* (with her husband). The Lyons had a daughter,

Barbara, in 1932, and later adopted a son, Richard. They moved to London in 1936 and decided to stay there after an American kidnapping threat to their daughter. Bebe made four British films before the outbreak of World War II; it was during that war that the couple really won the hearts of their adopted country. They refused to leave London during the Nazi Blitz, performing for civilians and troops alike; their radio show, *Hi, Gang*, was wildly popular. Ben joined the Armed Forces while Bebe traveled to France and Italy, singing and clowning for the soldiers—she was the first woman to land on Normandy after D-Day and was awarded the U.S. Medal of Freedom for service under fire.

The Lyons returned to the United States after the war, settling in Santa Monica. Ben became a casting director for Fox and helped promote starlet Norma Jeane Dougherty, whom he renamed Marilyn Monroe. Bebe became a producer for her old boss, Hal Roach. But the Lyons missed London and returned for good in the 1950s. The couple and their children became the Lucy and Ricky Ricardo of England with their popular domestic sitcom *Life with the Lyons*, which ran on BBC-TV from 1950 until 1962. Bebe's last films were big-screen versions of that show, *Life with the Lyons* (1954) and *The Lyons in Paris* (1956).

Bebe suffered a severe stroke in 1963. She stayed out of the limelight thereafter, struggling to regain her health. She gave occasional interviews and was well on the road to recovery within a few years. But another stroke hospitalized Bebe in late 1970. She died at her London home on March 16, 1971, with her husband and children at her bedside. Shortly after Bebe's death, Ben married Marian Nixon, an old friend (Nixon had been a Fox starlet whose career stretched from 1923 to the later 1930s). Ben died while the couple was cruising on the *Queen Elizabeth II* in 1979. The second Mrs. Lyon survived him by four years.

Marion Davies

When *Citizen Kane* was released in 1941, it was no secret that the film was Orson Welles's pseudobiography of newspaper tycoon William Randolph Hearst. It followed, then, that the stupid, talentless singer Susan Alexander Kane (played by Dorothy Comingore) must have been Hearst's mistress, actress Marion Davies. That slap caused more outrage than the rest of the film, for not only was Marion Davies a considerable talent but possibly the nicest and most-loved actress in Hollywood.

Marion Davies was no unknown chorus girl when she met Hearst; she had already gained a foothold on Broadway. She was born Marion Cecilia Douras to a large, eccentric Brooklyn family on January 3, 1897 (she later claimed 1905). All three of her sisters (Irene, Rose, and Ethel) went on the stage but, despite their beauty, never became big stars (though Irene's son Charles Lederer became a well-known writer).

The Douras family (soon stage-named Davies) moved to Manhattan, and little Marion began finding the theater more fascinating than school (she was never very bright, but her good heart more than made up for her lack of learning). She certainly had the looks to succeed: Marion Davies bore an amazing resemblance to an eighteenth-century Boucher pastel. She had gold hair, porcelain skin, china-blue eyes, and a tiny rosebud mouth. There are very few periods in which Marion would not have been considered a beauty. But she was no china doll—a sports-happy tomboy, she adored romping with friends and pets, swimming, playing tennis, and enjoying a good healthy meal.

Her first engagement was in *The Bluebird* (1910). She went on to appear in *Chu Chin Chow*, *Oh, Boy!*, *Miss 1917*, and the 1915 through 1917 *Ziegfeld Follies*. It was during her run in the 1917 *Follies* that she caught the eye of the married, powerful newspaper publisher William Randolph Hearst. It was lifelong love at first sight for the fifty-four-year old Hearst. The innocent twenty-year old showgirl's reaction can only be imagined, but, within a few years, she was as dedicated to him as any wife could be. The legal Mrs. Hearst, however, steadfastly refused him a divorce.

Hearst built Marion an enormous home, San Simeon, which stands today as a museum to their love and his wealth. There was also a huge castle-like "beach house" in Santa Monica (built in 1926), a castle at Wyntoon, and stopping places the world over. By the early 1920s all of Hollywood knew of their relationship, and soon all but her most naive fans did, as well. It's a measure of Hearst's power that Marion was not banned by the Hays office.

Marion had made her film debut in 1917 in *Runaway, Romany*. The reviews were good, and Marion seemed well on her way to becoming another Mary Pickford or Mabel Normand. Then Hearst stepped in to "guide" her career in earnest. William Randolph Hearst knew a lot about newspapers but little about the entertainment business. His taste ran to overblown period films and hearts-and-flowers romance. Ironically, though, his mistress was a brilliant comedienne with limited dramatic skills.

In 1919 Hearst formed Cosmopolitan Pictures, a subsidiary of Paramount, through which the films were released (and, of course, reviewed favorably in the Hearst press). In 1924 Cosmopolitan changed its affiliation to Goldwyn, and thereby to MGM when the studios merged. These films were so expensive and visually breathtaking that many were successes without Marion having to do more than wander around looking decorative; a Marion Davies cut-out doll would have sufficed as well. Marion was an indifferent (if sincere) dramatic actress, and audiences eventually tired of seeing her in frills (and, quite often, in military drag). Many critics resented having Marion Davies shoved down their throats by Hearst and Metro, so even when she did turn in a clever performance, non–Hearst reviews could be brutal.

Marion Davies early in her film career.

Among Marion's more successful costume dramas were *The Belle of New York* (1919), *When Knighthood Was in Flower* (1922), *Little Old New York* (1923), *Yolanda* (1924), *Janice Meredith* (1924), *Lights of Old Broadway* (a 1925 hit, both financially and critically), *Beverly of Graustark* (1926), *The Red Mill* (1927, directed by Marion's friend Roscoe Arbuckle under the pseudonym William Goodrich), and *Quality Street* (1927). Scattered throughout the decade, Marion also starred in a few modern-era films of varying quality. She was put upon by spies in *The Burden of Proof* (1918; "Miss Davies is no dramatic actress," said *The Motion Picture News*); was an heiress in *Getting Mary Married* (1919); was an author in *April Folly*

The flower-like beauty of Marion Davies in the early 1920s.

(1920); and played flappers in *The Restless Sex* (1920), *Enchantment* (1921), and *Adam and Eva* (1922).

Later in the decade she was finally given a few opportunities to show off her comic skills. Particularly good were *Tillie the Toiler* (as a comic stenographer) and *The Fair Coed* (as a college basketball star, both 1927). As a put-upon kid sister in *The Patsy* (1928), she did hilarious, dead-on imitations of Mae Murray, Lillian Gish, and Pola Negri; as an autograph hound in *Her Cardboard Lover* (1928), she did a wicked parody of costar Jetta Goudal. Altogether, Marion appeared in thirty silent films between 1917 and 1929.

Finally, in 1928, came a suitable showcase for Marion's talents. She gave a goofy, endearing performance as hopeful actress Peggy Pepper (renamed "Patricia Pepoire") in *Show People*. The film boasted a witty script, high production values, and walk-ons by nearly every star on the lot (including Marion Davies, in a delightful bit of postmodernism). She showed great comic timing and the rare ability to poke fun at both herself and her profession. *Show People* is one of Hollywood's funniest looks at itself, and happily, the film is available today on video. It was Marion's finest hour. Sadly, she never thought of herself as an actress. "All my life I wanted to have talent," she said in later years. "Finally I had to admit there was nothing there."

But it was as a hostess that Marion was best known to her friends. Hollywood was far from shocked by her relationship with Hearst, and the Hearst/Davies costume parties were hot tickets: Stars, executives, and visiting royalty dolled up as babies, cowboys, Bavarians, circus performers, and antebellum Southerners and grinned for the cameras. Marion frequently shanghaied friends for extended vacations (Anita Page recalls going up for a weekend and staying for five months). Some may have been jealous about her career (especially as Marion herself didn't seem to take it seriously), but no one could dislike her. Her bubbly, unpretentious personality won over all but her severest critics.

Despite her slight stammer, Marion had nothing to fear from talking film technology. It was the quality of her scripts which gave her trouble. She did an indifferent song and dance in 1929's *Hollywood Revue*; *Marianne* and *Not So Dumb* (both 1929) and *Florodora Girl* (1930) were downright unbearable. Even her better films were no match for what MGM was giving its other stars: *The Bachelor Father* and *It's a Wise Child* (both 1931) came and went without making much of an impression.

Finally, things began looking up, at the behest of Hearst (whom even Louis B. Mayer couldn't afford to ignore). *Five and Ten* (1932) was an agreeable soap opera costarring Leslie Howard; Marion was teamed with an up-and-coming Clark Gable (as a Salvation Army man, of all things) in the silly but amusing *Polly of the Circus* that same year. She was a showgirl opposite Robert Montgomery in *Blondie of the Follies* (1933, and costar Billie Dove's swan song). Other leading men included Bing Crosby (in the charming musical *Going Hollywood*, 1933) and Gary Cooper (in *Operator 13*, a terrible 1934 spy drama). Hollywood gossips later hinted that Marion had affairs with some or all of these leading men—but it's unclear how much truth and how much anti–Hearst venom there is in these statements.

Marion Davies had the best of both worlds: She was a film queen who also lived the life of actual royalty. "I used to go to Europe for three months every summer [bringing twelve to twenty-two guests], then I'd come back and do about three pictures a year." Marion was also smart enough not to make waves at her studios: "I had a really good time at MGM," she said later. "And we had no quarrels much, except once in a while, I'd go up to the front office and say I thought I should be doing something big, like washing elephants."

Hearst, however, did fall out with Mayer; and, in 1934, Marion, Hearst, and Cosmopolitan moved bag and baggage to Warner Brothers. That studio dolled her up in stiff platinum-blonde wigs and starred her in four films: as a starlet in the terrible *Page Miss Glory* (1935), as a Napoleonic sweetheart in

Marion Davies, gilded by Warner Bros., mid–1930s (Robert K. Klepper).

Hearts Divided (1936), as a singing star in *Cain and Mabel* (with Clark Gable, also 1936), and finally, as a put-upon stenographer in *Ever Since Eve* (1937). None of the films was a success, and only *Cain and Mabel* really had any merit.

Marion had enough and at the age of forty, she retired once and for all. "I wanted to take life easy," she said, "and once you get used to the lazy way of living, you find out that you rather enjoy it." She spent the next fourteen years as Hearst's wife in all but name. She and Hearst continued throwing parties and traveling the world, moving from castle to castle to castle. By this time, Marion was a full-fledged alcoholic, despite Hearst's constant efforts to keep her away from liquor. Her looks and health began to fade, but not her charm.

After Hearst's death in 1951, Marion was unceremoniously chucked out on the sidewalk by his family, who had never accepted their relationship. But Marion had her memories: "I liked to think that W.R. was at his happiest when he was with me," she later said. "Companionship and love. That was our pact." She quickly wed old friend Captain Horace Brown, more for companionship than for love. The marriage was a stormy one, but it endured. Marion threw herself into charity (endowing a children's hospital) and politics (she was a good friend of the Kennedys and did all she could to aid in John's 1960 election). After suffering from jaw cancer for three years, Marion succumbed on September 22, 1961.

Marion Davies was much better treated by posterity than she probably expected. With the dreaded Hearst gone, it was Marion's niceness that was remembered. The two books published on her since her death are superb: Fred Lawrence Guiles's 1972 biography is respectful and well researched; Marion's own highly imaginative notes were published in 1975 under the title *The Times We Had*. Both are well worth the read. It's a shame that more of her silent films are not available to the viewing public; still, Marion Davies can hardly be viewed as a tragic figure. A few years before her death, she said, "I can't say I was ever unhappy, not at all. It was a big, gay party, every bit of it."

It's not often the story of a long-dead film star has a sequel, but Marion's does. Her beloved and pampered "niece," Patricia van Cleve Lake, died in her early seventies on October 3, 1993, in California. Shortly thereafter, her son Arthur Lake, Jr. (son of the late actor Arthur Lake), announced that his mother was the daughter of Marion Davies and William Randolph Hearst, born in Paris sometimes in the early 1920s. Officially the daughter of Marion's sister Rose, Patricia was told of her true parentage when she was a teenager, and she later told her own family, swearing them to secrecy. She was buried near her mother and asked that her post-mortem announcement be kept "discreet."

JEANNE EAGELS

Jeanne Eagels was the Marilyn Monroe of the 1920s: beautiful, blonde, talented, vulnerable, mercurial—and a complete and utter mess. Indeed, Marilyn was a model of emotional stability compared to Jeanne. Yet, there's only been one (slightly dubious) biography and one (hilariously awful) film on Jeanne Eagels since her death in 1929. One of the most acclaimed stage actresses of the 1920s, she only made eight films—but she was quite a character, and she deserves more notice.

According to her own accounts, Jeanne Eagels was born in Boston, the daughter of a Spanish architect. Actually, she was from Kansas City, and her father was a carpenter of Pennsylvania Dutch origin. Amelia Jean Eagles (she would later adopt the spelling "Eagels") was one of six children (three boys and three girls) born to Edward and Julia (Sullivan) Eagles, on June 26, 1890 (most sources give a later year, but her only biographer, Edward Doherty, stated 1890). By the age of eleven she was acting in school plays; she was too poor to afford drama school but shone as Puck in a local production of *A Midsummer Night's Dream*. By the time she'd reached her teens, Jeanne was working as a cashier at a local department store. She seemed rather bitter about her childhood, telling a reporter, "My father was a dreamer, who never made enough money to support us in comfort. In all my life I have had only a year and a half at school. I have got my education as I went along—got it from life; and life, as I have known it, has sometimes been a queer business."

At the age of fifteen, she joined the Dubinsky Brothers' touring stock company. For the next seven years she played one Midwestern whistle-stop town after another, at $25 a week. It was a tough life, but a great acting school. Rising slowly, steadily from chorus girl and bit player to leading lady, Jeanne played everyone from Camille to Little Lord Fauntleroy—both classics and penny-dreadful melodramas. It was the same school of hard knocks that produced Mary Pickford and the Gish sisters. But, sadly, Jeanne didn't have the close family ties those other girls enjoyed. She

Jeanne Eagels in her early ingenue phase.

was on her own, dealing with rowdy patrons, coarse companions, crooked managers.

She married the eldest of the three Dubinsky brothers, Morris, and had a baby boy during this period. But the marriage quickly fell apart and the baby—who was to be her only child—was given up for adoption. Jeanne learned to roll with the punches and keep her eyes out for the big break. When one actress refused to perform a part in *Hamlet*, Jeanne jumped at it. "We played several months on the road," she recalled, "and when the first company came back to New York to play the subway circuit, I was given the role in that company."

It was 1911 when Jeanne hit New York, full of ambition and brimming with talent. She was also a knock-out, as lovely as any of Ziegfeld's Glorified American Girls. She had delicate, refined features, was as fashionably slim as a tango dancer, and her brown hair was newly dyed a pale blonde, She was as modern as jazz and bobbed hair, but with a sweet Valentine's face. Her first New York show was *Jumping Jupiter* (1911), with Ina Claire. Next, Jeanne was given two lines in Billie Burke's *The Mind-the-Paint Girl* (1912) and went on tour in *The Crinoline Girl*, a 1914 comedy starring female impersonator Julian Eltinge.

In 1915 the rising young starlet signed with Pathé to enter films. Charles Pathé had come to the United States in 1914 and was trying to strengthen the New York branch of his French company. Jeanne got good notices and positive reaction from fans, but none of her Pathé films were classics; *The House of Fear* (1915), *The World and the Woman* (as a bad girl turned faith healer, 1916), *The Fires of Youth* and *Under False Colors* (both 1917) came and went without causing much of a ripple. As they were filmed on the East Coast, Jeanne was able to appear in shows at night while filming during the day. During this time she also appeared on Broadway in *Hamilton*, and as Lady Clarissa in George Arliss's *Disraeli*.

Jeanne's last Pathé film was *The Cross Bearer* (1918). That same year, she finally had her first starring hit on Broadway, *Daddies*. Producer David Belasco spotted Jeanne in one of her small roles and snapped her up. "Her eyes were hard and bitter but shining with ambition," Belasco later wrote. "Thousands of girls have come to me, but never such a girl as Jeanne Eagels, with the air of a Duse, the voice of an earl's daughter, and the mien of a tired, starved little alley cat." With *Daddies*, Jeanne became the toast of Broadway. But she stormed out of the show halfway through its run, not a promising omen for her future in show business. Not yet thirty, Jeanne already had the demeanor of a major diva: "Never deny. Never explain. Say nothing and become a legend," she told a reporter in one of her rare interviews.

She had a lot to explain, too. By this time, Jeanne was an alcoholic and was growing dependent on sleeping potions as well. She began seeing one Dr. Edward Cowles, who tried to cure her of her habits—as the years went on, Jeanne spent more and more time drying out in sanitariums, to no avail. By the mid-1920s she was also using heroin. Her career didn't suffer, not at first. She starred in several more Broadway shows: *A Young Man's Fancy*, *In the Night Watch*, *The Wonderful Thing*. But she was only marking time.

Jeanne Eagels finally became a major star on November 7, 1922, when *Rain* opened in New York. "I felt I would die if I missed the chance to play that role," she said during the show's run. "Every time I sit down to put on my make-up, I have as great a thrill as if I were doing it for the first time." *Rain* was, of course, the story of Sadie Thompson, a good-natured prostitute locked in mortal combat with a hypocritical preacher. It was a dark, bitter play (John Colton had based it on a story by Somerset Maugham). Jeanne took Broadway by storm with her portrayal of the tough, humorous Sadie Thompson. It was a scandalous play for the time (and, indeed, might cause protests even today). She toured in it for five years, missing only eighteen performances in all that time.

She also cashed in on her stardom—Tallulah Bankhead recalled in her autobiography that Jeanne was paid $10,000 to endorse a cigarette. Her theatrical friends were horrified by this cheapening of her fame, but when Fanny Brice heard of her paycheck, she snorted, "For $10,000, I'd endorse an opium pipe!" Sadly, Jeanne Eagels never filmed *Rain*. Gloria Swanson and Joan Crawford did bang-up jobs with it, and poor Rita Hayworth struggled through a musical adaptation. But audiences were denied a lasting, filmed performance of Jeanne in her greatest role.

Toward the end of the run, Jeanne—long since divorced from Dubinsky—married Edward Harris "Ted" Coy, a wealthy New York stockbroker and former football star at Yale. The couple wed in 1925 at the home of actress Fay Bainter; they fought like alley cats, and the marriage lasted barely four years. Jeanne's lifestyle had begun to take a toll on her constitution, and as she entered her thirties, her health began to break down: twinges from a previously broken arm and jaw, sinus attacks, kidney problems, infection after infection. Through all her emotional ups and downs, Jeanne remained close to her siblings and especially close to her mother (her father had died some years earlier). Jeanne spoke to her mother on the phone twice weekly, sent her frequent tickets to New York, and bought her houses in New York and Los Angeles.

Jeanne was still enthusiastic about her art, no matter how her career turns depressed her. "The thought of the audience always thrills me," she said, "and yet I never see the people out there in front. I am not really conscious of them—except when people cough! I want to do all kinds of parts," she said hopefully, "and I know I can do them: sweet young things, tragic Camilles, lovely old ladies—

A drawn and weary Jeanne Eagels in the mid-1920s (Robert K. Klepper).

everything that is as real and thrilling as life is." Jeanne returned to films with the 1927 MGM production *Man, Woman and Sin*. It was a pet project of John Gilbert's, who was Jeanne's costar. The dark story of a reporter's tragic affair with his boss's mistress, it was a hit, though more critically than at the box office. Jeanne—photographed in glorious MGM soft focus—looked like a goddess, and both she and Gilbert gave superb performances, mixing humor and drama.

She returned to Broadway in 1927. She rehearsed for the role of Roxie Hart in *Chicago* but walked out before opening and was replaced by Francine Larrimore. She then took over the lead in *Her Cardboard Lover* from Laurette Taylor (opposite Leslie Howard). She also embarked on her last romance, with actor Barry O'Neill, a cast member of *Her Cardboard Lover*. The play was successful enough to go on tour—but, in March 1928, she vanished during the Chicago run. Whether her walkout was due to ill health, drink, a fight with O'Neill, or "nervous exhaustion," Jeanne was suspended by Actor's Equity and fined $3,600. She took to vaudeville and toured on the Keith circuit, doing scenes from *Rain* and *Her Cardboard Lover*.

Films still beckoned, though, and even if Broadway wouldn't touch her, Hollywood would. Though she was in her late thirties (old by contemporary standards), Jeanne was signed to a $200,000, three-picture contract by Paramount's East Coast studios. Her first talkie was *The Letter* (1929, with Reginald Owen). It was one of those tea-cup dramas so popular with early talking films (stationary mikes made such plays easier to film). It wasn't a patch on Bette Davis's 1940 remake, but Jeanne got good notices and adjusted well to the new medium. Her second film was a horror to make: Jeanne's health was rapidly failing, and she looked frighteningly thin while filming *Jealousy*. Then her leading man, Tony Bushell, had to be replaced (by Fredric March) when his voice failed to register well on film. Jeanne refused to make her third picture, *The Laughing Lady*, and was replaced by Ruth Chatterton. Both the films and the stage had rejected her—or vice versa. "It's harder to stay at the top than to get there," she told a reporter.

Jeanne's work, she once said, "means more to me than anything else in life... It has been my companion in all kinds of experiences, the only companion that I've always had with me. It has given me my education, my living, my friends. It has been my real life and my dream life." Like Bette Midler's character in *The Rose*, Jeanne dreamed of returning triumphantly to her hometown. "Kansas City wasn't even aware of my existence when I used to go back there after one of our box-car pilgrimages. But I'd like to stand on its front doorstep some fine morning and say to the old town: Well! See who's here! Little Jeanne Eagels has come back to show you what she can do!" Of course, Jeanne actually had returned to Kansas City, several times, but she enjoyed such self-dramatization.

If Jeanne Eagels lived like Marilyn Monroe, she died like River Phoenix. Jeanne was not well when *Jealousy* opened in September 1929. She spent ten days in St. Luke's Hospital, where she underwent an operation for an eye infection, and she suffered from neuritis and breathing problems, exacerbated by her drinking and drug taking. On Thursday evening, October 3, Jeanne and her longtime secretary, Christina Larson, left her apartment at 1143 Park Avenue, arriving at Dr. Cowles's office at the Park Avenue Hospital around 8:00 P.M. Jeanne was hardly dressed for a doctor's appointment: She wore an evening gown and wrap, also $300,000 worth of jewelry (a pearl ring "as large as a penny," a six-carat diamond-and-platinum ring, two pearl necklaces, and several other pieces).

Dr. Cowles was not in, but Dr. Alfred Pellegrini showed Jeanne to a room. While she sat on a bed chatting with him, Jeanne suddenly collapsed and went into convulsions. She was dead within minutes. Death was immediately laid to "alcoholic psychosis," but an autopsy revealed that Jeanne's system contained not only alcohol but chloral hydrate (a sleeping potion) and heroin. It's amazing that she even reached the hospital.

She lay in state at Frank Campbell's Funeral Church at Broadway and 66th Street while thousands passed before her silver-and-bronze coffin. It was a replay of Valentino's obsequies at the same church three years earlier. Jeanne wore a peach velvet gown and wrap, and she was surrounded by flowers. In a suitably theatrical finale, Loew's Theater just across the street was premiering her final film, *Jealousy*.

Harrison Ford

Many performers have similar names: Maude Adams and Maud Adams, Michael J. Fox and Michael Fox, and of course the many Seniors and Juniors (Fairbanks, Chaney, etc.). But only two legitimate stars have had the exact same moniker: Harrison Ford (1884–1957) and Harrison Ford (born 1942). The latter, no doubt delighted to be known as the "younger" Harrison Ford, has had such success with films like the *Indiana Jones* and *Star Wars* series, *Working Girl*, *Witness*, and *The Fugitive*, that he will assuredly live on as more famous than his unintentional namesake. But the career of his predecessor—not known to be any relation—is not to be sneezed at, either. The original Harrison Ford spent the 1910s and early 1920s as a reliable leading man for some of the screen's most famous stars, and in the late 1920s he blossomed as a light comedian in the tradition of Harold Lloyd.

Harrison Ford was born in Kansas City, Missouri, on March 16, 1884. The actor rarely gave interviews and only talked about his professional, not private, life, so little is known of his background. He started acting in stock early—some reports have him onstage by the age of seven, though this seems somewhat unlikely. Another article states that he left school at fourteen to join a stock company, working his way up from stagehand to bit player.

George Katchmer, in a 1987 *Classic Images* article, did a wonderful job of tracking down Harrison Ford's stage career. It seems he worked a good deal with renowned dramatic star Robert Edeson (one magazine stated that Edeson discovered young Harrison working as a shoe-store clerk, again a somewhat dubious tale). Harrison acted in Edeson's Broadway production of *Strongheart* (1905), and within a few years he took over the leading role of the romantic American Indian from the star, on tour. Harrison also attached himself to actor William H. Crane's company, appearing with him in *Excuse Me* (1911), *U.S. Minister Bedloe,* and others.

In 1913 Harrison was one of the actors chosen to appear with Holbrook Blinn's New York company, which put on such one-act plays as *The Fountain, Fancy Free, Any Night,* and George Jean Nathan's *The Bride.* Among his other Broadway shows were *Father and the Boys* (1908) and *Fear* (1913). In 1914 he was playing leading-man roles at the Harlem Opera House. He also spent a lot of time acting in stock companies, even after his film career had taken off; he appeared in Baltimore (*Brewster's Millions* and *Madame Sherry*, 1914), Los Angeles (*Come Again, Smith*, 1916), New York (*Rolling Stones, The Bubble,* and *A Night Off*, 1915), and Syracuse (*Charley's Aunt*, 1920).

In 1913 Harrison spoke to the *Syracuse Post Standard* about the gritty downside of acting, the "...anxiety, weariness of mind and body from a new production... The nervousness attending a first performance which some of us never overcome... While the play is in full swing, a life of constant restraint and self-denial in view of the coming performance is necessary. The public is a very exacting judge. An actor is human—he can be ill but the show must go on—and an ill actor's performance may not be his best. The patron simply says, 'so-and-so was rotten.'"

By the mid–1910s Harrison had reached a plateau in his career as a stage actor. He took his first-known film role, in the Pathé version of his stage show, *Excuse Me*, in 1915, and the following year he played in Paramount's *Anton the Terrible*, directed by William de Mille. Harrison was, by this time, in his early thirties and decided to throw his lot in with the new medium.

After one film at Universal (Lois Weber's *Mysterious Mrs. M.*, 1917), he signed with Paramount, where he made twenty films over the next four years. He got good exposure as the second lead in two Fannie Ward films, *The Crystal Gazer* and *On the Level*, both directed by George Melford and costarring Ward's husband Jack Dean. For the first time—though hardly the last—Harrison was teamed with a star actress. He made seven films with girlish blonde Vivian Martin from 1917 to 1919. In such fare as *The Sunset Trail* (1917), *A Petticoat Pilot* and *Unclaimed Goods* (both 1918), and *You Never Saw Such a Girl* (1919), Paramount built their new acquisition into a popular leading man. He also costarred with the studio's top male star, Wallace Reid, in *The Lottery Man* and *Hawthorne of the USA* (both 1919).

In 1918 Harrison made five films with Constance Talmadge, all directed by Walter Edwards. In *Sauce for the Goose, Good Night Paul, A Pair of Silk Stockings, Mrs. Leffingwell's Boots,* and *A Lady's Name*, the two cavorted through light marital escapades, mostly based on Broadway comedies. Harrison provided a steady, sensible counterpoint to Constance's feathery flapper wives, and the two went on to costar in another seven films through 1922: They married in haste in *Who Cares?,* tried an *Experimental Marriage* and verged on divorce in *Happiness à la Mode* (all 1919); they also fought and reconciled through *Wedding Bells* (1921) and *The Primitive Lover* (1922, their last pairing).

Enhancing their onscreen chemistry, the two became good friends. Each film with Constance, Harrison told a reporter, "was a holiday. She is the squarest girl to work with you ever saw! Constance has a distinct gift for always keeping comedy on a high, sparkling plane, and she has created a wonderful screen personality." In 1921 Harrison switched leading ladies but stayed in the same family, making his first of four

Harrison Ford in 1920.

films with Norma Talmadge. *The Passion Flower*, *The Wonderful Thing*, and *Love's Redemption* (all 1921) were fairly typical Norma Talmadge society dramas, but *Smilin' Through* (1922) was a huge hit, a four-handkerchief romance of love carried throughout the generations. By the time it was remade with Norma Shearer and Fredric March, it was somewhat old hat, but in 1922 *Smilin' Through* packed them in the aisles.

By this time, Harrison Ford's reputation with the leading ladies was settled: He was handsome (but not unsettlingly so), talented (but not a scene stealer), and easy to work with and reliable ("He is never a minute late on the set," noted one magazine). Like George Brent and David Manners a decade later, he made actresses look good without distracting fans from their charms. Among the stars who took advantage of Harrison's services were Bebe Daniels (*Oh, Lady! Lady!*, 1920), Gloria Swanson (*Her Gilded Cage*, 1922), Alma Rubens (*Find the Woman*, 1922), Clara Bow (*Maytime*, 1923, and *Three Weekends*, 1928), Corinne Griffith (*The Marriage Whirl*, 1925), and Bessie Love (*The Song and Dance Man*, 1926, and *Rubber Tires*, 1927).

Some actresses latched onto him as a good partner through several films. His more frequent leading ladies included such sparkling comediennes as Marion Davies (*Little Old New York*, 1923, *Janice Meredith*, 1924, and *Zander the Great*, 1925), Phyllis Haver (*Up in Mabel's Room* and *The Nervous Wreck*, 1926, *No Control* and *The Rejuvenation of Aunt Mary*, 1927), and Marie Prevost (*Up in Mabel's Room* and *Almost a Lady*, 1926, *Night Bride* and *The Girl in the Pullman*, 1927, *Blonde for a Night* and *Rush Hour*, 1928). As it had with Constance Talmadge, Harrison's no-nonsense, big-brother persona counterbalanced these actresses' girlish, jazzy charms.

As he jumped from one leading lady to another throughout those years, Harrison Ford also frequently switched studios. He made nine films for Select (1918–19), five for Realart (1920–21) and seven for First National (1921–25), as well as freelancing for Metro, Goldwyn, Fox and such little-remembered companies as Kenma Corporation, Rosemary Films, and CC Burr Pictures, Inc. Few of these films came to be classics, but Harrison kept busy—he starred or co-starred in a total of thirty-five films from 1920 to 1925. Some of his more popular were *Miss Hobbs* (with Wanda Hawley, 1920), *A Heart to Let* (with Justine Johnstone, 1921), *Shadows* (with Lon Chaney, 1922), *Vanity Fair* (with Mabel Ballin and Eleanor Boardman, 1923), *The Price of a Party* (with Hope Hampton, Mary Astor, and Dagmar Godowsky, 1924), and as an orchestra leader in D. W. Griffith's *That Royle Girl* (with Carol Dempster and W. C. Fields, 1925).

For all his success, Harrison remained an unknown quantity as far as his personal life was concerned. "A rather serious, secretive chap," one reporter called him. "The Hermit of Hollywood" soon became his nickname. "When discussing a question," wrote journalist William McKegg, "Mr. Ford has the trick of looking far away, or down on the ground, or glancing behind him, as though he might find the explanation in any of these directions." Harrison himself complained, "What I can't make out, though, is what you people see in any of us [actors] interesting enough to keep writing about." If Harrison ever married or had any romance, it remained unreported. The few private glimpses into his life involved his love of gardening and his large collection of books, many of them first editions.

A character shot of Harrison Ford from a 1920s fan magazine.

Harrison's career had reached another plateau by 1926. At forty-two (thirty-four, according to his press releases), he had a reputation as a reliable prop for star actresses: agreeable, handsome, a bit dull. He seemed resigned to the situation, telling one reporter that "I remember what has happened to other leading men who decided to star... When you become a star, your troubles begin. The star is the cause of a picture's failure, if it fails, and if it's a success, the star is bound to that sort of role from then on... So much is made to depend upon the individual performance of the star that spontaneity is almost impossible."

The same reporter compared Harrison to other second-tier leading men and noted that "Kenneth Harlan, James Kirkwood, Conrad Nagel and the temperamental House Peters all have their streaks of heavy popularity, but none has been so consistently employed as young Mr. Ford." Then, for some unknown reason, Al Christy picked Harrison to star in his film version of the 1923 Broadway hit, *The Nervous Wreck* (later reworked musically as *Whoopee!*, with Eddie Cantor).

Suddenly, the stolid leading man burst forth as a comic delight. Playing a timid hypochondriac who regains his self-composure and finds love on a dude ranch, Harrison turned in a jittery, funny performance. He became a handsomer and slightly more virile version of Edward Everett Horton, and his marketability skyrocketed. Explaining his comedy success, he modestly said that "A good situation, worked out well enough to carry you into the drift of the action, is all you need with a good director. When you have these aids, you can't go wrong in putting over a scene." Harrison added diffidently that "I do not know that I'd care to play consistently in farce comedy. I like it, and I'll play in it as long as they'll let me. But I have no particular preferences. I like both comedy and drama. I'm afraid I don't know enough about either to decide which I like best."

That typecasting he'd foreseen earlier in his career came to pass. He made eleven films in 1926 and 1927, most of them as a madcap farceur. He supported Madge Bellamy in one of her most successful films, *Sandy*, filmed another Broadway hit, *Up in Mabel's Room*, crossed the country with Bessie Love in *Rubber Tires,* and got into more risqué scrapes in *The Girl in the Pullman* and *Night Bride*. For those two years, Harrison was Big Man on Campus, his services requested by many top studios.

But, by 1928, the party was about to end for Harrison Ford. He appeared in seven films that year, and some of them were quite good: For Paramount he made *Just Married*, and he costarred with Clara Bow and Neil Hamilton in *Three Weekends* (though, significantly, he lost the girl in the final reel). He made three films for Pathé, including two delicious comedies with Marie Prevost (*Blonde for a Night* and *Rush Hour*). But he was also reduced to such low-budget fare as Columbia's *Golf Widows* and Tiffany-Stahl's *A Woman Against the World* (both with starlet Sally Rand, soon to become a famous fan dancer).

When talking films came into popularity, Harrison Ford simply left the screen and returned to the stage. It's unclear why he did not try his hand at talkies; after all, he had a good, stage-trained voice. Perhaps producers didn't find the now-middle-aged actor marketable, or perhaps he was simply tired of films. He is rumored to have appeared in a handful of shorts, but his last film (and his only talking feature) seems to have been the low-budget *Love in High Gear* (1932), with Alberta Vaughn.

Little more was heard from Harrison Ford. He appeared in Shaw's *Man and Superman* at the Pasadena Community Playhouse in 1929, joined the Henry Duffy Stock Company, and did a bit of stage work in England. In the 1940s he worked for the USO, and he directed some plays at a stock company in Glendale, California. But Harrison's name stayed pretty much out of the newspapers until 1951, when he was struck by a car near his Glendale home. He was hospitalized in critical condition with a concussion and a broken ankle. Harrison never fully recovered from his injuries and spent his last years as a semi-invalid at the Motion Picture Country Home. He was seventy-three when he died there on December 2, 1957. By that time, he was almost completely forgotten by the public at large, and his obituaries were sketchy and brief. They probably went unnoticed, except perhaps by another Harrison Ford, then a fifteen-year-old in Chicago, still nine years away from his own film debut.

Dorothy Gish

Anyone who's followed a straight-A sibling through school can appreciate Dorothy Gish's position in film history. A talented dramatic actress and one of the silent screen's most brilliant comediennes, she has been unjustly neglected by film historians in favor of her sister Lillian. Unlike many show-business siblings, however, the Gishes remained the best of pals from beginning to end. Lillian was always her younger sister's champion ("Dorothy was always the most talented of the Gishes," she once said). Lillian would have been the first to admit that even had she herself been just an Ohio housewife, Dorothy Gish would still be remembered as one of the screen's immortals.

Dorothy Elizabeth Gish was born on March 11, 1898, in Dayton, Ohio, five years after her sister. By 1902 the girls were earning their living in stock companies. Their father having failed in business, Mrs. Gish took to the stage with her daughters. Among Dorothy's early successes were as Little Willie in *East Lynne*, and parts in *Her First False Step*, *Dion O'Hare*, and other plays—everything from the worst penny dreadfuls to more high-toned fare.

A tough life for a little girl, but it was the best school any actress could have. Both girls were quick learners, and their resilience, strength, and humor helped them through this period. Trouping in stock seems romantic from a distance, but it often meant cold, strange towns, dull train rides, sleazy hotels, and unbearable loneliness. Those shows reuniting all three Gishes were a particular treat. "I have never for a single day lamented my lost childhood," Dorothy later said. In fact, she claimed that theatrical life brought the family closer together.

As of 1912, they were boarding on Eighth Avenue in Manhattan. A friend—another theatrical child named Gladys Smith—had changed her name to Mary Pickford and found employment in films. Dorothy and Lillian visited her at Biograph Studios on 11 East 14th Street (about a twenty-minute walk from their apartment), and she introduced them to director D. W. Griffith. The sisters were lucky enough to land in the birthplace of

Dorothy Gish in the mid-1920s.

film's true golden age. While Hollywood in the 1920s and 1930s may have had more glamour, New York in the 1910s was the fun, rough-and-tumble, inventive spawning ground of the industry.

In those pre-union days, anyone wandering into the studio had a chance. With the right look (extremely youthful), talent, and a pitch-in spirit, almost anyone could get a break. When Griffith asked the girls if they could act, Dorothy drew herself up haughtily and informed him that they "were of the legitimate theater." He gave them the benefit of a doubt. Both sisters were great beauties, though Dorothy never saw herself that way. "I have a crooked face," she'd laugh ruefully. "I always think of myself as a squirrel, with two nuts stored in one cheek and only one in the other." She had blue-gray eyes and dark gold hair, although she occasionally wore black wigs in her films as a kind of comic disguise.

After playing extras in an unremembered film, the Gishes made their official debut being menaced in *An Unseen Enemy* (1912). They were off and running: The film industry entered its adolescence along with the younger Gish. Lillian went on to star in more than one hundred films, mostly dramas, but rambunctious Dorothy began making her mark in comedy. In 1912 and 1913, she appeared in nineteen films, first in tiny roles, later in larger ones. Among these—many still surviving—were *The Musketeers of Pig Alley*, *Oil and Water*, *The Perfidy of Mary* and *The New York Hat*. In the amazing Biograph stock company, she costarred with her sister Lillian, Mary Pickford, Robert Harron, Mae Marsh, Wallace Reid, Lionel Barrymore, Blanche Sweet, and Henry B. Walthall. She worked under several directors (Griffith, James Kirkwood, Donald Crisp, and others), and one of her more promising screenwriters was young Anita Loos.

In 1914 Dorothy Gish made thirty films, which is only slightly less astonishing when one recalls that these were about the same length as a modern situation comedy and were filmed in as little as a day or two. The sisters by this time had become teen idols—their photos appeared in fan magazines, colored postcards of them sold well, and a series of children's books (*The Moving Picture Girls*, by Laura Lee Hope) was based on them. Dorothy's roles were widely varied: She played a crippled beggar in *Judith of Bethulia*, a chorus girl in *The Floor Above*, a nun in *Her Mother's Daughter*, a spinster servant in *Silent Sandy*, a political activist in the startlingly titled *The Suffragette's Battle in Nuttyville*, and a silly deb in *A Lesson in Mechanics*.

Dorothy was becoming one of the

Dorothy Gish and her husband, James Rennie, in *Remodeling a Husband* (1920, directed by Dorothy's sister Lillian).

best-loved actresses on the lot. Her impish sense of humor and utter lack of pretension made her scores of friends, many of whom mothered her to death. She and Constance Talmadge were the rollicking puppy dogs of the company, amusing Griffith (who intimidated everyone else) with their jokes, giggles, and irrepressible carryings-on. Dorothy was also something of a hero: She was seriously injured in 1915 when she pushed Mae Marsh out of a speeding car's path and was herself hit.

The production company shifted from Biograph to Majestic-Mutual to Triangle-Fine Arts, and from coast to coast—but Griffith remained the star director. By 1915 and 1916, the films were getting longer and fewer, as one-reelers (about eleven minutes) were being replaced by more elaborate two- and three-reelers. By that time, Dorothy was also the unchallenged star of her films, which still varied between drama and comedy. She was the female lead (a role later played by Norma Shearer) in *Old Heidelberg*, a put-upon immigrant in *Gretchen the Greenhorn*, a backwoods daughter in *Children of the Feud*—a total of twenty films in those two years. Only three followed in 1917 (*The Little Yank*, *Stage Struck,* and *Her Official Fathers*), but Dorothy had her biggest hit yet in 1918 with *Hearts of the World.* Made partly in England and France during the war, this impressive film also featured Lillian, Robert Harron, Kate Bruce, and a teenaged Nöel Coward. It featured perhaps Dorothy's greatest performance—one of her own favorites—as a rowdy French peasant girl.

Impressed, Paramount signed Dorothy in 1918; she made fourteen films for them over the next four years. Among the most successful were *Battling Jane* (1918); *I'll Get Him Yet* (a proto *It Happened One* Night with Richard Barthelmess, 1919); the comic western *Nugget Nell* (also 1919—Dorothy "did right by her men and drank her whiskey straight"); and *Remodeling a Husband* (1920, the only film purportedly directed by her sister Lillian, also boasting a script by Dorothy Parker). Dorothy discovered a young bit player named Rudolph Valentino and cast him in *Out of Luck* (1919). Sadly, these films all seem to be lost.

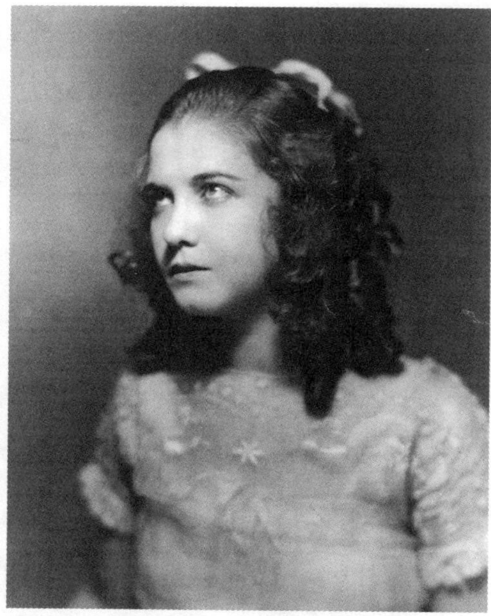

Dorothy Gish during her Biograph days, about 1915.

Tragedy touched Dorothy during her Paramount years with the death of close friend and costar Robert Harron on September 4, 1920. The twenty-six-year old actor—still at the peak of his career—died of a self-inflicted gunshot wound in New York. His death was probably accidental but has been understandably clouded in mystery ever since. Dorothy was shattered. Their relationship has variously described as platonic or romantic; the truth will never be known, as neither Gish sister was ever fond of making her private life public.

Dorothy married almost immediately after Harron's death. On December 26, 1920, she and Constance Talmadge eloped to Connecticut with their fiancés. Dorothy's beau was thirty-year-old actor James Rennie, who had co-

A more glamorous Dorothy Gish in the late 1920s (Jerry Ohlinger).

starred with her in *Remodeling a Husband* and *Flying Pat.* Dorothy later insisted she'd eloped just to keep Connie company; she had to be gently coerced out of her mother's home and into her husband's. The Rennies separated in the early 1930s and divorced in 1935, though they remained friendly. Indeed, the most serious charge she could bring against him was giving her hiccups. Rennie later remarried, and he died in 1965; Dorothy remained single.

Dorothy returned to Griffith in 1922 for *Orphans of the Storm*, perhaps her most-revived film. As a blind waif in revolutionary France, she gave her character both strength and pathos, a far cry from her usual light comedies. She followed this with another deft tragic role in *Romola* (1924, also with Lillian, directed by Henry King): Seduced by William Powell, she committed suicide by drowning herself in the River Arno ("She proved a problem as she kept bobbing up like a cork," Lillian told this author). Dorothy proved herself one of the most versatile actresses of her generation, just as comfortable in these high dramas as in roustabout comedies. She shied away from being labeled a comedienne, claiming that audiences did not like their women funny. She was right, too: Chaplin, Keaton, and Lloyd were free to be as comic as they liked, but Dorothy, Mabel Normand, and Constance Talmadge were accused of being "unfeminine." It wasn't until talkies allowed women to mouth comic lines that the barriers began to fall.

Dorothy worked steadily through the 1920s for First National and Paramount (in New York and London). Her career never faltered: Among other roles, she played a Cuban dancer in *The Bright Shawl* (1923); a nagging wife in *Clothes Make the Pirate* (1925); the title role in *Nell Gwynn* (1926, the first British film to find worldwide success); and a cabaret star in *Tip Toes* (1927, costarring Will Rogers). British producer Herbert Wilcox called Dorothy "undoubtedly ... the wittiest woman I have met." By the late 1920s, she was also quite a world traveler, immersed in her journeys almost as much as in her career. Then she suddenly had to deal with the popularity of talking films.

Rather than diving straight into talkies, Dorothy returned to the stage with *Young Love* (1928–29), a light comedy which she played in New York and London. She took a deep breath and filmed her first talkie in 1930. Her voice was deep, stage-trained, and musical.

But *Wolves*—a British thriller costarring Charles Laughton—was such a disaster that she never let her sister see it, and she abandoned her film career for fourteen years. Indeed, she always thought of herself as a better stage than film performer.

She picked up her theatrical work with stunning success. Dorothy spent the 1930s appearing in thirteen shows, many produced by the Westport Repertory Company in Connecticut, others in the great Broadway theaters such as the Empire, Morosco, and Longacre. She performed in Gogol's *The Inspector General*, Shaw's *Getting Married*, Boucicault's *The Streets of New York*, as Emily Dickinson in *Brittle Heaven*, and in Paul Osborne's *Mornings at Seven*. She also performed in a great many radio plays, greatly enjoying the use of her voice after so many years in silents.

After several other shows (including a three-year tour in *Life with Father*), Dorothy Gish returned to films with *Our Hearts Were Young and Gay* (1944), a delightful period comedy based on Cornelia Otis Skinner's memoirs. In her mid-forties, she proved a warm and lovely character actress, yet she only made three more films: as Constance Bennett's sister-in-law in *Centennial Summer* (1946), as a mill owner's widow in *The Whistle at Eaton Falls* (1951) and as the title character's mother in *The Cardinal* (1964). "You miss the old feeling," she said of modern filmmaking. "Making movies used to be fun. A medium is always more fun when it's new." She also appeared onstage in such shows as *The Magnificent Yankee* (1946), *The Story of Mary Surratt* (a great 1947 success), and—her last role opposite Lillian—in Enid Bagnold's *The Chalk Garden* (1956).

Dorothy spent much of her time traveling: extended trips to England, Italy, Africa, Yugoslavia, Stockholm, and Israel, often with friends, family, and of course, Lillian, in tow. Shortly after her last film, Dorothy's health began to fail, and she moved to the Villa Chiara in Rapallo, on the Italian Riviera. She died of bronchial pneumonia there on June 4, 1968. Her sister was at her bedside.

In 1987 Lillian Gish's final movie, *The Whales of August*, was released. It was one of her best films and best performances. Costar Bette Davis was also brilliant, but the memory of Dorothy Gish hung like a veil of regret over the film. Fans who recalled *Orphans of the Storm*, *Hearts of the World*, and *An Unseen Enemy* couldn't help but wish that Lillian's blind sister had been played by her own Dorothy.

William Haines

William Haines's life and career have been overshadowed in retrospect by his open homosexuality. But that really had little—if any—effect on his acting career, which lasted from his debut in 1922 until his retirement in 1934. His coworkers and friends knew "Billy" was gay, but the public was largely ignorant of this until scandal hit in 1936. By then, he was well established in another career.

Charles William Haines had the rare distinction of being a child of the century, claiming to have been born on January 1, 1900 (his biographer, William J. Mann, was unable to either confirm or deny this through records). He was the oldest of five (two brothers and two sisters), born into an old, wealthy Staunton, Virginia, family. His early childhood was bucolic; the family cigar business brought in money, and Bill seemed to get along well with everyone. "My mother was lovely and aristocratic," Bill said later, "everything that a boy could wish of a mother… My father I liked tremendously, not just because he was my father, but because he was such a good scout."

An indifferent student and born wiseacre, Bill barely got through school. His life turned around in his early teens. In a surprisingly revealing 1931 interview, he said, "The things that happen after one is fourteen are so much more important. After that age one is sex-conscious, and it is always an important discovery. When I was fourteen I ran away from home… A boy friend, another would-be adventurer, stole some old coins and went with me." The boys got work in a powder factory in Hopewell, Virginia, eventually with the grudging Haineses' consent. According to Bill, he and his friend briefly ran a dance hall, though they were not yet fifteen years old. Bill moved to New York, where he got a job at a rubber company, until family reverses forced him back to Virginia to work at a dry goods store.

Around 1920 Bill moved back to New York to make his fortune. He clerked in a department store, then got a job as an office boy at S. W. Straus, a bond company. Despite his ineptitude, he was promoted to assistant bookkeeper. "They must have liked me in

William Haines at the time of the talkie revolution.

spite of my faults," he said. "I stayed there for more than a year, but I can't recall a single instance when my books ever tallied." Living in a Greenwich Village boarding house with several other ambitious young men, Bill entered a New Faces contest sponsored by Goldwyn Studios. He and Eleanor Boardman, the winners, were shipped off to California with beginner's contracts in 1922.

Bill made only five films for Goldwyn in two years: *Brothers Under the Skin* (his 1922 debut, as a butler), *Souls for Sale* (with Barbara La Marr, 1923), *Three Wise Fools* (also 1923), and *Three Weeks* (1924, a small role in a heavy-breathing Elinor Glyn romance starring Aileen Pringle). If Goldwyn had lost interest in the newcomer, Columbia took notice. The brand-new studio needed cheap, talented players and borrowed Bill Haines for *The Midnight Express*. It was his first leading role, as the son of a railroad president.

Universal next borrowed Bill for another lead, in *The Gaiety Girl* (1924). Bill was beginning to hope Goldwyn would sell his contract to a more appreciative studio. But in 1924 Goldwyn merged with Metro to form Metro-Goldwyn-Mayer. It was a whole new ball game. Sam Goldwyn no longer had much say in the studio's running, and Bill's star began to rise. Louis B. Mayer and Irving Thalberg saw something in him that Goldwyn had missed. Bill's first film under the new regime was promising: He was part of a romantic triangle with Eleanor Boardman and Ben Lyon in *Wine of Youth* (1924). Later that same year, he was one of Mae Murray's admirers in *Circe the Enchantress* and Eleanor Boardman's brother in *Wife of the Centaur* (with John Gilbert).

By 1925 Bill was swiftly edging his way upward toward stardom, appearing in eight films, including three more on loan-out to Columbia (*A Fool and His Money*, *Who Cares?*, and *Fighting the Flames*), and one for United Artists (as good-hearted street tough in Mary Pickford's popular hit, *Little Annie Rooney*). For his home studio, Bill appeared that year in *The Denial* (as a casualty in a war film), *A Slave of Fashion* (supporting Norma Shearer), *The Tower of Lies* (with Shearer again, and Lon Chaney), and *Sally, Irene and Mary*. The latter film was his first of five with Joan Crawford, who became a lifelong pal.

In 1926 Bill Haines fell in love for the first and only time. He and twenty-one-year-old Jimmie Shields moved in together and became, as Joan Crawford once said, "the happiest married couple in Hollywood." Shields was put on the MGM payroll as Bill's secretary and stand-in. The two stayed together for nearly fifty years, until Bill's death—an impressive marriage in or out of the film business.

Meanwhile, Bill's career continued apace; he made another six films in 1926. The first two, *Memory Lane* and *The Thrill Hunter*, came and went without causing a stir. But *Brown of Harvard*, released in April, finally made Bill a full-fledged star. It was the classic college tale of the full-of-himself athlete, and Bill's breezy, youthful demeanor meshed perfectly with his character. For the rest of his career, no matter what the role, he was "Brown of Harvard." "I didn't have to act," he later said of this role, "I was just myself. 'Brown' was the sort of fellow I am ... kind of lazy, good-natured, wise-cracking." But 1926 was far from over: That same year, Bill starred in *Mike*, *Lovey Mary*, and *Tell It to the Marines* ("Brown" joins the Marines, with Lon Chaney and Eleanor Boardman).

By now, the fan magazines were knocking at his door, publicizing Hollywood's most eligible bachelor. Bill gave good interviews: Chatty, funny, self-effacing, he charmed reporters, fans, and coworkers alike. "He has a reputation in Hollywood for wisecracks that is second to none," said reporter Dorothy Spensley. "Hostesses have been known to postpone dinner parties because Bill Haines was out of town." Bill himself took a more modest view of his wit. "After establishing a reputation for wise-cracking it isn't hard to keep it up," he told *Photoplay*. "I don't have to do homework by reading joke books. People just laugh at anything I say from force of habit."

Bill Haines was the perfect male flapper for the latter half of the 1920s. While Valentino represented dangerous love and John Gilbert played noble, tortured heroes, Bill Haines exemplified the sunny, collegiate self-confidence of the Jazz Age. Like the characters played by Clara Bow, Joan Crawford, and Colleen Moore, Bill's screen heroes were the happy-go-lucky fellows his fans thought themselves to be. And Bill's generally cheery offscreen personality fitted perfectly with this.

In 1928 Bill played a go-getting reporter in *Telling the World*, his first of five films with Anita Page, who today recalls him as the lovable big brother she never had. "He'd come onto the set singing 'Nothing could be sweeter than to be with my Anita in the morning,'" she laughs. "I'd say, 'Bill, I am *not* your Anita,' and he'd pick me up and swing me around. I remember his wonderful smile—it was just like a big horseshoe." He also played a polo champ (*The Smart Set*) and a vaudeville acrobat (*Excess Baggage*) in 1928, but his big hit—indeed, his biggest since *Brown of Harvard*—came with *Show People*, released in October of that year. *Show People* was the best

Dashing leading man William Haines in the mid–1920s.

showcase for another of Bill's friends, Marion Davies. A scathingly funny look at Hollywood and the star factory, it featured Marion as Peggy Pepper, a small-town girl who becomes overblown star Patricia Pepoire. Bill played Billy Boone, a lowbrow slapstick comic who loses Peggy when she becomes too big a star. It was another perfect role for Bill, and he and Marion made a great team.

As the silent era inevitably drew to an end, Bill Haines was one of MGM's biggest romantic male stars. John Gilbert was already on the outs with Louis B. Mayer, and upcomers Johnny Mack Brown, Bill Bakewell, and Douglas Fairbanks, Jr., were not yet bringing in big money. Audiences were still undecided on MGM players Lars Hanson and Conrad Nagel. Ironically, MGM's other big male draw, Ramon Novarro, was also gay, though not as comfortable with it as was Bill. Mayer was far from happy about Bill's private life, but he was not about to kill a goose while it still laid golden eggs. Bill was professional, cooperative, and friendly, and Mayer was quite willing to suppress his disapproval.

Talking films came comparatively late to MGM, but Bill was their first star to take the plunge. In January 1929 he played the soft-hearted safecracker in *Alias Jimmy Valentine*, which had been a big Broadway hit in 1910 and a Bert Lytell film in 1920. Only the last few moments of Bill's version had a talkie sequence, which seems quite jarring now but was rather common in 1928 and 1929. Bill appeared in two more part-talkies in early 1929, *The Duke Steps Out* (with Joan Crawford) and *A Man's Man* (the title of which caused much merriment among those in the know).

Bill also costarred with every other MGM player (sans Chaney and Garbo) in the all-star *The Hollywood Revue of 1929*, released in June of that year. Filmed largely at night so as not to disrupt other schedules, it was one of the variety shows produced by all major studios of the time to introduce their stars and supporting players to talkie audiences. The films were varied in their quality; MGM's had a few dazzling numbers, but overall it was rather stuffy and stilted. Bill appeared in a brief (and not terribly funny) comedy sketch with Jack Benny.

After one last silent (*Speedway*, with Anita Page, had synchronized sound effects but no dialogue), Bill's first all-talkie feature was *Navy Blues* (released in December 1929). Bill played a sailor romancing a dime-a-dance girl (Page, again). But Bill's star was beginning to fade; his "Brown of Harvard" character didn't translate to talking pictures.

What was adorably pushy and cocky in silence seemed obnoxious to the point of disturbing when dialogue was added. Bill's pursuit of Leila Hyams in *The Girl Said No* (1930) was particularly obsessive. The Girl eventually said Yes, of course; but a normal woman, faced with Bill's character, would have taken out a restraining order and bought a gun. Additionally, Bill simply didn't enjoy making talkies. Like Clara Bow, he was a bumptious, off-the-cuff performer, and learning lines and hitting marks was no fun. In his early thirties, he'd put on about twenty pounds and no longer looked like a fresh college kid.

It was a vicious circle: The less money Bill brought in at the box office, the less MGM was willing to expend on him to restore his luster. Of the seven films he made at MGM in 1930 and 1931, none were much good. He was a fast-talking con man in a comedy western, *Way Out West*, and a radio announcer in *Remote Control* (both 1930). In 1931 Bill played an ambitious young businessman in *A Tailor Made Man*, a pushy playboy in *Just a Gigolo,* and yet another con man in *The New Adventures of Get-Rich-Quick Wallingford*. None of these films were up to much as far as dialogue or plot.

A rare exception was *Are You Listening?* (1932), a low-budget *Grand Hotel* concerning the tangled lives of radio workers. Bill, as an unhappily married writer, gave a quiet, convincing dramatic performance, assisted by the excellent supporting cast (Anita Page, Wallace Ford, Madge Evans, Karen Morley). Bill made one last film for MGM in 1932, *Fast Life*, again with Evans. He dropped out of sight for a year before resurfacing at the low-budget Mascot Studio, where he appeared in two 1934 films: *Young and Beautiful* (as a manic PR man) and *The Marines Are Coming* (as a manic Marine). With that, the film career of William Haines came to an end.

But life went on. Bill had been interested in decorating since at least 1931, when he worked as art director on *Just a Gigolo*. Joan Crawford hired Bill to decorate her home, and the results were so impressive that Carole Lombard, George Cukor, Constance Bennett, Lionel Barrymore, Claudette Colbert, and other Hollywood clients were soon lined up at his door. Jimmie Shields became partner in William Haines, Inc., one of the country's most successful interior decorating firms.

Disaster loomed only once, in 1936. Bill and Shields owned a house at Manhattan Beach, a fashionable California resort town. They'd befriended a neighbor's child, named Jimmy Walker. When the child's parents found out he was associating with the gay couple, all hell broke loose. Despite the six-year-old's protestations that nothing untoward had happened, Bill Haines, Jimmie Shields, and fourteen other known—or suspected—homosexuals were attacked by lynch mobs in early June. A crowd of fifty to one hundred men and women surrounded Bill and Shields outside a restaurant and told them, "We don't want you to live here—and we'll give you just an hour to get out." The couple was severely beaten and run out of town. "How such things can happen in a civilized country is beyond me," said Bill the next day. "There was absolutely no reason for such an attack and it was caused only by false, malicious gossip." Years later, a grown-up Jimmy Walker told Haines's biographer that Jimmie Shields had, indeed, molested him.

But the furor settled down, and William Haines, Inc., continued to accrue clients and prestige. Indeed, Bill was a much more respected and successful decorator than he'd been an actor. A 1949 article called him "one of the leading interior designers for Hollywood homes." He turned down a cameo role in *Sunset Boulevard*, telling a reporter that "It's a rather pleasant feeling of being away from pictures and being part of them because all my friends are. I can see the nice side of them without seeing the ugly side of the studios." Bill's success continued through the 1960s, when he designed The Mocambo Club and the London residence of U.S. Ambassador Annenberg. His work was featured in *Architectural Digest*, and Bill was generally acclaimed one of the country's leading designers. He remained socially active until shortly before his death of cancer on December 26, 1973.

On March 6, 1974, Jimmie Shields committed suicide, leaving a note that "It was just no good anymore without Billy." Thus ended one of the longest and happiest marriages Hollywood ever knew.

ROBERT HARRON

With everything written about actresses discovered or nurtured by D. W. Griffith, one tends to neglect the actors he helped develop. On the one hand we have the Gishes, Mary Pickford, Mae Marsh, and Blanche Sweet. But one should not forget Henry B. Walthall, Arthur Johnson, Richard Barthelmess, and of course Robert Emmett Harron, who appeared in fifty-four Griffith films between 1909 and 1919.

Bobbie Harron (he preferred that spelling to "Bobby") was born into a large Irish Catholic family; he had two brothers and six sisters. The Harrons—not wealthy people—lived in New York's Greenwich Village. Bobbie, who was born on April 24, 1893, attended St. Joseph's Parochial School and retained strict religious beliefs for the rest of his brief life.

Bobbie got into films early, but not as an actor. The American Mutoscope and Biograph Company (better known simply as "Biograph") was located at 11 East 14th Street, quite nearby St. Joseph's. The company frequently put "help wanted" signs up at the school. One day in 1907, Bobbie and his pal Jimmie Smith headed to Biograph after school and got jobs as gofers (Smith later became a film cutter). Bobbie Harron—only fourteen when he went to work—spent his days sweeping floors, hammering sets together, delivering film reels around the city, and going out to get lunch for the crew. His starting salary was $5 a week. Bobbie also did a little acting: He appeared in three Wallace McCutcheon films: *Dr. Skinum* (1907), *At the Crossroads of Life,* and *Bobbie's Kodak* (both 1908). Soon he was earning an impressive $25 a week as Biograph's shy, good-natured Jack-of-all-trades.

In early 1908 D. W. Griffith joined Biograph, and he and Bobbie quickly became friends. Griffith—who never had children—looked upon Bobbie as a son. While his relationships with other actors could be fractious and his relationship with actresses fraught with romantic tension, Griffith loved being around bumptious teenagers like Bobbie, Dorothy Gish, and Constance Talmadge. While most coworkers respectfully called

Bobbie Harron with Lillian Gish in *Hearts of the World* (1918).

their director "Mr. Griffith" and spoke in hushed tones in his presence, Bobbie would dash up to him with a "Hey, Griff!" Griffith loved it, though such a greeting from anyone else would have resulted in instant dismissal.

Bobbie's first role in a Griffith film was in *The Lonely Villa* (1909). His acting career, however, didn't really take off until 1911, when Bobbie appeared in four films. Thirteen more followed in 1912 (including *A Girl and Her Trust*, *The New York Hat*, and *The Musketeers of Pig Alley*), seven in 1913 (including *Oil and Water* and *The Battle at Elderbush Gulch*), and twelve in 1914 (including *Judith of Bethulia*, *The Battle of the Sexes*, and *Home Sweet Home*). Bobbie Harron's roles in the Griffith shorts were many and varied; like other company members, he jumped from bit part to lead and back again. He was a villain in *Fate* (1913, with Lionel Barrymore); a caveman in *Man's Genesis* and its sequel *Brute Force* (both 1912); a hillbilly peacemaker in *The Great Leap* (1914); and a demented sadist in *The Escape* (1914). Mostly, though, Bobbie played the homespun young lover, often one unjustly accused of a crime or cowardice. In the Gish sisters' film debut, *An Unseen Enemy* (1912), he charmingly played Lillian's boyfriend.

The slim, dark-haired Bobbie made a perfect, unthreatening leading man for the Valentine-like Griffith actresses. Among his more frequent female costars were Mary Pickford (eight films),

Bobbie Harron, still looking adolescent well into his twenties.

Lillian Gish (fifteen films), Dorothy Gish (five films), and Blanche Sweet (seven films). The prize, however, goes to the sweet-faced innocent Mae Marsh—she and Bobbie Harron co-starred twenty-seven times, from *Man's Genesis* (Marsh's 1912 debut) to *Sunshine Alley* (1917). Today, Bobbie Harron is best-known for his roles in Griffith's feature-length films. He worked in several capacities on *The Birth of a Nation*. As Lillian Gish later recalled, he served as one of Griffith's many assistant directors and "might play my brother in the morning, and in the afternoon put on blackface and play a Negro."

As Griffith moved from shorts to features, Bobbie Harron's career continued to rise. Griffith took Bobbie to Reliance-Majestic with him when he left Biograph in 1913, and later to Triangle in 1916. Possibly his best performance was as Mae Marsh's young husband in the modern sequence of *Intolerance* (1916). His role was not as showy as Marsh's or Constance Talmadge's, but Bobbie gave a delicate and amazingly natural performance as the young small-town man corrupted by the big city and redeemed by love. Only twenty-three when *Intolerance* was filmed, Bobbie Harron was already a brilliantly talented actor. The Harron-Marsh segment was later padded and rereleased as *The Mother and the Law*, in 1919.

Bobbie was very shy and soft spoken, avoiding interviews whenever possible. "Harron isn't a typical actor," one coworker said. "He is a regular boy. He will go to a football or a baseball game and have just as keen an interest about it as about a scene at the studio. He will be just as absorbed over the mechanism of an automobile as over the script of his next picture." One story—perhaps apocryphal—had a press agent showing Bobbie one of his newspaper clippings. Bobbie laughed at the comic strip on the back and never bothered to glance at his own notices. "He has always refused to be the hero in strutting fashion," said one of Bobbie's reviews. "He is as casual as a good movie." Fans made him nervous: "Don't know what to do with my hands when people begin to look at me," he all but blushed.

More and more people were looking at him: Success after success followed Bobbie Harron in the late 1910s. Another great role was as the soldier in love with Lillian Gish in *Hearts of the World* (1918). Along with the cast and crew, Bobbie sailed for Europe in May of 1918 through dangerous waters and filmed near the front lines before returning to the States. He looked very adult and dashing in his mustache and sideburns, and he gave a moving performance, holding his own against

By
FREDERICK JAMES SMITH

Biograph Company secured its minor employees by applying to the academy. In the course of events, Harron and a lad named Jimmie Smith were sent over to the Biograph studio by the good fathers. That was in 1907. They went to work in the film cutting room. Jimmie Smith is now Griffith's chief cutter.

Harron moved on to doing all sorts of odd jobs around the studio. Acting, however, was far from his thoughts.

"Then Griffith came," he says. "I remember those first days very well. At the start, he wrote scenarios and played as an extra. Then he developed to 'heavies' under the direction of Wallace McCutcheon's father, at that time a Biograph director. Soon he was given a chance to direct and, with his first picture, 'The Adventures of Dolly,' he established himself. That first picture was staged up near City Island, not far from the new Griffith Mamaroneck studios."

From the entrance of Griffith, fortune began to shape Harron's career. He was literally pushed into success. "That boy," as they called Bobbie, was pressed into service in tiny rôles. Lillian Gish once told us that her earliest memory of Bobbie was of a queer lad acting a bit and devoting the rest of the day to sweeping up and doing odd chores around the Fourteenth Street studio.

Harron takes himself far from seriously. He is a difficult subject to interview, for he simply wont talk about himself. Yet his story is a fascinating one, for he is a veritable prodigy of the photoplay

Thus it comes about that a mere boy can speak like a white whiskered patriarch about the screen's palmy days. For instance, he remembers when he "delivered films to a man named Loew running a little place over on Second Avenue." The man named Loew turned out to be Marcus Loew.

He remembers one decidedly interesting incident. It seems that the outer portals of the old Biograph studio were then guarded by an iron-willed feminine tartar who never relented an inch.

One day, David Griffith was coming down the studio steps when he heard the dragon saying in sugary tones, "But, honey, I cant!" Griffith paused in amazement and listened. Then another—and very girlish voice—protested. "How is he ever going to know whether or not he wants me when he isn't allowed to see me?" And then the dragon responded: "Well, dearie, I'll do what I can."

Right then and there Griffith says he decided to engage the unknown.

(Continued on page 71)

Bobbie Harron poses for a July 1920 *Motion Picture Classic* story.

both Gish sisters at their best.

Bad luck, however, also dogged the Harron family at this time. In December 1915 Bobbie's older brother Charles died in an auto accident. In November 1918, his nineteen-year-old sister Tessie—who had started a film career of her own—died during the Spanish flu epidemic. Several Harrons had gone into show business: Sisters Mary and Jessie made a few appearances, and brother Johnny became a successful character actor in the 1920s and 1930s.

Bobbie Harron shortly before his death.

Although Bobbie Harron is closely associated with D. W. Griffith, he did work for other directors as well. Christy Cabanne directed Bobbie in *The Great Leap* (1914, with Mae Marsh) and *The Rebellion of Kitty Belle* (also 1914, with Lillian Gish). Jack O'Brien directed *Her Shattered Idol* (1914), and Lloyd Ingraham directed *Hoodoo Ann* (with Mae Marsh, 1916). Other directors flocked to work with the talented and cooperative young leading man: Paul Powell (*The Wild Girl of the Sierras*, 1916), Chester Withey (*The Wharf Rat*, 1916), and John Noble (*Sunshine Alley*, a 1917 Goldwyn film, on loan-out).

One member of the Griffith company was closer to Bobbie than the rest, though: Dorothy Gish. The two spent much time together, and the company looked with amused affection at the blossoming romance. What was their relationship? Dorothy herself never spoke of it, but Lillian Gish later wrote that "It was a childlike love affair, but I think they had unspoken dreams of marrying." The Gishes and Bobbie would often go riding with young bit player Rudolph Valentino, whom Bobbie had befriended. But for all the romance with Dorothy, it was Lillian Gish Bobbie courted onscreen. The two were again lovers parted by the war in *The Great Love* and *The Greatest Thing in Life* (both 1918), and they played bucolic sweethearts in the charming small-town *A Romance of Happy Valley* (1919).

The Girl Who Stayed at Home (1919) added another costar to Bobbie's world:

Clarine Seymour played the title role, a showgirl named Cutie Beautiful who waits for her man to return from war. Later that same year, Clarine played a baby vamp who steals Bobbie away from Lillian Gish in *True Heart Susie*. Bobbie and Seymour worked together wonderfully, their dark, youthful exuberance making them the hottest team till Garbo and Gilbert met in the 1920s. Sadly, they only costarred twice; Clarine Seymour died in 1920, at the age of twenty-one.

Bobbie Harron's last film with Griffith was the odd, dark *The Greatest Question* (1919), with Lillian Gish. Some feel he was being ousted by Richard Barthelmess, who had already appeared in several Griffith films (most notably *Broken Blossoms*) and was being groomed for the male lead in *Way Down East*. When Bobbie died, some writer speculated that he was heartbroken at Barthelmess's usurping his career. But, actually, Bobbie's career was on the upswing when he and Griffith parted amicably. Bobbie Harron signed on with Metro early in 1920. He had his own company within the studio, with Griffith's financial and emotional support.

His first film under the Metro banner was *Coincidence*, a comedy costarring June Walker. In July 1920, *Motion Picture Classic* magazine ran an article stating that "Bobbie Harron is soon to be a star ... Dame Fortune has literally pounded upon the Harron doors and, finding no response, climbed in a window." His career was in no trouble—indeed, the decade to come seemed very promising for the twenty-seven-year old actor. By this time, he had moved to Los Angeles and bought a house which overflowed with Harrons. In late August 1920 he took a train to the East Coast for the New York premiere of *Way Down East*. It's a sign of how close he was with Griffith: Bobbie had not even appeared in the film but wanted to remain part of the "family."

The only account of Bobbie Harron's death came from Lillian Gish, who would certainly not have written anything reflecting badly on her old friend. According to her, Bobbie (who was staying at the Hotel Seymour) had bought a gun from a man who needed the money. "He had put the gun in the pocket of his dinner jacket and forgot about it," said Gish. Then, on September 1, "as he took his dinner clothes from the trunk, the gun had fallen to the floor and gone off." That sequence of events stretches plausibility a bit, but it's all we have. The bullet tore through Bobbie's right lung. He managed to summon the hotel's switchboard operator, who called an ambulance. He was rushed to Bellevue Hospital and placed in the prison ward, for possession of an unlicensed gun. A Metro employee paid his bail, and Bobbie's handcuffs and guard were removed; he was transferred to a normal room.

He lived four days. Again according to Lillian Gish, a Catholic priest asked him if the injury had been intentional; Bobbie assured him it was not a suicide attempt. Certainly a Catholic funeral would have been out of the question if Bobbie had killed himself on purpose. When Bobbie Harron died on September 5, 1920, the official certificate listed his death as accidental.

While most Griffith actresses went on to long and successful careers, the Griffith actors seemed cursed. Henry B. Walthall was reduced to playing small parts by the 1930s (you can spot him in *42nd Street* if you don't blink), and

Arthur Johnson died an alcoholic in 1916. Had Bobbie Harron lived, he would doubtless have given Richard Barthelmess and Charles Ray a run for their money in the 1920s. But he was fortunate enough to leave behind a handful of brilliant performances in films which will live forever.

May Irwin

Florence Lawrence is generally given the title of "the first movie star," but May Irwin—who only made two films—should really be given precedence. The jolly, roly-poly comedienne was the first stage star to appear in a hit film in the United States, even though that film was less than thirty seconds long.

The future film pioneer was born on June 27, 1862, in Whitby, Canada. She and her sister Flo sang in amateur shows and local pageants while still small children. That talent soon came in handy. "I went on the stage because I had to do something," May later recalled. "My father failed in business. He died soon afterward ... Money had to be earned, and we drifted naturally into the theatrical business. I was eleven years old when my mother took my sister and me to Buffalo to make our first appearance on the stage."

The young Irwin sisters worked their way up in vaudeville in the 1870s, making their first hit as a two-act at Tony Pastor's in New York. When May was twenty, in 1882, she was discovered by producer and director Augustin Daly, who determined to make a legitimate star out of her. "Mr. Daly told me he thought I was capable of better work, and I believed him," said May. "He said I was a diamond in the rough, and he implied that he would take off the rough." Sister Flo went off to a less successful career of her own, and she was still appearing in vaudeville until shortly before her death in 1930.

Under Daly's management for the next five years, May appeared in such shows as *Boys and Girls* (her first), *She Would or She Would Not*, *Red Letter Nights*, *After Business Hours*, *A Night Off*, and *Nancy & Company*. Among her costars were John Drew, Otis Skinner, and William Gillette. Legitimate theater, she said, "was hard for me, coming from Pastor's, where there was no discipline." Money was also a problem—vaudeville paid so well that May returned to it in 1887. She had to support two young sons, Harry and Walter, since her husband, Frederick Keller, had died the previous year. After another few years in vaudeville, May was signed by

Stage star May Irwin in the 1890s.

producer Charles Frohman, who—like Daly before him—saw star material in her. What was her particular appeal? "May Irwin is a personality rather than an artist," said writer Lewis Strang, "an entertainer more than an actress." Blonde haired and blue eyed, she was jolly and buxom, with a clear, strong alto singing voice. She was "untouched and untouchable by any of her imitators," according to *Variety*.

She didn't have a smash hit until

the 1894–95 season, with the comedy *The Widow Jones*, in which she popularized "The Bully Song." A pioneer in more than one medium, May recorded that number (the racist lyrics make it quite unplayable today, though another recording, "The Frog Song," is delightful and shows off her strong voice). *The Widow Jones* had a good run on Broadway and toured the country through the late spring of 1895. After a summer break, it re-opened in the fall for another successful run. Her costar was the blonde, mustachioed comic John C. Rice, who had also come up through vaudeville to legit.

By the spring of 1896, *The Widow Jones* was ready to wrap up its second season on Broadway and head off for another tour. At the behest of a theatrical reporter for the *New York World*, May and Rice went to Thomas Edison's now-dilapidated Black Maria film studio in West Orange, New Jersey, in mid–April 1896. The Black Maria had been constructed in late 1892, and the first-known American films were shot there early the next year. Edison employee Frank Gammon later recalled the difficulty in getting New York stage performers out to New Jersey "dressed in their thin silk costumes, as it was just like going out into an open field in midwinter." May wore a white frilly dress, Rice a plain dark suit.

Present at the shoot were William Heise and William Gilmore. Heise—who directed the shoot—had joined Edison as W. K. L. Dickson's assistant in 1890 and had helped devise a new camera. Gilmore acted as Heise's assistant. The performers rehearsed the scene several times: It was a comic kissing scene that had been a high point of the show. The scene was shot only once: As described by the Edison catalog, "They get ready to kiss, begin to kiss, and kiss and kiss in a way that brings down the house." That pretty much sums it up. The film has been listed as either forty-two or fifty feet long, and lasts less than half a minute.

It also gives modern audiences a turn: "Were they supposed to be *sexy*?" is the most-frequently heard remark. Well, no—May Irwin and John C. Rice were comics; they weren't supposed to be Greta Garbo and John Gilbert. Think, rather, of Bette Midler and Danny DeVito, or even Marie Dressler and Wallace Beery. Had this been a sexual, rather than comic, kiss, it never would have been distributed nationwide. And it was distributed. When *The Kiss* showed in San Francisco in May, one paper raved, "The figures were so large that one could almost tell what Rice was saying to May Irwin and what Miss Irwin was replying. The facial expression was the widow to a T, and ditto Rice, and the real scene itself never excited more amusement than did its vitascopic presentment, and that is saying much." *The Illustrated American* called the film "a formidable challenge to the legitimate drama."

May Irwin was the first star to draw audiences to film theaters: Through word of mouth and the few newspaper mentions, fans clamored to see the Broadway favorite onscreen. Copies of *The Kiss* circulated throughout the country, and by 1900, Edison replaced the worn-out prints with a new version, filmed with another cast. By that time, May Irwin had moved on with her career, having given *The Kiss* not a second thought. As famous as her appearance later became in retrospect, it was considered barely a blip, a publicity stunt, in the 1890s. Her film costar John C. Rice went on to enjoy a successful vaudeville career with his wife, Sally Cohen, and died in 1915.

Nearly every theatrical season for the next few years featured a successful May Irwin comedy: *The Swell Miss Fitzwell* (1897), *Kate Kip, Buyer* (1898), *Sister Mary* (1899), *The Belle of Bridgeport* (1900), *Madge Smith, Attorney*, and a revival of *The Widow Jones* (both 1901). She announced her retirement in 1902 and turned down an offer by Weber and Fields, but she returned with another smash hit, *Mrs. Black Is Back*, from 1904 to 1906.

May was a popular figure in the theatrical world, intelligent, well spoken, and as jolly offstage as on. When kidded about her increasing girth, she said, "I am glad to be known as a stout woman, for I like stout people ... Most lean persons give me the shivers." A smart businesswoman, she was worth $200,000 by 1898, attributing this to "hard work and horse sense ... I have always looked a long way ahead. I made up my mind years ago that I would be a star someday. I knew that my turn would come, and I was always preparing for it. And I made up my mind, too, that I should not work all my life. I know exactly when I shall retire from the stage and spend the rest of my life enjoying the fruit of my labor. And I mean to live in luxury."

May caused something of a scandal in 1907 when she married her thirty-nine-year-old manager of two years, the Viennese-born Kurt Eisenfeldt (May was forty-five at the time). But Eisenfeldt turned out to be a good manager and a good husband, and the marriage thrived. May played in vaudeville in 1907, toured Europe in 1908, and starred in a few more Broadway shows: *Getting a Polish* (1910), *Widow By Proxy*, and *33 Washington Square* (both 1913).

In 1914 May starred in her second and final film, a version of her stage play *Mrs. Black Is Back*. Filmed by Famous Players and released on November 30 through Paramount, it ran for four reels (about an hour in length). May, at fifty-two, played a "fair, fat and forty" mail-order bride trying to pass herself off as a sweet young thing in her twenties. There was much weight-loss and age-disguising comedy, as May also tried to pass off her grown son as the kitchen help. Finally, of course, her new husband (played by Charles Lane) learns to love her for herself. May only agreed to make the film because it was shot at her summer home in Clayton, New York. She didn't need the money and recognized that she was too old to begin a film career. *Mrs. Black Is Back* received polite reviews, but May was never tempted to make another film.

She finally retired to her farm in Clayton, an extremely wealthy woman (partially from investments in real estate). The only dark spots in her life were an unsuccessful attempt to open a theatrical summer home and a feud with her sister Flo. A gourmet cook, May had published the humorous book *May Irwin's Home Cooking* in 1904. Although she'd retired nearly twenty years earlier, her death on October 22, 1938, received a great deal of press notice. By this time, the film industry was old enough that her historic 1896 debut was given a good amount of space in her obituaries.

Despite all her success, May Irwin had few illusions about her career. "All the genius I have is work," she once said, "and all the luck is good, sound, common sense ... The stage has been good to me, and I am happy." Unlike some actresses, she'd had no desire for drama, no wish to tear her audiences' hearts: "I am a believer in comedy," she affirmed. "I think it is more beneficial, on the whole, than emotional or tragic plays. There cannot be too much laughter in the world."

ARTHUR JOHNSON

Arthur Johnson was one of the screen's first matinee idols—before Francis X. Bushman, before Maurice Costello. Johnson made his debut alongside D. W. Griffith and was his equal in dedication, if not talent: actor, writer, director. But his death in 1916 erased him from film history. Griffith called Johnson "matchless in everything—modern, romantic, comedy. He would have been a great film leader had he lived."

Arthur Vaughan Johnson was born in Cincinnati, Ohio, on June 1, 1876, the son of a pastor. His family moved to Davenport when Arthur was a child so his father could preside over Trinity Church. It was then that Arthur began showing an interest in the theater, much to his father's dismay: The boy was promptly packed off to military school. A few years later, the Johnsons relocated to Chicago, and there Arthur followed up on his ambitions, running away with a theatrical company. He made his stage debut at eighteen as Tybalt in *Romeo and Juliet.*

Arthur spent fourteen years onstage, from 1894 to 1908. But despite his dark good looks, hard work, and obvious talent, he never became a star. He continued acting in Shakespearean roles in William Owen's company and also supported stars Marie Wainright and Robert Mantell. He befriended ingenue Mary Pickford while in a Chicago company of *The Gentleman Burglar* with Jim Corbett; she was appearing in *The Warrens of Virginia.* Arthur was exposed to all kinds of roles: classics, comedies, period dramas, tragedy, and light farce. But by the time he'd reached his thirties, he realized his career had stalled.

In the summer of 1908, Arthur later recalled, "I had heard that the Biograph company wanted people, so I went down to their studio in New York City." As chance would have it, failed actor D. W. Griffith was planning his first directorial effort and was impressed with Arthur's good looks and background. "You're too tall," he told Arthur, "but if you could cut the heels off your boots you might do." Arthur demurred at ravaging his only pair of boots, but Griffith hired him nonetheless. He costarred with the director's wife, Linda

Arvidson, in *The Adventures of Dollie* (1908).

Arthur Johnson stayed with Biograph for three years, becoming the company's romantic lead (Henry B. Walthall was just as good looking, but he was nearly a foot shorter and was often assigned character parts). Arthur's costar in many of these films was buxom blonde Florence Lawrence. Among their appearances together were *The Bandit's Waterloo*, *The Red Girl*, *Where the Breakers Roar*, *The Vaquero's Vow*, *The Planter's Wife*, *After Many Years*, *The Test of Friendship*, the famed labor drama *The Song of the Shirt* (all 1908), *The Curtain Pole* (Mack Sennett's directorial debut), *The Drunkard's Reformation*, *Confidence*, Tolstoy's *Resurrection*, *Her First Biscuits* (Mary Pickford's film debut), and *The Way of All Man* (all 1909).

His other Biograph films included *The Gibson Goddess* (a 1909 comedy with Marion Leonard, Mack Sennett, and James Kirkwood), *The Unchanging Sea* (1910, with Arvidson), and *In Old California* (1911, with Walthall). But then he and Griffith came to a parting of the ways. In some aspects, they were too much alike to work together: Arthur, at thirty-six, was anxious to expand his duties into writing and directing. Griffith was not too thrilled with the idea, so Arthur moved on to the small, independent Reliance Studios, an arrangement that lasted only four months.

Later in 1911 Arthur found a happier home base, Philadelphia's Lubin Company. Lubin was run by the kindly, popular Sigmund Lubin, who'd made his first film in 1897. Lubin joined the Motion Picture Patent Company in 1909 and soon became a major, successful producer. Among the stars Arthur joined there were Lottie Briscoe, Ethel Clayton, Ormi Hawley, Earl Metcalf (who died in a freak airplane accident in 1928), and House Peters. By the mid-1910s, the company was joined by Yiddish star Jacob Adler, Anita Stewart, Earle Williams, dashing Crane Wilbur, Marie Dressler, and Evelyn Nesbit Thaw, the infamous "girl in the red velvet swing." Also on board was Arthur's wife, actress Florence Hackett; dark and rather unphotogenic, Hackett never broke through to stardom. Johnson's first costar, however, was his old friend Florence Lawrence, who had also been company jumping. The two costarred in forty-eight films in 1911 and 1912, including *His Friend, the Burglar* (their first), *The Two Fathers*, *The Fascinating Bachelor*, *That Awful Brother*, *His Chorus Girl Wife*, and *A Surgeon's Heroism* (their last, early in 1912).

The movies' first leading man, Arthur Johnson.

When Florence left Lubin for

Arthur Johnson, with frequent costar Florence Lawrence, in *Resurrection* (1909).

Victor, Arthur was teamed with pert, dark-haired Lottie Briscoe. The two became good friends, although Briscoe good-naturedly complained that her costar was a hard task master. His post–Lawrence films included *The Wooden Bowl* (a 1912 character role) and *The Burden Bearer*. He was already showing signs of the obsession for work which would lead to his downfall: When a reporter caught up with him in 1912, he had to literally chase the actor from office to office. "What do you do on vacations?" asked the reporter. "Don't take any," snapped Arthur.

Lubin gave Arthur Johnson what Griffith wouldn't: From 1914, he directed most of his own films, also writing many of them. Of course, Lubin insisted that Arthur stay in front of the camera as well; he had the same kind of dark, saturnine looks that Walter Pidgeon and Gregory Peck later used to their advantage. He worked hard in 1914, starring in (to name just a few) *Lord Lucy*, *Behind the Footlights*, *The Inventor's Wife*, *The Man with a Future*, *The Golden Hope*, and the enormously successful fifteen-part serial *The Beloved Adventurer*. Arthur's personal life wasn't going as smoothly; that June, Florence Hackett sued him for divorce, although she dropped the suit and the two remained married. At least one fan magazine said that the sympathies of the film community were on Mrs. Johnson's side, a surprisingly frank comment for 1914.

By the time Arthur made *Who Violates the Law* in May 1915, rumors of ill health were beginning to plague him.

Lottie Briscoe, interviewed at this time, said that "He is not a physically strong man. His spirit wears out his body." That summer, Arthur vanished from the screen and the Lubin lot. He turned up in Atlantic City, New Jersey, where he gave a revealing interview. "Please tell my friends that I had a nervous breakdown," he said. "Not a very serious one. I have been working very hard for the past few years and have needed a vacation. The doctors told me this some time ago, but it's hard for me to keep away from the studio…"

His prognosis was not good, as he told the departing reporter; "I expect to write a number of photodramas while I am taking it easy at the seashore." Arthur's first film upon his return in August was *Country Blood.* By December of that year he was back at the seaside, "recuperating from a dangerous illness." The nature of that illness remains frustratingly unclear after more than seventy years. Overwork, a nervous condition, and tuberculosis were mentioned during his lifetime. But in almost every posthumous article it is stated that Arthur Johnson was a chronic alcoholic. There is no contemporary evidence to either prove or disprove this; stars did not air their personal woes to the press in 1915. Arthur Johnson may or may not have suffered from alcoholism. It's doubtful we will ever know for certain.

In any case, he all but vanished from the screen, contenting himself with writing and trying to regain his quickly failing health. Arthur Johnson died in Philadelphia at the age of thirty-nine on January 17, 1916, of "tuberculosis and the effects of a recent accident," according to the press. The "accident" went unreported at the time and may well have been a polite evasion. His death certificate lists pulmonary trouble as the primary cause of death, though what led up to that remains a mystery. He was survived by his wife and young daughter (Florence Hackett Johnson died in 1954). The Lubin Company was out of business by 1917. And by the 1920s, Arthur Johnson was almost completely forgotten.

Alice Joyce

Alice Joyce was like the calm in the eye of a storm. No matter how vivid the plot she was given, no matter how harried or put-upon her character, there was always something ladylike and serene about the actress. "D. W. Griffith told me that I reminded him of a cow," she was fond of recalling. "So perhaps that accounts for my placid disposition." But she was hardly bovine; Alice Joyce was one of the silent screen's more intelligent and respected actresses.

She was born in Kansas City on October 1, 1890, the daughter of an Irish-French smelter and a Welsh seamstress. Alice's brother Frank also entered show business, eventually teaming up with Myron Selznick as an agent. Alice was educated at a convent in Annandale, Maryland, but took off for New York while still a teenager. Her first steady work was as a telephone operator, or "hello girl," as they were called then. Attempts to break into films came to naught; as we have seen, D. W. Griffith was far from impressed with her. But Alice's looks did get her much work as an artist's and photographer's model. According to film historian Dewitt Bodeen, Alice, Mabel Normand, and Anna Q. Nilsson were among the top supermodels of 1910.

She was lovely, in an odd way. Her eyes were her most noticeable features: brown, large, and unusually wide set. She had an aristocratic bone structure, a long nose, and an oddly shaped mouth, similar to Bette Davis's. In 1909 and 1910, Alice made good money posing for such top artists as Harrison Fisher, Charles Dana Gibson, and Neysa McMahon. In late 1910 the film studios came calling. Alice was signed by director Keanan Buel of Kalem, a thriving studio founded in 1907. Both director and studio are now long forgotten but, in the early 1910s, both were established workhorses. Alice was sent to Kalem's West Coast offices, where she began her career in westerns and outdoor adventures (the studio's specialty).

The actress later known for her roles in well-dressed society dramas spent the years 1911 through 1915 playing cowgirls (*Slim Jim's Last Chance* and *The Peril of the Plains*, both 1911), Spanish

Alice Joyce

maidens (*A Princess of the Hills* and *The Bell of Penance*, both 1912), gypsies (*Fantasca*, *The Gypsy*, 1912) and Indian maidens (*The Love of the Summer Morn* and *The Trail of the Pomos Charm*, her 1911 debut). Alice Joyce made an impressive 105 films for Kalem during those years, slowly gaining the loyalty and admiration of movie fans.

It wasn't all horses and six-shooters, of course; her roles increased in variety as time went on. Alice appeared as Betsy Ross (*The Flag of Freedom*, 1913), a crime-busting heiress (*In the Grip of a Charlatan*, 1913), an Orthodox Jew in love with a Christian (*The Pawnbroker's Daughter*, 1913), Lady Teazle in *The School for Scandal* (1914), and a chorus girl (*The Girl of the Music Hall*). But she was most popular in her society girl and heiress roles, and she was cast in more of those as her contract wore on. Alice had a serene, ladylike quality which made her stand out in even the most frenetic of films. A 1913 reporter called Alice "a woman of vast silences," adding that she was "not an easy person to interview. Unlike many of her sister artists, she shrinks from rather than courts publicity."

One of her most frequent leading men at Kalem was Tom Moore, brother of actors Matt and Owen Moore, and brother-in-law of Mary Pickford, Owen's wife. Alice and Tom were married in May 1914 while filming on location in Florida. When their daughter, Alice Joyce Moore, was born November 23, 1915, Alice opted to take a year's maternity leave. She and Moore moved into a large Long Island estate, and Alice settled down to become a mother and housewife.

In 1916 she told a visiting reporter that "This past year has been the happiest of my whole life. It is the first vacation I have ever had, and I had worked from eleven years ... But I'm getting restless now ... Motion picture work, to one who loves it and has been given measure of success, finds a place in one's heart that can never be taken by anything else." She also didn't like the idea of her husband being the only breadwinner in the house. "I could never be dependent," Alice insisted. "I believe every woman should have some work in life ... I could never see a gown in a Fifth Avenue shop window and then hurry home to ask the lord of the manor for the wherewithal to buy it."

Not surprisingly, Alice Joyce was ready to resume her career by the end of 1916. But during her retirement, Kalem had undergone reverses and been purchased by Vitagraph. Already twenty years old in 1916, Vitagraph was still at its peak, boasting such stars as Norma

Alice Joyce in *Cousin Kate*, 1921 (photograph: The Metaluna Collection).

Talmadge, Maurice Costello and his daughters Helene and Dolores, Anita Stewart, and Clara Kimball Young. It was at Vitagraph that Alice Joyce's career—and popularity—really took off. From 1916 through 1921, she starred in thirty-one feature films, all from five reels (about an hour) to nine reels (about 110 minutes). Most of Alice's Vitagraph films were directed by Tom Terriss, though she went through every director on the lot, from cofounder J. Stuart Blackton to Mrs. Sidney Drew to actor Edward José.

Vitagraph found Alice's specialty—heavy, tearful drama—and exploited it. Not until the 1920s was she given any films with even a hint of comedy (*The Sporting Duchess*, 1920; *Cousin Kate*, and *Her Lord and Master*, both 1921). Her audiences loved to see Alice in trouble, and that's what the studio provided. She made about six or seven films a year, appearing as put-upon heiresses, betrayed country girls, wronged fashion models, noble prisoners, and poor but honest working girls. Among her biggest Vitagraph hits were *Whom the Gods Destroy* (her first, 1916) and *Within the Law* (from a Broadway hit and novel, 1917).

For all her fame and popularity, Alice had a level-headed opinion of her own talents. "I'm not a great actress. I realize all that," she told a fan magazine at the height of her career. "I'm at my best in simple, direct roles—roles that avoid over-emotionalism." Most screen stars, she added, "simply play themselves—with now and then a moment of over-acting, called 'the big scene.' Perhaps that's why I love Mae Marsh. She lives a part." A smart woman, Alice saved her money and, in 1919, she opened the Hotel Joyce at 31 West 71st Street, New York. Divorced from Tom Moore, she married hotel magnate James Regan in 1920; their daughter Margaret was born in 1921. At that point, Alice left Vitagraph and was not seen onscreen for another two years. When she returned, it was as a freelancer, a risky business move. She starred in another sixteen silent films for nearly as many studios, big and small. Her comeback film, the adventure/romance *The Green Goddess* (1923), was a huge hit, which helped get her off and running.

She made *The Passionate Adventurer* in England in 1924, with a script by twenty-five-year-old Alfred Hitchcock. After several more films, Alice accepted a supporting part in *Stella Dallas* (1925, with Belle Bennett). She then settled in at Paramount for five successful films,

Alice Joyce in 1914.

all released in 1926. Probably her best was the ultrasophisticated *Dancing Mothers*, in which Clara Bow made an early hit as her flapper daughter. Alice played a society woman who walks out on her selfish family to live her own life—a very modern, feminist tale.

She next appeared in the rough-and-tumble *Beau Geste* and opposite W. C. Fields in one of her few comedies, *So's Your Old Man*. Her Paramount stint ended with *Sorrell and Son*, costarring Nils Asther and ill-fated Ziegfeld Girl Mary Nolan. In her last silents, all released in 1928, Alice played a snobbish society woman in *Washington Square* (Universal-Jewel), a noble governor's wife in *The Noose* (First National), and a rather eccentric mother in *The Rising Generation* (for the British Westminster company).

Alice Joyce was in her late thirties when talkies arrived, and hardly a flapper. *Photoplay* said of her in the mid-1920s, "She is what visitors from the provinces expect to see when they have luncheon at the Ritz or tea at the Plaza ... Money can't buy nor finishing schools bring the ease and grace of the Joycean type. You're either born that way or you're not." According to film historian Dewitt Bodeen, Alice prepared for talkies by touring with the play *The Marriage Bed*, saying that despite her fears, "friends like Gloria Swanson and Erich von Stroheim came backstage afterwards to praise me and say that I had nothing to be afraid of in talking films."

Alice's first talkie was *The Squall* (First National, 1929). It was not a propitious move. She starred as the warm and wise matriarch of a Rumanian family torn apart by evil gypsy Myrna Loy. Alice managed to turn in an intelligent performance, given the low quality of the script and the vague, meandering plot. She made only three more talkies, all for different studios. For Warner

Alice Joyce

Brothers, Alice appeared in a not-bad remake of *The Green Goddess* (1930), once again costarring George Arliss (who never seemed to get any older or younger). In *Song o' My Heart* (Fox, 1930), she played the mother of Maureen O'Sullivan. The schmaltzy sentiment and nonstop singing of costar John MacCormack gave this film a limited appeal. Finally, Alice played a society matron in a tea-cup drama called *He Knew Women* (RKO, 1930), with Lowell Sherman and David Manners. With that, the still lovely forty-year-old actress retired to raise her daughters, then nine and fifteen.

She and James Regan divorced in 1932, and the following year Alice wed MGM director Clarence Brown, best known for his seven films with Greta Garbo. That marriage lasted until 1945, after which Alice opted to stay single. She was hardly a social butterfly in her later years, but neither was she a recluse, showing up occasionally at parties and friends' dinners. Both her daughters married, and Alice socialized with her in-laws. But she was a name from the past, forgotten by the public and giving virtually no interviews. When she died of a heart attack on October 9, 1955, aging fans were startled to see her large-eyed face staring out at them again from newspapers for one last time.

Florence LaBadie

"No young artist of the screen is more widely known," said a fan magazine of a lovely blonde film star in 1916. That same Griffith-trained actress came in tenth in a popularity poll around the same time, below Mary Pickford and Theda Bara, but above Lillian Gish, Blanche Sweet, and Mabel Normand. Florence LaBadie was one of the most beautiful and talented actresses of her era, an enormously popular star. Yet today, more than eighty years after her death, most of her films are crumbled to dust, and her name is completely forgotten.

Florence LaBadie was born Florence Russ in Manhattan on April 27, 1888. Her mother, Marie Russ, gave her up for adoption (for unknown reasons) to Joseph and Amanda LaBadie, who raised her as a pampered only child. Educated at the Convent of Notre Dame, she became proficient in French and German, as well as excelling in painting and sculpture. She also became an accomplished athlete. Whether under the patronage of her parents or the nuns, Florence was soon an avid swimmer, rider, and all-around outdoor girl. With her thick golden hair and perfect features, she was the ideal Gibson Girl: healthy, sporty, and cheerful.

In 1908, when Florence and her parents were living on New York's Upper West Side, she began her acting career. Her debut was as a fairy in a touring company of *Ragged Robin*. The following year she appeared in *The Blue Bird*, toured in stock with future screen star Ethel Grandin, and worked as an artist's model and magazine cover girl. It wasn't long before the aspiring actress began arriving at local film studios looking for work.

Fellow actress Mary Pickford introduced Florence to Biograph's D. W. Griffith in the summer of 1909, where she picked up several bit parts. Pickford was a one-woman talent agent: She also ushered the Gish sisters into the studio. Although she spent a year at Biograph and was chosen to work on their periodic West Coast productions, Florence felt slighted. Griffith rarely gave her featured roles, and she found herself in competition with Pickford, Florence

Lawrence, Blanche Sweet, and two Dorothys (Bernard and West). Among her noticeable roles was as Bobbie Harron's sister in the two-reel *Enoch Arden* (1911). She also appeared in Biograph's *After the Ball*, *Her Sacrifice*, *Madame Rex*, *Bobby*, *The Coward*, and about a dozen other films.

By the summer of 1911, Florence decided it was time to look around at less-exalted but more-nurturing studios (indeed, had she stayed much longer, she'd have had the Gishes and Mae Marsh to contend with). Biograph was a "very seriously competing studio," she told a fan magazine—one of the few discouraging words heard about the legendary company. Florence took the train up to the three-year-old Thanhouser Film Corporation in New Rochelle, New York. Studio manager Dave Thompson gave her a polite brush-off, and she returned to Biograph.

But less than a month later, Edwin Thanhouser himself spotted Florence in one of her minuscule Biograph roles. He got in touch with her, and Florence had the supreme satisfaction of breezing successfully back up to New Rochelle. Florence was joining a very successful company. Thanhouser was known for filmed versions of classics as well as more popular fare; its stars included James Cruze, Harry Benham, Mignon Anderson, Irving Cummings, and Boyd Marshall—they even had their own dog star, Shep. Popular, charming Charles Hite—acting on behalf of an investment group—bought the studio from Edwin Thanhouser in 1912, and its fortunes continued to skyrocket.

Florence quickly became popular on the Thanhouser lot, especially with child actors Helen Badgely, Marie Eline, and the Fairbanks twins, to whom she read German and French fairy stories. "Ever since I was a little girl I have liked weird stories," said Florence, "queer, ghoulish creations of the brain, who were always doing miserable, unlooked-for, uncalled-for things." The reaction of the children's parents to these grisly bedtime tales was not recorded. One of Florence's closest friends was ingenue Muriel Ostriche, who also lived in Manhattan. "Each day we would take the train together from the 125th Street station," Ostriche told author Q. David Bowers in 1986. "She was a wonderful girl, a great actress, and my dearest friend at Thanhouser."

Among Florence's early Thanhouser films were *The Last of the Mohicans*, *The Baseball Bug*, and *Cinderella* (all 1911); *Dr. Jekyll and Mr. Hyde*, *Jilted*, *The Merchant of Venice*, *Through the Flames*, and as Mary in the biblical *The Star of Bethlehem* (all 1912); she later called this last role her favorite. Florence appeared in an impressive forty-five films in 1912 and another thirty-eight in 1913 (when her roles became bigger and her films longer).

Pearl White's *The Perils of Pauline*, while not the first action-adventure serial, was by far the most successful, and Thanhouser was quick to jump on the bandwagon. Early in 1914 Florence was given the leading role in the twenty-two-part *The Million Dollar Mystery*, cementing her position as her studio's top female star. She portrayed put-upon heroine Florence Gray and was joined by James Cruze and Marguerite Snow. Florence's daredevil tendencies came to the fore during filming. Although no stars did all their own stunts, Florence did as many as Charles Hite would allow her. She jumped from a speedboat while crowds cheered, later telling a

The lovely Florence LaBadie (The Metaluna Collection).

reporter, "I only remember I lost my breath when I struck the water. The rest of it was fine." She was also side-swiped by a car while filming a chase scene. Director Howell Hansell said, "If I were to say to her, 'Miss LaBadie, go and jump out of that window, there'll be someone down below to catch you,' she'd do it without even going to the window to look ... She's pure steel."

Florence herself elaborated. "If [I] were to go up in an aeroplane," she said in 1915, "and Mr. Hansell said he wanted me to fly upside down and drop within four feet of the earth and then right the machine, I'd feel that I had to do it." Was LaBadie afraid of anything, asked her somewhat dubious interviewer? "Snakes! Ugh! I detest them! When they brought out that Mexican gopher in the *Mystery*, I thought I'd die, and I plainly showed my fright."

The Million Dollar Mystery was a huge success—helped, perhaps, by a little audience participation: Viewers were invited to write in with a proposed ending. While the serial remained Florence's biggest success, she continued working steadily in starring roles and gaining critical raves as well as fan loyalty. Her press agent claimed that she received four hundred marriage proposals a month and sent a tiepin to every one hundredth suitor (Florence herself declined comment on this bit of PR fluff). She was popular on the set as well, though director Hansell sighed that "There's nobody who can give as many reasons for not ... being around when they're wanted as Flo LaBadie and Peggy Snow. I asked them the other day how they managed to have their excuses so ready, and Flo said they had a whole series of them numbered and that when they had tried No. 23 they would bring out No. 87, and so on; all peachy excuses."

Florence made another twenty-two films in 1915; among them were *The Six Cent Loaf* (as a poor factory worker), *God's Witness* (a four-part serial), *The Adventures of Florence,* and *Her Confession*. She continued to be a risk taker and daredevil; her pursuit of thrills seemed almost self-destructive at times. She occasionally rode a motorcycle to the studio, and she took aviation lessons on Long Island. She became known as "the hero of Coney Island" for her love of the scarier rides, and she laughed about being thrown from her horse while filming *Ward of the King*. "I'm crazy about swimming," Florence told another reporter. "I love to ride—fast! Anything with an element of danger in it appeals to me." One vacation Florence "improved by getting arrested for speeding."

In 1915, with her fame and salary

increasing, Florence and her parents moved to the St. Andrews Hotel on Broadway and 72nd Street. Around the same time, she began keeping company with Daniel Carson Goodman, a former medical student turned scriptwriter (who stole her away from former boyfriend, actor Hal Hush). She also added to her collection of pets, which by now included six dogs and a cat (the last sent to her—goodness knows how—by a young fan).

On August 22, 1914, Charles Hite, only thirty-nine years old, died in a car accident, shattering Florence LaBadie and the other Thanhouserites. Indeed, Florence cried for days and was useless before the camera. Edwin Thanhouser resumed ownership of the studio. Hite's death and the failure of the expensive serial *Zudora* put the studio on a slow decline, and it began releasing films via Pathé. Many stars jumped ship, but Florence stayed put. Among her latter-day films were *The Fugitive*; *The Pillory; Saint, Devil, Woman; The Five Faults of Flo* (a marital comedy); and a five-part "moral serial" called *Divorce and the Daughter*. In *The Fear of Poverty*, Florence played a dual role, which she called "exacting and wearing. A double exposure picture tests the actress as nothing else in pictures." More fun was the prison drama, *Her Life and His* (1917), which gave Florence the opportunity to wear a ragged tramp costume.

After nearly a decade of acting, Florence was still enthusiastic about her profession and was constantly praised for her talent as well as her looks. She did, however, find her career emotionally wearing at times. "Often when the next picture is presented I go to it with misgivings," she admitted. "But something gets in your blood and you play as

Florence LaBadie in a 1915 fashion spread from *Motion Picture* magazine.

you felt you could never play again." Unlike many stars, she admitted that she enjoyed watching her own films, and, "As silly as it may seem, I really have stage fright. I sit with my hands clenched and watch myself, seeing where I might have done better and longing to walk into the picture again and improve my acting."

Florence enjoyed her relations with the press and was called "an experienced interviewee" by reporter George Vaux Bacon. She teased and deadpanned through Bacon's 1916 interview. When asked about her favorite country, she smiled sweetly, "Iceland. I think the volcanoes and glaciers and sagas and things are perfectly sweet." Although Florence tried to steer clear of controversial issues, she did lash out in print against censorship and against one Rev. Albert Parker Finch, who called films immoral. She was forgiving of people who mispronounced her name, but drew the line at "la-body." "Sounds like a coroner's inquest," she shuddered. Turning serious when quizzed on her philosophy of life, she said, "I am an indifferentist. I don't care what happens," then brushed off the whole subject with a curt, "Life is too short for that sort of thing."

In April 1916 Florence signed a new star contract, and, that June, Edwin Thanhouser rewarded her loyalty by presenting her with a new car. Florence picked out an ivory Pullman coupe with brocade interior and rose-colored silk curtains. The press said that the car "was noted for its ease of control and beautiful motor." Florence promptly tested it out by taking off on a mountain vacation. As popular as she was, Florence had a realistic view of screen stardom. "Everyone should know how to do two or three things, so that if one should fail, one would have something to fall back upon." Florence herself took typewriting courses and spent three weeks in a booth training herself as a projectionist. By this time she was involved in the war effort, making patriotic films and encouraging rationing on the home front. "It's up to us all to help out during wartime," she said. "I am going to try and persuade every woman I know to have a vegetable garden this summer." She lectured for the Peace Society, showing slides of the front lines of France, and raised money for the Statue of Liberty Illumination Fund.

Florence made only thirteen films in 1916 and 1917, as Thanhouser began to wind down its operations. In the late summer of 1917, she appeared in a war drama called *The Man Without a Country*. Shortly after its completion, she and Goodman took off on a motor trip. On August 28, outside Ossining (about thirty miles north of Manhattan), the car's brakes failed on a hill. Some reports later said that Florence and Goodman were pinned under the wreckage, others said they were thrown free. The results were the same. Florence's injuries were mortal, but she didn't have the luxury of a quick death. She lingered painfully in the hospital for two months before succumbing to internal injuries on Saturday afternoon, October 13, 1917. She is buried in Brooklyn's Green-Wood Cemetery.

Goodman survived the wreck (he went on to marry and divorce another ill-fated actress, Alma Rubens). Another victim was Thanhouser. The company, which had been crippled by Charles Hite's death, found the loss of its biggest star a fatal blow. Less than a year after Florence LaBadie's death, Edwin Thanhouser sold the studio, and it ceased production.

Max Linder

Although primarily a European film star, Max Linder had a profound effect on American comedy. Indeed, many routines he originated were shamelessly lifted by Charlie Chaplin, Laurel and Hardy, Abbott and Costello, and Lucille Ball, among others. But Linder did them first and, some feel, best.

Gabriel "Max" Leuvielle was born on December 16, 1883, in a beautiful little village near Bordeaux; his parents ran a successful vineyard there. The rebellious, energetic Max was sent to boarding school, where he discovered his love of sports, girls—and the theater. In 1902 he enrolled in drama school and began making the rounds of local theaters. He joined various regional companies and eventually made his way to Paris as a classical actor. Despite his talent, athletic physique, and youthful good looks, his height—5'2"—and his irrepressible mischievousness ruled out a career as a serious stage actor. Like many another future star, he posed for postcards (where his height didn't matter). He briefly acted with the Théâtre des Variétés, but "he turned heavy drama into high comedy," as his daughter later said. "The audience was delighted, but the director wasn't the least bit pleased."

By 1905 Max (adopting the stage name "Linder") entered the film industry, already booming in France. He signed on with Charles Pathé. Daughter Maud Linder claims his first film was *Learning to Skate*, though Jack Spears, in his superb *Films in Review* article, claims that Max's debut was actually *The Collegian's First Outing*. Regardless, Pathé was quite happy and signed Max on to act in more comedies. Despite his status as a comic, Max was much handsomer than most leading men, sort of a pocket Errol Flynn. Soon Max Linder was starring in, writing, and directing his own films. By 1907 he'd hit upon the screen character which skyrocketed him to international fame: Max, the dapper but hapless boulevardier in impeccable morning coat and silk topper.

Amazingly, some of these films were made in as little as one day—even Mack Sennett rarely matched that record for speed. Max was as talented and subtle a director as he was an actor. It's

The ever-dapper Max Linder.

impossible to believe how haphazard filming was, but he later claimed, "I told my story to the actors, I acted it out, I explained it—we rehearsed it once, and then we shot." More thought must have gone into his films, for his camera angles, sets, and lighting were far superior to anything being done in America at the same time. In an amazing three hundred sixty films over the next eight years, he wrote the emerging language of silent comedy. The titles are self-explanatory: *Max Takes a Bath* (an extremely funny and risqué 1906 film); *Max in a Dilemma* (a great 1910 success); *Max Is Afraid of Dogs* (a one-joke film perhaps, but a very good joke); *Max's Duel* (fought with swords on horseback in a parlor); *Max on Skis* (as athletic as any of Douglas Fairbanks's films). He worked particularly well with animals, as in *Max and His Dog* (1912), in which the pup unmasks his mistress's affairs.

Despite his film success, Max didn't completely give up the stage, making personal appearances in sketches to appreciative crowds. He was also happy to share the spotlight with other acts which he'd discovered and nurtured (Maurice Chevalier appeared in one of Max's early films, as did future director Abel Gance). Before talkies, movies were a universal language, and Max became a popular star worldwide. In the early 1910s he made hugely successful tours of Spain, Italy, Greece, Germany, and Russia, using the opportunities to film on-location comedies (of particular historic interest today). *Max the Toreador* was filmed at an actual bullfight, and was very funny—at least until the bull is gruesomely killed. In a bizarre film made on the Riviera, Max's shoes fall in love with those of a female guest, through the magic of trick photography.

Many of Max Linder's short comedies rate alongside the best of Keaton and Lloyd. *Max Doesn't Speak English* was a brilliant, subtle piece of screen acting: He and an English girl communicate by scrawling pictures on a notepad, creating a touching and believable love story in only a few minutes of screen time. *Max Takes a Rest* was filmed in his childhood villa and costarred his parents and sister. It's a charming bucolic romp, worthy of Griffith's better comedies. In *Max and the Lady Doctor*, the patient becomes a very impatient and jealous husband.

Max was not shy about his success. "My salary on my last trip to Russia was 3,000 francs a day for two months," he bragged to a reporter in the summer of 1914. "This year I go abroad for 80,000 francs a month. My next Russian trip brings me in 120,000 francs for a single month." He added that he was not going to renew his current Pathé contract because "I can do much better." Settled happily on his large estate in Varennes, he was "The King of Europe's Movies," the world's highest-paid film star.

Then came World War I. Max enlisted in September 1914 and was seriously wounded three times—he was hit by shell fire in the battle of the Marne, hit by machine-gun fire in the battle of the Aisne, and suffered a collapsed lung while in France's primitive air force. He nearly died, spent much time in hospitals, and his emotional and physical health began declining from this point. This period also marked the rise of Charlie Chaplin, Max's chief rival. While Max was (much later) called "the French Chaplin," the comparison doesn't hold up. Chaplin called himself Max's disciple, but his comedy was both more maudlin and crude than Max's ever was. If Chaplin was a sad little clown, Max was a puppy dog with a rag in its mouth.

Max Linder

Still recuperating from his war wounds, Max made a trip to America in 1917 at the behest of Essanay Studios. This trip resulted in three films costarring starlet Martha Early, who later went on to fame as Martha Mansfield. *Max Comes Across*, *Max Wants a Divorce*, and *Max and His Taxi* (all 1917) did well, but not well enough to keep Max in the United States. None, sadly, have survived. He returned, physically worn out, to Europe, where he entertained

Max Linder mugging furiously in *Max Comes Across* (1917).

troops and eventually returned to films (*The Little Cafe*, 1919).

A second trip to America was more successful, resulting in *Seven Years Bad Luck* (1919). This is probably his best-known feature and contains the famous fake-mirror sequence later used by the Marx brothers and Lucille Ball. He designed the costumes for his next film, *Be My Wife*, and gave interviews in hilariously fractured English, while he attempted to learn the language. Max settled down happily in Hollywood, befriending Chaplin and Fairbanks, throwing parties, and buying an impressive home. He made a few more films, the best of which was probably *The Three Must-Get-Theres* (1922), a delightfully absurdist parody of Douglas Fairbanks's hit, *The Three Musketeers*—the good-natured Fairbanks loaned sets and costumes. Once again, Max's fragile health forced him to return to his native country.

Max never suffered a shortage of female companionship, but he didn't marry until 1923, at the age of forty. His bride was a teenaged model and actress, Helene Peters. Despite his apparently happy marriage, his health continued to decline, and he suffered from increasing depressions. As Spears reports in his *Films in Review* article, there were rumors of suicide attempts. A yellowed and crumbling news clip in Max's Lincoln Center file reports Linders's recovery from "accidental" overdoses of barbiturates. Max built his own theater in Paris and was named President of the Association of Filmographers. But the next Max Linder film wasn't until 1924's *Au Secours!*, a feature-length comedy with dark overtones of horror and tragedy. Significantly, Max no longer felt up to directing himself: Abel Gance took over. Another long hiatus ended with *The King of the Circus* (1925), a comedy filmed in Vienna. That summer, he started working on another film, *Le Chevalier Barclas*, with René Clair assisting. It was never completed.

On October 30, 1925, Linder checked into a Paris hotel with his young wife and baby daughter. After taking morphine, Linder slashed his wife's wrists and his own. They died a day later. Although two suicide notes were found, Helene's degree of enthusiasm for the final act was never determined. "There was never any real explanation for this tragedy," his daughter said decades later, "and I have never tried to find one." In 1983 Maud Linder compiled and narrated a loving tribute to her father (*The Man in the Silk Hat*), which is available on video. It took her decades of legal wrangling and searching through flea markets and attics for crumbling films. She managed to save eighty-two. Hers is a great gift to her father: His surviving films reveal him to be a comic genius, his routines holding up wonderfully after nearly a century.

Ormer Locklear

One of the most touching moments in Kevin Brownlow and David Gill's 1979 documentary *Hollywood* came when actress Viola Dana reminisced about her romance with actor and stunt pilot Ormer Locklear. "He had green eyes, too, and I want to tell you, we looked at each other ... and that was it. I guess we fell in love immediately." More than fifty years had passed since Locklear's death, but Dana's eyes welled up as she said brokenly, "I don't even like to talk about it," and turned from the camera. Ormer Locklear has vanished from film history; it's nearly impossible to find him mentioned in books on the silent screen. Art Ronnie's superb 1973 biography (*Locklear: The Man Who Walked on Wings*) is long out of print. His is an undeserved anonymity, for Ormer Locklear was one of the era's most electric and fascinating characters.

Ormer Leslie Locklear was born into a large Scottish-Irish family on October 28, 1891, in Greenville, Texas. He was a daredevil from an early age, regularly risking his neck in youthful escapades. He married Ruby Graves, a Texas girl, in 1915, but his bride proved unsuitable for such a roustabout. Locklear delighted in pushing cars, motorcycles, and airplanes to their limit, and he was soon pushing his bride to hers. When the United States entered World War I in 1917, the twenty-six-year-old Ormer wasted no time in enlisting. Although he never left the flying fields of Texas, Ormer soon made lieutenant and began his romance with stunt flying. By the time the war ended in late 1918, Ormer Locklear had mastered wing walking and was the first recorded person to leap from plane to plane during flight. "When I'm standing on the plane," he enthused, "the wind is so strong that I can lean against it just as if it were a brick wall."

Despite his wife's entreaties, Ormer was not about to ground himself after the war. Along with stunt pilots [Mr.] Shirley Short and Milton Elliott, he criss-crossed the country. In barnstorming shows and county fairs, Ormer made headlines, perfecting his wing-walking stunts. He was on the cutting edge of the stunt craze of the Roaring Twenties, which included everything from flagpole

Ormer Locklear, ready for action (Art Ronnie).

sitters to human flies. By the summer of 1919, Ormer Locklear's national press had reached the notice of Hollywood, and he flew west to consider offers. Ruby Locklear remained in Fort Worth. The marriage had proven a failure, but Ruby refused her husband a divorce.

Ormer Locklear descended on the rough-and-tumble Hollywood of 1919 like a whirlwind. Tall, slim, sexy, and athletic, Ormer's brash personality made him an instant hit with the younger set, who lined up for airplane rides. Studio heads and stuffier residents turned their

Ormer Locklear in *The Great Air Robbery*, 1919 (Art Ronnie).

noses up at his antics, but actress Leatrice Joy recalled, "He took all the stars up. I succeeded very tactfully in avoiding him ... I was havin' too much fun on earth!" He eventually charmed Joy into a flight in "a little crackerbox, so help me heaven." Misunderstanding Joy's frantic gestures of dismay, Ormer spun her delightedly into a "falling leaf" maneuver, telling her, "'You're the only one who asked for the falling leaf!" "I didn't have the heart to tell him that was my sponge I was throwin' in," Joy later laughed. He also became close friends with Jack Pickford, one of the most self-destructive and irresponsible residents of Los Angeles. Pickford was hardly a good influence.

Around the same time, Ormer met actress Viola Dana, a popular twenty-two-year-old Metro star. The two fell madly in love, and much of their romance was airborne. "We'd chase our friends down Hollywood Boulevard," she recalled for Brownlow and Gill. "I guess I've done everything in a plane that's to be done—one day we did 25 consecutive loops ... We'd go between telegraph poles under the wires." The two buzzed friends on the highway, tossing Dana's old lipsticks at them. Dana and Ormer were soon known around town as a couple; only Ruby stood in the way of their marriage.

Ormer modestly described himself as "homely as a mud fence, and I've only got two or three strands for hair." Actually, he had an athlete's physique, great camera bones, and a dazzling smile. His thinning hair mattered little under a dashing flight helmet. Universal signed Ormer to start shooting his first film, *The Great Air Robbery*, in the summer of 1919. Ormer played United States mail pilot Larry Cassidy, in love with debutante Beryl Carruthers (Francelia Billington) and pursued by the wicked Chester Van Arland (Ray Ripley). The film, of course, made liberal use of Ormer's airborne stunts.

Never one to sit still for a moment, Ormer (accompanied by Short and Elliott) was off performing in air shows as soon as filming wrapped. *The Great Air Robbery* opened just as 1919 became 1920. It proved quite popular: The press praised not only the plot and pacing but the handsome leading man as well. With the ailing Wallace Reid's career slowing down, the industry had a new rising star on its hands. Ormer's impact was much the same as Errol Flynn's when *Captain Blood* opened fifteen years later.

Surprisingly, Universal didn't pick up Ormer's option. Perhaps his offscreen antics worried them (besides his extramarital affair with Dana, he'd nearly gotten himself arrested for mischievously buzzing a Los Angeles parade). William Fox, however, snapped him up, signing Ormer in the spring of 1920 to star in *The Skywayman* (his costars were Louise Lovely and Sam De Grasse). Ormer portrayed Norman Locke, an amnesiac flyer who becomes involved in a gang of jewel thieves. At the film's close, the emotionally distraught Locke attempts suicide in a crash dive and—in an unlikely turn of events—not only survives but regains his memory, winding up in Louise Lovely's arms.

Ormer enjoyed acting, although no one claimed he was a Barrymore waiting to happen. He was tired of local fairs and wing walking for crowds. Biographer Ronnie states that Fox did not have another film waiting for him and that Ormer was extremely depressed at the prospect of a return to barnstorming. On the night of August 2, 1920, Ormer (with co-pilot Elliott) was scheduled to film one last stunt, the suicide dive. An oil field on what is now Wilshire Boulevard and Third Street was chosen for the site. Most of the cast, and girlfriend Viola Dana, showed up to watch Ormer's "death dive." Both Dana and Jack Pickford wanted to go along on the ride but weren't permitted.

Dana recalled that Ormer "said to the director, 'when I get down to the level of the oil wells, take the lights off me, and I'll know where I am. I can come out of it.' And he went into the tailspin and they never took the lights off him ... I guess there was practically nothing left of him, because those Jennies, you know, were very fragile. I started to run for the plane and somebody said, 'Grab her!' I guess I was kinda crazy. I couldn't believe what had happened. When you're young, those things are very shocking..."

Ormer Locklear's *Variety* obituary reported that the fatal footage was promptly exhibited in theaters to avidly morbid fans. After noting that Mrs. Locklear was on her way west to claim her husband's remains, the article added coyly that "Locklear had been a great favorite in the film colony here, and one noted screen actress has donned mourning because of his death." *The Skywayman* opened around the country in early September, one of the first times a star appeared posthumously to the public—though far from the last. Ormer Locklear was buried in Texas and was promptly forgotten by the film industry and his fans. There were so many tragedies in the opening years of the decade: William Desmond Taylor, Olive Thomas, Roscoe Arbuckle and Virginia Rappe, Wallace Reid, Martha Mansfield, Bobbie Harron, Clarine Seymour ... Viola Dana married twice, but never really got over Ormer Locklear. No prints of his two films are known to have survived.

Douglas MacLean

When the comic greats of the silent screen are discussed, the "big three" always head the list: Chaplin, Keaton, and Lloyd. Close on their heels are Laurel and Hardy, Harry Langdon, Mabel Normand and others. But virtually forgotten today is Douglas MacLean, who starred in nearly thirty comedies in the 1920s, most of them for Paramount and First National. His acting career ended with the talkies, and MacLean went on to even greater success as a producer and writer. But his success as an actor is not to be sneezed at.

Douglas MacLean was born in Philadelphia on January 10, 1890, though his family moved to Dixon, Illinois, when Douglas was a teenager. His father, a minister, was a friend of President McKinley, and young Douglas became a pet of Mrs. McKinley's. "I remember very well the stories she used to tell me," he recalled, adding that he used to sit atop the head of her white bearskin rug. Planning to become a mechanical engineer, Douglas went to Northwestern University and the Lewis Institute of Technology in Chicago. He eventually drifted into bond sales. While vacationing with a friend in New York, Douglas met producer Daniel Frohman, who kindled an interest in acting. Douglas enrolled at the American Academy of Dramatic Arts, while his father sighed that "three months would cure him." Instead, it started Douglas on a whole new path. After his graduation, Frohman cast the young actor in small roles, supporting Maude Adams in *Peter Pan*, *The Legend of Lenore*, and *Rosalind*. He acted in stock companies in Los Angeles and Pittsfield, Massachusetts, and played opposite Alice Brady in his first film, *As Ye Sow* (1914).

He met fellow stock player Faith Cole, playing a love scene with her before even being introduced. The two dated for three months, then married on a Wednesday—traditionally matinee day in the theater, but Faith's "lucky day." "We went out to her home on Long Island," Douglas later recalled, "where my father married us, and then I had to hurry back for my evening performance." Douglas was making only $35 a week, which troubled his new in-laws. "Our parents didn't object greatly, though Father Cole did think it his duty to make a mild remonstrance. But we won him over."

Perhaps it was this new family responsibility that impelled Douglas to go into films, where a steadier income was possible. Paramount's Thomas Ince cast him in a small role in *Fuss and Feathers* (1918), after which William Desmond Taylor picked him to support Mary Pickford in *Captain Kidd, Jr.* and *Johanna Enlists* (both 1918). Douglas worked in several undistinguished films, including *The Hun Within* (with Dorothy Gish, 1918) and *The Home Breaker* (1919) before his big break came.

In 1919 Douglas starred as a sailor in *23½ Hours Leave*, costarring eighteen-year-old Doris May. The film was a huge hit, and Paramount signed Douglas to a long-term starring contract. He made another five romantic comedies with May, many directed by Lloyd Ingraham: *What's Your Husband Doing?* (1919), *The Jail-Bird*, *Let's Be Fashionable,* and *Mary's Ankle* (1920), and *The Rookie's Return* (1921). Ince spoke of MacLean's winning screen persona and films, the "high spirits, the rollicking humor, the reckless dare-deviltry of our young hero and heroine." By 1921 one reporter stated that "Mr. MacLean has established himself as a star of the first screen magnitude."

He was certainly handsome enough to be a leading man, but he chose the comedy route. His screen character was not unlike that of Harold Lloyd: the all–American go-getter, brash but skittish, trying to win the girl, the job, or just to get out of trouble. His studio dubbed him "The Man with the Million-Dollar Smile." Trouble was rumored between Douglas and his costar, which he went so far as to refute in a newspaper story. "Doris is one of our best friends," he insisted. "She is coming to visit Mrs. MacLean and we are looking forward to showing her New York. She is like a child and will be so enthusiastic over everything." The MacLean-May partnership ended in 1921, and he was never teamed with another actress for more than a film or two.

Douglas MacLean, "The Man with the Million-Dollar Smile."

Like Lloyd and Buster Keaton, MacLean was an architect of comic scenes and made himself useful behind the camera. A mechanic at heart, he told a reporter that "There's no such thing as a pretty good bridge or a pretty good comedy. The test of a bridge is to stand up, and the test of a comedy is just as direct: it's got to make people laugh. An audience can go away from a dramatic picture and say, 'Oh, it was fair,' but if a comedy doesn't make them laugh, it is a failure." He even built and designed sets to help the gags along. "Laughs are like firecrackers," he said. "The fuse must be just the right length and they must be thrown just at the right time. You have to build sets to key with the action." Douglas's "help" was not always appreciated by the crew.

From 1922 through 1929, Douglas starred in fourteen films, mostly released through First National or Paramount (he also had a cameo appearance as himself in *Mary of the Movies*, 1923). He played modern, peppy go-getters in such long-forgotten comedies as *The Hottentot* (1922, with Madge Bellamy), *Bell Boy 13* (with Margaret Loomis, 1923), *The Yankee Consul* (with Patsy Ruth Miller, 1924), *Hold That Lion* (with Margaret Morris and a horde of tame lions, 1926), and *Let It Rain* (as another sailor on leave, 1927). One of his few films adapted from a stage hit was a 1925 remake of George M. Cohan's comic thriller, *Seven Keys to Baldpate*.

Douglas's films were not slapstick comedy; he liked to think out story lines and characters. "Make your audience feel superior to you," was one of his rules, "but don't let them feel superior to the picture. I don't try to make my pictures 'comic.' I try to make them entertaining. I try to put humor into them, not obvious comedy." It's not surprising that when talkies arrived, the thoughtful "architect" Douglas MacLean decided to move behind the camera, never missing the thrill of acting. "I was always planning to quit acting next week or at the very latest the week after next," he said. While he had a large and loyal audience, Douglas MacLean never achieved the cult standing of his contemporaries Keaton or Lloyd.

Douglas MacLean toward the end of his acting career (The Metaluna Collection).

After appearing in one talkie, *Divorce Made Easy* (1929, also released in a silent version), Douglas put away the greasepaint and became a writer and producer, first for RKO, then Paramount. He supplied stories for Wheeler and Woolsey's *Caught Plastered* and *Cracked Nuts* (both 1931), and the Mary Boland–Charlie Ruggles comedies *Mama Loves Papa* (1933) and *Six of a Kind* (1934). In 1932 Douglas made his debut as a producer, with *Ladies of the Jury*. He produced a total of eight films for Paramount, including *Tillie and Gus* (with W. C. Fields, 1934), *Ladies Should Listen* (also 1934, with young Cary Grant and "Clara Lou" Sheridan, later re-named Ann), and *Accent on Youth* and *Two for Tonight* (both 1935). He moved later to Grand National, producing *Great Guy*

(1935, with James Cagney and Mae Clarke), and finally a remake of his early success *23½ Hours Leave* (1937), starring James Ellison in his old role.

Douglas thoroughly enjoyed himself. "Producing is fascinating and delightful," he said. I still am an actor, playing the scenes vicariously. And, in addition, I follow the production through from purchase of the story to arrangements for advertising and distribution. It's a perfect set-up." When working with the high-strung stage great Pauline Lord in *Mrs. Wiggs of the Cabbage Patch* (1934), Douglas put her at ease by hugging her and calling her "Toots." "It became a gag line," he recalled. "Every time things went wrong thereafter, someone would call her Toots. She liked it. Miss Lord's a grand trouper."

After his marriage to Faith Cole ended, Douglas wed again in 1931. This marriage, too, failed, as did his third, to actress Barbara Barondess, which lasted from 1938 to 1946. Douglas MacLean retired from film producing in 1937, not yet fifty years old. Through the 1940s and 1950s he freelanced, writing for films and television, but his time as a "player" was over. He suffered a stroke in 1962 and died at his Beverly Hills home on July 9, 1967, at the age of seventy-seven. His obituaries lauded him more as a producer, mentioning in passing that "He'd once been an actor."

Douglas MacLean himself would probably be just as happy that his work as a producer and writer survives, rather than his work as an actor. His films for Wheeler and Woolsey, W. C. Fields, and Mary Boland and Charlie Ruggles live on in TV and video. But his starring films, once so enjoyed and anticipated, are mostly gone and forgotten. Only his photos remain: That million-dollar smile, the flashing eyes, athletic build, and strong hands give some hint that here was an actor worth watching.

Martha Mansfield

Something about Ziegfeld Girls seemed to invite tragedy, in a "beautiful and damned" scenario. Olive Thomas poisoned herself in France. Allyn King threw herself from a window. Hilda Ferguson died of heart failure at thirty. Edith Carper died of carbon monoxide poisoning on the eve of her first show. Bessie Poole died in a speakeasy fight. Lillian Lorraine, May Day, Jessie Reed, Kay Laurell, and others ended up broke and alone. But perhaps the most horrific finale was that of poor Martha Mansfield, who burned to death at the dawn of a promising film career.

She was born Martha Ehrlich in Mansfield, Ohio (thus her stage name) on July 14, 1899. It's not clear if her father, Morris Ehrlich, died or was divorced, but by 1911 or 1912, Martha and her mother, the former Harriet Gibson, were living on 158th Street in the Bronx, north of Manhattan. "When I was 14 years old I made up my mind that I should become an actress," Martha said in 1920, "and therefore immediately went to see Mr. [William] Brady, who was at the time casting for *Little Women*. He poked fun at me because I was so young and earnest and finally told me that I would receive notice at the end of the week if he wanted me." Eventually, Martha was cast in that 1912 Broadway show (which starred Brady's daughter Alice), but in a small role, as a boy.

Martha also began getting work as an artist's and photographer's model, becoming quite successful in the mid–1910s. Commercial photographer Alfred Cheney Johnson took more than three hundred photos of her, and she was a favorite of illustrator Harrison Fisher. Speaking of her modeling career, Martha said that "I tired of this within a year's time. It was so inactive and did not call for the use of one's facilities. I wanted to be more than a mere doll. So I got a small part as one of Hop's brothers in the pantomime *Hop o' My Thumb*" (1913, starring DeWolf Hopper). Martha continued working on Broadway, in such shows as *The Century Girl* (1916) and *On with the Dance* (1917). "I was at the Century Theater when Hazel Dawn told me that a girl of just my type was wanted for a star part in a new picture,"

Martha later recalled. French comic Max Linder had just come to the United States and signed with Essanay to make three films. He'd wanted Dawn to appear with him, but she was unable to break previous contracts. She recommended her friend Martha.

Billed as Martha Early, she co-starred with Linder in the comedies *Max Comes Across*, *Max Wants a Divorce*, and *Max and His Taxi* (all 1917). The films received a polite reception but not enthusiastic enough to keep Linder in America. In 1919 Martha told *Motion Picture Classic* that filming with Linder "really was lots of fun. We had many a picnic out of it—and much exasperation, too" (due to Linder's lack of English skills and Martha's equal ignorance of French). Linder had been directing and acting in films since 1905, and despite the language problem, he and Martha clicked. Getting her feet wet in films, Martha noted that "I learnt then and have seen since that a good director is everything. You can rave a great deal about a movie actress's beauty and charm and vivacity, but if she is without intelligence, a spark of imagination, and a sympathetic director to bring it all out, she is nothing and will never get anywhere on the screen."

Martha Mansfield in 1920.

In the meantime, though, she returned to the stage. She became a glorified Ziegfeld Girl with the *Follies* of 1918, also appearing in Ziegfeld's rooftop *Midnight Frolic* of 1918 and both the *Frolic* and the *Nine O'Clock Revue* in 1919. Martha would get out of work at 2:00 A.M. and—42nd Street stage-door Johnnies notwithstanding—take the subway home to the Bronx. She also made the occasional film, such as the Northwest drama *Broadway Bill* (1918, with Harold Lockwood), *The Hand Invisible*, *Should a Husband Forgive?*, and a Fox film with Miriam Cooper. There may have been others; her shifting billing—Martha Ehrlich, Early, or Mansfield—makes her hard to pin down.

Martha was still appearing in the *Frolic* when she was cast in the Paramount production of *Dr. Jekyll and Mr. Hyde*, starring John Barrymore. Filmed in late 1919 and released in April of 1920, it was Martha's big break—she portrayed the innocent, menaced fiancée of Dr. Jekyll, while fellow showgirl Nita Naldi played the more colorful vamp role. "I'll tell you something funny," Martha said to a reporter during filming. "I have been kissed in the first scene of every picture I have made. I thought that record would be broken in the *Dr. Jekyll and Mr. Hyde* picture. But no—in the very first part Mr. Barrymore had to kiss me." Immediately on finishing *Jekyll and Hyde*, Martha followed up at

Martha Mansfield (The Metaluna Collection).

Paramount, playing a Salvation Army lass in the war drama *Civilian Clothes* (1920), costarring Thomas Meighan. While filming in Cuba, she worked in mud-filled trenches and said that "If this is the sort of life the soldier boys had to live through during the war, then God bless them for coming out of it."

In June 1920 Lewis J. Selznick signed Martha to be groomed as an "understudy" for his biggest star, Olive Thomas (ironically, Thomas would be dead within three months). Martha Mansfield seemed like star material. Dark haired and blue eyed, she had soft, almost childlike features, rather resembling her contemporaries, Mary Miles Minter and Marguerite Clark. She gave typically fluffy starlet interviews to the press: "I like work and even if it is rough I enjoy it just the same," she said prettily. "I am very fond of all kinds of sports, especially horseback riding. I am a very poor swimmer, which I do not like to admit, and some time I am going to sneak off by myself and learn." For Selznick, she appeared in four films: She costarred with Eugene O'Brien in *Gilded Lies* and *The Last Door* (both 1921) and *The Wonderful Chance* (1922), and she played a supporting role in *The Man of Stone* (1921). For some reason, Selznick decided not to mold Martha for stardom; she was loaned out and freelanced until being signed by Fox in late 1923.

Still, Martha kept busy. She made only three films in 1922, but one of those was a star part: As *The Queen of the Moulin Rouge*, she played an unusually flashy role. She had given up on her theatrical career and moved west ("California is my heaven," she exulted). Enthusiastic about her future in films, she told a reporter, "I care for pictures—good ones—a great deal. Oh, there is no excuse for some of the pictures we see nowadays. There is not a reason in the world, at this late cinema date, for a bad picture." Keeping all bases covered, she added that "I believe in throwing my heart and soul into everything. There's no success in any line of work without spontaneous enthusiasm. It's the whole secret ... I am aiming for the legitimate stage, of course, although I find picture making absorbing work."

Despite her troubles at Selznick, Martha worked steadily, making eight films in 1923. She starred in *The Little Red Schoolhouse*, for Arrow, but most of her roles were supporting ones in small, independent films. She worked for such second-string studios as Lee-Bradford

(*Is Money Everything?*), Amalgamated (*The Woman in Chains*), the ailing Vitagraph (*The Levenworth Case*), and Hodkinson (*Youthful Cheaters*, with Glenn Hunter). One of Martha's bigger successes was in the low-brow ethnic comedy *Potash and Perlmutter* (First National, 1923), which also featured newcomer Ben Lyon in a small role. Finally her hard work paid off, and at the age of twenty-four she was signed to a long-term contract by Fox. Her first film was *The Silent Command*, in a small role supporting Edmund Lowe and Bela Lugosi. In the fall of 1923 she was cast as the female lead in *The Warrens of Virginia*, from the popular Broadway show. She played the Confederate fiancée of a Union soldier in this romantic, big-budget costume picture; the role might have made her a star.

But disaster struck while the company was filming in San Antonio, Texas. Martha was sitting in a car on the set when a smoker carelessly tossed a match in her direction. Her voluminous 1860s costume went up in flames, despite the frenzied efforts of costar Wilfred Lytell to smother the fire. She was rushed to a hospital with severe burns; there was virtually no chance of survival. She died at noon the following day, November 30, 1923. When *The Warrens of Virginia* was finally released late in 1924, Martha's role had been edited down, and Rosemary Hill was promoted as the female lead.

It's difficult to tell what direction Martha Mansfield's career might have taken had she lived; not enough of her work survives to judge her talent. She might have been overtaken by the jazz babies about to appear on the horizon: Clara Bow, Joan Crawford, Colleen Moore. As it stands, Martha was part of that brief transition period between the becurled, girlish actresses of the 1910s and the sleek flappers of the late 1920s.

Mae Marsh

All film historians agree without pause that Lillian Gish was the greatest actress the silent screen produced. But there's always that little addendum: "Oh, except maybe for Mae Marsh." The Griffith-trained actress's career was essentially over by the time talkies arrived, and she was largely forgotten by the public. Unglamorous, unambitious, and self-effacing, Mae Marsh has unjustly been neglected by all but the most knowledgeable of film fans. Yet her talent was truly remarkable.

Mary Warne Marsh was born in Madrid, New Mexico, on November 9, 1895, the daughter of a large, wealthy Scottish-Irish family. The twentieth century did not start out promisingly for the family: Father Charles Marsh died in 1899, and the remaining Marshes lost their home and possessions in the San Francisco earthquake in 1906. Mrs. Marsh took her five daughters and one son to Hollywood, a fortuitous choice. Little Mary Warne—later abbreviated to "Mae"—was educated at The Convent of the Immaculate Heart, while her older sister Marguerite took to the stage. By 1911 Marguerite was acting with D. W. Griffith's Biograph company, which was spending winters in California.

"I had been begging my sister for weeks to let me come along to the studio with her," Mae told Robert Cushman in 1967. It was 1912 when Marguerite introduced the seventeen-year-old to Griffith, who was less than impressed. Surprisingly, Mae made her debut not for Griffith but as a Mack Sennett bathing beauty. She sat in the background of a Mabel Normand film: "I knew how to sit; and that was my first day in the movies."

Mae was an extra in another film or two before her first acting role in *Lena and the Geese* (1912), with Mary Pickford. She later described her first acting lesson. "[Griffith] said, 'Now, I want you to go sit over there on the wall. Don't do a thing, just sit there. And if I tell you to do something, you can do it, but all I want you to do is sit there and think that this fellow beside you—you're terribly in love with him…' Evidently, I must have been acting all over the place, because I *was* so in love with him. And finally Mr. Griffith said, 'Well, that's fine. I think you might be an actress some day.'"

Mae's big break came later in 1912 with *Man's Genesis* and *Sands of Dee*. Mae volunteered to do the first film—as a scantily clad cavewoman—when Mary Pickford refused it. As a reward to Mae and a slap to Pickford, Griffith handed Mae the coveted role of the heroine in *Sands of Dee*. Mae spent 1912 working for directors Griffith and Tom Ince and with the Kalem Company, before heading east with her sister to appear in Biograph's New York films (Marguerite's own film career languished, and she died in 1925 at the age of thirty-three). Beginning in 1914 Mae Marsh worked exclusively with Griffith. In the four-reel *Judith of Bethulia*, she was a peasant girl in love with Robert Harron. She was a poor Western girl in love with an Eastern boy (Harron again) in *Home Sweet Home*. She was accused of murder in *The Outcast* and threatened by hillbillies in *The Great Leap*.

The soulful Mae Marsh, in a 1915 portrait.

Then came 1915 and *The Birth of a Nation*. It's a problematic film: the first "great" American movie, with many touching and effective moments. But Griffith's unapologetic racism and glorification of the Ku Klux Klan make it impossible to watch without embarrassment today. Mae Marsh walks off with *The Birth of a Nation*, outshining such talented costars as Lillian Gish and Henry B. Walthall. Her performance as Walthall's beloved, doomed Little Sister is a well-rounded, emotional, and believable portrayal of a childlike, trusting girl of the pampered pre–Civil-War South. During the filming, "I resigned four times and was fired once," she later laughed. "My temperamental days were over. I realized that pictures meant indefatigable effort and sacrifice. I was never fired again nor did I ever resign."

Griffith was well known for encouraging competition among his actresses, and he commended Mae for being a more intuitive actress than Lillian Gish. "You didn't have to study nearly as hard as Gish," Mae later recalled the director telling her. "She can't act at all." Mae herself said of Gish, "I like to do things perfect, but I like to have fun, too. She works too hard." There seems to have indeed been a little bad blood on the Griffith lot: "The Gish girls used to tell me my hair looked

An ethereal-looking Mae Marsh (The Metaluna Collection).

as though I put it up with a bellows," Mae said.

Mae's next film began as a feature called *The Mother and the Law*, in which she and Robert Harron played a newlywed couple dealing with urban crime and child care. Their little film was incorporated into Griffith's masterpiece *Intolerance*, released in the autumn of 1916. While Constance Talmadge steals the spotlight in the Babylonian sequence, Mae and Harron give startlingly modern, heartfelt, and moving performances in the modern portions of the film. The actress refused to prepare for her harrowing courtroom scene, wanting the set to come as a surprise to her. "When I went to the courtroom scene," she said, "I was really feeling as if I was in my first courtroom, and I was scared, very frightened. And to add to the fright, having no lines, I had to make my hands go, I had to make my face go, and I had a handkerchief, and I thought, 'Well, this would be good for that business—nervous, scared.'" It was indeed good, and the scene is still shattering today.

Mae made another six films for Griffith's then-current studio, Triangle, in 1916, though none were directed by Griffith. In *Hoodoo Ann*, Mae played a poor, put-upon orphan, opposite Harron again. It was a great hit—indeed, it made more money than *Intolerance*, as it didn't have to support huge road companies. She was an Irish colleen in *The Marriage of Molly O* (again with Harron) and played the title roles in *The Wild Girl of the Sierras*, *A Child of the Paris Streets*, *The Little Liar*, and *The Wharf Rat*. The last film—again with Harron—had Mae on the lam from the law dressed as a boy, a stunt later reprised by Louise Brooks, Katharine Hepburn, and Veronica Lake, among others.

It was at the end of 1916 that Mae Marsh was signed (at $3,000 a week) by the brand-new Goldwyn company, formed by Samuel Goldfish and Edgar Selwyn. Goldwyn trumpeted its new stars in ads around the country: Mae Marsh, Mabel Normand, Jane Cowl, Maxine Elliott, Mary Garden, and Madge Kennedy were featured as the jewels in the studio's crown. Mae starred in an unlucky thirteen films for Goldwyn from 1917 through 1919. "Oh, they were terrible, those Goldwyn pictures," she bemoaned, making an exception only for her first two, *Polly of the Circus* and *The Cinderella Man* (both 1917). "It was my fault, too, I should have realized that." She refused to break her contract, as Griffith advised her to do. "I just don't feel like I could break my word with anybody, no matter what they have done to me ... I just made money, and that was all there was to it." Well, not quite all—while working for Goldwyn, Mae met journalist and publicist Louis Lee Arms. The two wed on September 21, 1918, and stayed married until Mae's death.

When the 1920s dawned and Mae's Goldwyn contract lapsed, she was at loose ends. Mae Marsh was not a glamour girl. Her face was that of a dramatic actress: Her pale eyelashes and eyebrows gave her face a naked, vulnerable look, and she was able to mirror emotions brilliantly. But in the age of the flapper and jazz baby, Mae's image was still that of an Edwardian Valentine. She got scores of angry letters once after wearing a "daring" dress in a film: "It was taffeta with a bodice that ended under the arms—and had one shoulder strap of rosebuds," she later recalled. Even after Goldwyn took over her publicity, though, Mae never became a "star" like Theda Bara or the Talmadge sisters. She was shy and soft spoken, more interested in her family, knitting, and painting than in discussing acting or looking glamorous for photographers. Everyone admitted her great talent, but offscreen, Mae Marsh was a little gray mouse.

Mae freelanced for three years, appearing in five indifferent films, none of which did anything to re-establish her. She mostly played orphans and put-upon waifs; her only "grown-up" role was in the British-made *Flames of Passion* (1922), in which she played a wronged society girl. Griffith came again to her rescue, offering Mae a role in *The White Rose* (United Artists, 1923). Costarring Carol Dempster and Ivor Novello, the film was a huge success and helped put Mae back on top. She once again played a poor little orphan girl, but that's what the public wanted. "I was always in trouble, homeless, abandoned or dying," she summed up her career. "How they loved to play lights on my hair and have me weep!"

She next made another high-budget film, this one for Warner Brothers. *Daddies* (1924) was a change of pace for Mae: In a role originally played on Broadway by Jeanne Eagels, she was a girl "adopted" by a bachelor's club. Mae traveled to inflation-wracked Germany to appear in *Arabelle* (also 1924), a horse story; then she came back to the United States for *A Woman's Secret* (1924) and *Tides of Passion* (1925). The latter film was one of the very last produced by Vitagraph, which had formed in 1896. J. Stuart Blackton, a founder of the dying company, directed Mae in this tale of a deserted wife. Mae's last silent film was *The Rat*, filmed in England in 1925. She costarred with her old *White Rose* pal Ivor Novello in a story of the Paris underworld. The film was a mild success.

Then Mae abruptly retired from the screen, settling down with her husband and children (Mary, Brewster, and Marguerite). "When I'm home with my family around me, I'm the happiest woman in the world," the unambitious ex-star said. But the 1929 stock market crash played havoc with the Armses's fortunes, and in 1932 Mae returned to acting as a poor old scrubwoman in 20th Century-Fox's *Over the Hill*. Mae was only thirty-seven, but looked twenty years older, with the help of makeup and lighting. The 1930s were tough years for the family, as they were for the rest of the nation. Mae very nearly died of a ruptured appendix in 1935, and she and her husband filed for bankruptcy in 1939. Happily, things picked up, and the family was soon back on its feet. Director John Ford gave Mae a role in *Drums Along the Mohawk* (1939) and continued to cast her in his films over the years: *The Grapes of Wrath* (1940), *Three Godfathers* (1949), *The Sun Shines Bright* (1953), *The Wings of Eagles* (1957), *Sergeant Rutledge* (1960), *Two Rode Together* (1962), and *Donovan's Reef* (1963). She had the best of words for Ford, whom she compared to Griffith: "He works out a scene like you'd work out a piece of embroidery."

Indeed, Mae Marsh was one of the busiest and most effective character actresses of the 1940s and 1950s. The ex-sweetheart of the early Griffith films can be briefly glimpsed in—among many others—*Young People* (1940, as a prim small-town woman), *A Tree Grows in Brooklyn* (1945), *The Snake Pit* (1948), *The Gunfighter* (1950), *The Robe* (1953), *Prince of Players* (1955), *While the City*

Sleeps (1955), and *Girls in Prison* (1956, as a tough con, of all things). Her last "big" moment onscreen came in Doris Day's *Julie* (1956). After Mae completed her cameo as a nervous airplane passenger, the cast and crew burst into impromptu applause. "I'm anything from a scrubwoman to a face in a train window," Mae said of her later character work. "I don't suppose many people even recognize my name today."

After *Donovan's Reef*, Mae again retired, to nurse a heart condition. She enjoyed a quiet life with her husband, children, and nine grandchildren until her death on February 13, 1968. To the end, Mae Marsh was philosophical and unstarlike. "I love being a grandmother," she said shortly before her death. "Every year has its beauty and its love, the same as a flower."

Colleen Moore

She epitomized the jazz-crazed 1920s, with her severely bobbed hair, wild eyes, and carefree demeanor. She was also one of the smartest women to ever set foot in Hollywood, and her story was one of the happiest in all of film history.

She was born into a comfortable upper-middle-class home in Port Huron, Michigan, on August 19, 1900 (some sources say 1902). Kathleen Morrison was the older daughter of Charles and Agnes (Kelly) Morrison; she was also the darling of her six aunts and her uncle, who happened to be the editor of *The Chicago Examiner*. Kathleen described herself as "some punkins, and [a] happy child," but she was also of that first generation to be impressively movie struck. By the time her family had resettled in Tampa, Florida, the youngster was obsessed by Mary Pickford, the Gish sisters, and Mabel Normand.

In was in 1917 that the teenager made her first entrance into the film world—then, as now, connections were everything, and it was her influential newspaperman uncle who contacted D. W. Griffith to give the lucky girl a tryout. "I wonder at my audacity in dreaming that I could become a movie star," she later said. Colleen Moore—as she was soon renamed—had a point. She was no great beauty, like Pickford or Gish. Her amusingly perky face was no one's idea of a pageant winner. She had a turned-down, almost beak-like nose, a small mouth, and her eyes were two different colors (though that, happily, did not photograph). But her supportive family let her drop out of high school to follow her dream to Triangle Studios in California.

Though it is sometimes written that Colleen made her debut in *Intolerance*, that film had already been released by the time she arrived on the West Coast. The outgoing girl immediately befriended the Triangle actresses she'd admired from afar: the Gishes, Mildred Harris, Bessie Love, Carmel Myers. "No one I ever knew could look or be so imperial as Mr. Griffith," Colleen recalled. "When I met him I had an impulse to curtsy." Her debut was as a second lead in *Bad Boy* (1917), and she did well enough to win herself sizable parts in the Triangle films *An Old-Fashioned Young Man* and *Hands Up!* before finding herself out of a job. At this point, Colleen happily admitted, "acting" was a skill totally beyond her, and she simply followed her director's instructions. "I loved it all," she wrote, "because I was doing ... the only thing I had ever wanted to do." But she didn't do it well enough to suit Griffith. Despite her head of dark, Pickford-like sausage curls, she was not the Valentine type of actress whom Griffith preferred. But "I was mighty lucky and very glad I was never a beauty," she said later in life. "The beauties suffered the most."

The late 1910s were exciting and busy for Colleen, as she learned her craft and worked steadily for a number of studios. But she was essentially spinning her wheels. No one knew quite what to do with her: Was she an ingenue, like Lillian Gish? An action heroine, like Pearl White? A comic, like Constance Talmadge? A dramatic leading lady, like Norma Talmadge? There was, as of yet, no "Colleen Moore type," though in a few years young starlets would be made over in *her* image.

She was an unrecognizable bit player in Mary Pickford's *The Little American* (1917), then played the lead in *Little Orphan Annie* (1919) for Selig, and had a sizable role in the baseball romance *The Busher* (with a young John Gilbert) for Paramount the same year. Colleen played leading lady to a number of stars while trying to find her forte. Tom Mix won her heart onscreen and became her first crush offscreen in *The Wilderness Trail* (1919) and *The Cyclone* (1920), both at Fox. "In my love scenes with him, I nearly swooned away," Colleen said, adding, "though I must say I didn't forget to keep the best side of my face toward the camera." She played opposite Sessue Hayakawa (*The Devil's Claim*, 1920), John Barrymore (*The Lotus Eater*, 1921), Richard Dix (*The Wallflower*, 1922), up-and-coming youngsters Warner Baxter (*The Ninety and Nine*, 1922), and Antonio Moreno (*Look Your Best*, 1923). She also got some much-needed comedy training by appearing in a handful of two- and five-reel comedies for the Christie Studios in 1920.

In 1921 Colleen met the man who—despite her later marriages—may have been the love of her life. King Vidor was twenty-seven when he directed Colleen, for the first and only time, in *The Sky Pilot* (her favorite director was actually the ingratiating and sometimes infuriating Marshall Neilan, who directed her in three films between 1921 and her last, in 1934). Colleen and *The Sky Pilot* cast and crew were conveniently snowbound in northern California during the shoot, and a passionate romance blossomed (probably several did, but the Moore/Vidor affair is the only one to survive in print). Colleen was still a blushing virgin up until that point, little more than a schoolgirl. The two remained friends until Vidor's death in 1982, dubbing each other "Professor LaTour" and "Madame Zaza" after a magic act they did to entertain the crew.

In 1923—after a two-year relationship—Colleen married First National press agent John McCormick (not to be confused with his contemporary, the Irish singer John MacCormack). He'd helped her get a four-picture contract at Goldwyn, which resulted in *Come On Over*, *The Wallflower*, *Broken Chains* (all 1922), and *Look Your Best* (1923). After seven tumultuous years (McCormick was a heavy drinker), the two divorced in 1930.

From her debut in 1917 till the end of 1922, Colleen had appeared in some thirty films and was well known to fans, but she was not yet a "star." She was still merely one of those struggling leading ladies who appears in one unremarkable film after another until eventually sinking down to bit player or retiring into marriage or a second career. Only in her early twenties, Colleen still knew that she was becoming old hat and needed a role to set her apart from the pack.

That role arrived in 1923 with the starring part in *Flaming Youth*, the First National adaptation of Warner Fabian's scandalous best-seller about the disillusioned, sex-mad, postwar generation. Colleen had just signed a long-term contract with First National, and when she saw this script, "I knew that here was my chance for stardom." To make herself look more like the book's heroine, Colleen chopped off her long curls and fashioned a severe Dutch-boy bob (actually modeled after the hair on a Japanese doll). The style was to become her signature and was copied by scores of actresses (notably Louise Brooks and Clara Bow) and, subsequently, by women around the world. Just as Colleen Moore soon epitomized the flapper, her hairstyle became a veritable caricature of the 1920s look.

Flaming Youth was the story of Pat, a good/bad girl, the kind who kicked up her heels but could still be considered a proper character for families to view (this was, remember, the dawn of the Hays Code). With Milton Sills as her leading man (and young Ben Lyon in a bit part), Colleen put everything she had into the role. "Never had I been so happy in a movie role," she wrote. "I loved every scene." The role of Pat allowed Colleen to show off both the dramatic and comedic skills she'd acquired over the last seven years, and it proved to be the star-making vehicle she'd predicted. As F. Scott Fitzgerald famously wrote, "I was the spark that lit up flaming youth, Colleen Moore was the torch. What little things we were to have caused all that trouble."

With the release of *Flaming Youth*, First National suddenly found that their reliable stock player had become a major star and one of the studio's most valuable properties. She was to stay with that company for the next six years and twenty-three films, taking only one loan-out for anyone else after her first year. The company's executives, to their credit, "tore up my old contract and gave me a new one for $50,000 a picture for the next four pictures, all of them to be made in a year. I didn't get excited until I broke it down and saw that it came to almost $4,000 a week."

Colleen starred in five films in 1924, three in 1925, and four in 1926—not that hectic a schedule in a time when films were made in about eight weeks. Between shoots, though, "I spent days having fittings for the next film and then having tests made to see how the clothes photographed and if they were suitable to the character I sought to portray," taking publicity photos, doing interviews, and going over scripts. Colleen thrived on this, even going to the studio on her days off just to hang around the set.

Her career nearly ended in 1925 while filming the western *The Desert Flower*: Colleen fell off a railroad cart and broke her neck on the tracks. Fortunately (in those days of relatively primitive medicine), it was one of the less serious forms of neck fractures, and Colleen was able to resume work after a few months of bed rest and traction. The difference between the 1920s and now can also be seen in the fact that Colleen didn't sue First National.

Most of Colleen's films were programmers, which showed her off to a certain extent but never became classics. Among her better mid–1920s films were the delightful rags-to-riches parody *Ella Cinders* (1926), the film versions of the stage hits *Sally* (1925) and *Irene* (1926), and the flapper follow-ups *Painted People* (1924) and *We Moderns* (1925). Colleen's own favorite was the old-fashioned *So Big* (1924), adapted from Edna Ferber's mother-love novel. The dramatic role, she said, "was a challenge, and I wanted to prove I could play it. I was a big enough star now to demand the story I wanted, and it was given to me."

Colleen Moore in her ingenue period.

Colleen's last big year of stardom was 1928, during which she appeared in *Her Wild Oat* (another flapper tale), *Happiness Ahead* (with Edmund Lowe and his wife, Lilyan Tashman), *Oh, Kay!* (from the Broadway hit), and *Lilac Time* (her last big success, a World War I tale opposite Gary Cooper). By the end of that year, everyone knew they had talking films to deal with, and Colleen was sent to aging theater star Constance Collier for vocal coaching. She hilariously recalled in the TV documentary series, *Hollywood,* how Collier took one whole day to teach her how to say "mother," another to teach her "father," and so on. "Cheer up, dollink," said one of her studio bosses. "Tomorrow maybe you vill loin a sentence."

Colleen made two more silent films, *Synthetic Sin* and *Why Be Good?,* while acquiring her new vocabulary. Her voice was actually quite good—high but not squeaky, with no discernible regional accent—but her first talkie, *Smiling Irish Eyes* (1929), was an unbearably lachrymose failure. "It was surely the longest, slowest, dullest picture ever made," she later groaned. Colleen's marriage and career simultaneously self-destructed. She made another five talkies, only one of them much good: *The Power and the Glory* (Fox, 1933) was a dark tale of ambition run amuck and showed off Spencer Tracy in one of his best early roles. But *Success at Any Price* (RKO, 1934) and an earnest but dull version of *The Scarlet Letter* (Majestic, 1934) helped end her career as a marketable actress. Her swan song was the Marshall Neilan-directed *The Social Register* (Columbia, 1934).

While her career slid downhill, Colleen's life did not stand still. Her second husband was New York businessman

Colleen Moore's later flapper incarnation.

Albert Scott, whom she married in 1931. This marriage soon ended in an amicable divorce, and the two stayed close friends. With all her energy to be rechanneled, Colleen found a new creative obsession. From 1928 to 1935 she poured her heart (and a good chunk of change) into the creation of a huge doll house. Though the term "doll house" really doesn't do it justice, this museum-quality creation is a huge castle, its detail work breathtaking. It contains elaborate furniture and paintings, tiny books signed by their authors, decor of real gold—even a tiny bearskin fashioned from a mouse. It has working electricity and running water and is now one of the most popular exhibits at the Museum of Science and Industry in Chicago.

After a few mediocre plays—*On the Loose*, *The Church Mouse*—Colleen officially retired from acting and devoted herself to the stock market and real estate. She married stockbroker Homer Hargrave in 1937, a marriage which lasted until his death in 1967. In 1971 Colleen married her building contractor, Paul Maginot. A tremendously wealthy woman, she traveled and wrote books about the stock market and her doll house, as well as a delightful autobiography (*Silent Star*, 1968). She kept her looks, health, and sense of adventure right up till the time she died, on January 25, 1988, at her ranch home in Templeton, California. In a 1983 interview with James Watters for his book, *Return Engagement*, the last of the flappers said happily, "Even at my age, I believe in looking forward more than looking backward."

Antonio Moreno

The phrase "Latin Lover" is a wildly misleading one, encompassing everything from Italians (Rudolph Valentino) to Mexicans (Ramon Novarro, Gilbert Roland) to Chicagoans (Rod La Rocque) and Brooklynites (Ricardo Cortez). One of the screen's first (and most charming) was Antonio Moreno, born in Madrid on September 26, probably in 1887.

Christened Antonio Garrido Monteagudo Moreno, his father Juan was a noncommissioned officer in the Spanish army. "My father considered me an attraction about on par with a bullfight," Antonio recalled. "He thought I was good entertainment." Juan Moreno died when his son was quite young, and Antonio's mother, Ana, moved to Seville and wed a local market gardener. Antonio—always "Tony" to his friends—spent his time avoiding school, charming odd jobs out of tourists, and, he later said, wooing the girl next door, Conchita Perres.

This is where Antonio's story takes an eyebrow-raising turn. While he was still in his early teens, he befriended two men, Benjamin Curtis and Enrique de Cruzat Zanetti, who were making The Grand Tour together. They took a liking to Antonio, and—with his mother's blessing—took him with them on the rest of their trip and back to America. Once in America, the handsome and charming young man lost no time in finding more patrons. One Charlotte Morgan—a lonely Civil War widow—paid for his tuition at the Williston Seminary in Northhampton, Massachusetts. Fan magazine writers likened it to a Horatio Alger book, but it sounds more like Moll Flanders to modern ears.

He took a job with the local gas and electric company, but by this time—around 1910—Antonio was getting bored with his settled existence. When Maude Adams hit town, touring with *The Little Minister*, Antonio showed up at the stage door and charmed his way into a job as a walk-on and gofer. He toured with the Adams company, then made his Broadway debut as a Spanish count in Mrs. Leslie Carter's *Two Women* (1910). Antonio spent the next couple of years playing small roles in the Shakespearean company of E. H. Sothern and

Antonio Moreno early in his career.

Julia Marlowe, touring in vaudeville and stock and showing up in such plays as *DuBarry* (Mrs. Carter, again), *Thais* (1911), *The Right to Happiness*, *The Man from Cook's,* and *The Old Firm.*

While he never became a leading player, it's amazing that Antonio got as far onstage as he did. Despite his stunning dark good looks and enthusiasm, he retained an attractive but noticeable Spanish accent, which severely limited the roles he could play. Not surprisingly, his thoughts turned to the silent drama of the photo-plays. He applied to both the Rex-Universal and Biograph Studios in Manhattan and was snapped up in 1912, when he was in his mid–twenties. After one film at Rex (*The Voice of the Million*), Antonio settled down at Biograph, where he made seven films over the next two years.

Several were directed by D. W. Griffith, though Antonio did not stay with him long enough to be labeled a "discovery." Griffith piloted him through *Two Daughters of Eve* (1912, with Lillian Gish), *So Near, Yet So Far* (1912, with Mary Pickford), and *By Man's Law* (1913, with Mae Marsh and Robert Harron). For some reason, he did not thrive at Biograph, which was known for its cutthroat competition. In 1914 Antonio signed up with Vitagraph in Brooklyn and stayed there learning his trade through 1917. Those make-or-break years proved to Antonio that he had a future in films. He saved his money and even managed to visit his mother in Spain while working his way up the ladder at Vitagraph in bigger and better roles. He appeared in nearly fifty films, supporting such Vitagraph Girls as Norma and Constance Talmadge, Edith Storey, Lillian Walker, and Muriel Ostriche. Nearly every director on the lot worked with him, most often Van Dyke Brooke, Lionel Belmore, and George Baker.

Unlike Rudolph Valentino, whose "ethnic" looks typed him as a villain, Antonio was most often cast as a stalwart hero and romantic lead. He was a newspaperman in *Politics and the Press* and a philandering artist in *Goodbye, Summer* (both 1914, with Norma Talmadge), Rodolf to Constance Talmadge's Mimi in *In the Latin Quarter* (1915), a department store heir in love with a shopgirl in *A Model Wife* (1915, a role he would reprise years later in *It*), an antebellum Southern beau in *Kennedy Square* (1916), and an old West cowpoke in *By Right of Possession* (1917).

By mid–1917 Antonio was getting dissatisfied again and moved to Pathé, making five films for them over the next year, including *The Mark of Cain* and *The First Law*, both with Irene Castle, and his first serial, the hugely successful *The House of Hate*, with Pearl White. Vitagraph lured him back in 1918 and, with *The House of Hate* as incentive, began pushing him into more and more adventure serials: *The Iron Test* (1918, a circus tale), *The Perils of Thunder Mountain* (1919, a particularly exhausting outing), *The Invisible Hand* (1920, a spy thriller), and *The Veiled Mystery* (1920, which Antonio codirected).

Antonio flat-out hated these serials, which involved little acting and were taking his career nowhere. Wanting to return to features, he got his friend, director William Desmond Taylor, to send out feelers for a Paramount contract. By the time Antonio was finally hired, Taylor had been murdered (author Sidney Kirkpatrick later hinted that Antonio knew a lot more about Taylor's death than he let on at the time). There was another change in Antonio's life besides studios: On January 27, 1923, he married thirty-five-year-old socialite Daisy Canfield Danziger, a wealthy divorcée with three children (all of whom later changed their name to "Moreno"). He had known Daisy, who often invested in films, since 1919. They moved into a huge Spanish-style showcase called Crestmount and became famed for their parties (besides his Spanish house, the homesick actor had a ring and cufflinks made with the colors of the Spanish flag).

Antonio had a lot of friends, including rival Latin Lovers Ramon Novarro and Gilbert Roland, youngsters whose early careers he helped along. Reporter Gladys Hall, interviewing Antonio shortly after his marriage, bemoaned, "What with Valentino in double harness, and Richard Barthelmess, and now you, what is there left for the poor girls to hope for?" "Ramon Novarro," answered Antonio, no doubt with tongue in cheek (Novarro's friends knew full well he was gay). For all his popularity, Antonio sometimes suffered from an inferiority complex. He referred to himself as "just a mutt," and when his hometown put on a celebration for him, he said that "I wanted to run away, my heart was beating so. I felt so damned unworthy of it all."

He was hardly unworthy in 1923, his first year at Paramount. The studio launched their new leading man with panache, starring him in no less than six big-budgeted films that year. He romanced Gloria Swanson in *My American Wife* and Colleen Moore in *Look Your Best*, was a swashbuckling pirate in *Lost and Found*, costarred with Mary Miles Minter in one of her last films, *The Trail of the Lonesome Pine*, knocked about with Bebe Daniels in *The Exciters*, and supported fellow Paramount freshman Pola Negri in *The Spanish Dancer*. Paramount was taking no chances, and, by the time 1924 dawned, Antonio Moreno was officially a star.

Oddly, though, he didn't stay with Paramount long; he never stayed with any studio very long. It may have been his discontented, adventurous spirit; certainly, Antonio did not have a reputation for being difficult or unprofessional. Audiences and critics adored him, but he was unable to maintain a relationship with a studio. He made another five films for Paramount in 1924 before jumping ship for First National. Again, his stay was short. After a mere three films in 1925 (including *Learning to Love*, with old pal Constance Talmadge), Antonio signed up with MGM.

Antonio Moreno in one of his more exotic roles (The Metaluna Collection).

Antonio's first MGM film was his best showcase. Happily, *Mare Nostrum* (1926) survives in a beautifully restored version. Starring Antonio as a restless sea captain and Alice Terry as a Mata-Hari–like vamp, it was directed by Terry's husband Rex Ingram on location in Madrid, Naples, Monte Carlo, and other European locales. Long and complex but still breathtaking, *Mare Nostrum* was the apex of Antonio's career and was his own favorite film. He told reporter Roscoe McGowen at the time that he actually spoke his lines in Spanish. "When an actor plays a foreign role and speaks his lines in English, it is plain to be seen on the screen ... One can watch actors speaking and practically tell what they are saying. So when I'm supposed to be French I speak French, and when I'm Spanish I speak Spanish."

Beverly of Graustark—a 1926 costume romance—was an enjoyable experience, as costar Marion Davies was full of fun and made shooting a holiday. But Antonio's next film, *The Temptress*, was a horror for all concerned. His costar Greta Garbo (in her second American film) was told of her sister Alva's death on the fourth day of shooting. Antonio and director Mauritz Stiller hated each other from the start, and MGM agreed to replace Stiller with Fred Niblo. This, of course, upset poor Garbo further. She couldn't yet speak much English, and losing her Swedish mentor Stiller didn't endear her to her leading man. Still, the film is a treat, with Antonio as an engineer vamped by the jinxed Garbo. A sadomasochistic whipping scene is particularly startling, even today.

Antonio made only two more films at MGM (the Elinor Glyn bodice-ripper *Love's Blindness,* and the color adventure *The Flaming Forest*, with Renee Adoree) before—true to form—decamping for greener pastures. For the rest of his career, Antonio freelanced. For the next few years, it looked like a good business decision. He went to Paramount and starred as the stuffy department store heir brought down to earth by shopgirl Clara Bow in *It* (1927). One of the funniest, sexiest films of the late 1920s, *It* was the movie that officially made Clara Bow a star. A brilliant publicity campaign had authoress Elinor Glyn dubbing Clara and Antonio among the few lucky possessors of "it," along with the Ambassador Hotel doorman and (in a bizarre glimpse into Madame Glyn's fantasy life) Rex, the Wonder Horse. Constance Talmadge reteamed with Antonio for the romantic jewel-robbery comedy, *Venus of Venice* (First National, 1927), after which he journeyed to England for *Madame Pompadour* (Paramount, 1927) with Dorothy Gish.

Antonio made another eight silent films in 1927 and 1928, working for major studios like Fox (*Come to My House*, a society thriller), Warner Bros. (*The Midnight Taxi*, a crime film with Helene Costello), and First National (the delightful comedy *Synthetic Sin*, with Colleen Moore). But he also wound up on Poverty Row for the first time: Tiffany (*Nameless Men*, as a prison spy) and FBO (*The Air Legion*, with Ben Lyon). He also journeyed south to Mexico, where he appeared in *En la Tierra del Sol*. Then, in 1929, Antonio encountered talkies, and his life as a leading man was over.

It happened to them all, real and fake Latins: Ramon Novarro, Ricardo Cortez, Gilbert Roland, Rod La Roque. Had Valentino lived, it would have happened to him as well. Due to accents and simply to changing tastes, the Latin Lovers became character actors. Antonio was in his early forties and had enjoyed a good run, so this turn of events was hardly tragic. Indeed, his ability to speak Spanish brought in work filming Spanish versions of American films. He starred in foreign-language roles played in English by William Boyd (*El Cuerpo del Delito/The Benson Murder Case*, 1929), Walter Huston (*El Hombre Malo/The Bad Man*, 1930), Neil Hamilton (*El Gato/The Cat Creeps*, 1930), Monte Blue (*Los Que Danzan/Those Who Dance*, 1931), and George Sanders (*Senora Casada Necesita Marido/My Second Wife*, 1937).

But his American roles dropped off in both quality and quantity. He was an unhappily married judge in *Careers* (his 1929 talkie debut), a villain menacing Warner Baxter in *Romance of the Rio Grande* (1929), a squadron major in *Storm Over the Andes* (1935), a gypsy in Laurel and Hardy's *Bohemian Girl* (1936), and a detective in the crime drama *Ambush* (1939). Realizing that his American career was waning, Antonio spent a good deal of time in Mexico, where he directed that country's first two talkies, *Santa* (no, not Claus) and *Aguilas Frente al Sol* (both 1932). He also travelled back to Spain, where he starred in *Maria de la O* (1936), playing, ironically, an American.

The perfect profile of Antonio Moreno (The Metaluna Collection).

Tragedy struck Antonio in the 1930s. He and his wife separated in mid–February 1933, due to "some of the usual minor family incompatibilities," according to a newspaper interview. They almost immediately announced a probable reconciliation, but Daisy Moreno was killed in a car accident on February 23.

She and a young Swiss visitor were driving through a heavy fog on Mulholland Highway when the car's lights failed and they plummeted down a 250-foot embankment. Mrs. Moreno died instantly; the driver survived, though with a broken back. Antonio, who collapsed when given the news, never remarried.

For the next two decades, Antonio was a very busy character actor, appearing in twenty-three films between 1940 and his swan song, the Cuban comedy *El Senor Faron y la Cleopatra* (1958). Some of these films were high-profile, big-budget successes, such as *Seven Sinners* (1940, as one of Marlene Dietrich's admirers), Alfred Hitchcock's *Notorious* (1946, as one of the spies chasing Cary Grant), *Captain from Castille* (1947, as Tyrone Power's father), *Dallas* (1950, supporting Gary Cooper), and John Ford's *The Searchers* (1956, his last American film). Many other films passed pleasantly enough through theaters but hardly achieved immortality: *Two Latins from Manhattan* (1941), *Lust for Gold* (1949), *Thunder Bay* (1953), and the like. Ironically, Antonio's biggest latter-day hit was the 3D camp horror film *The Creature from the Black Lagoon* (1954), portraying the scientist who discovers the "leading man" in an Amazonian swamp.

If Antonio is to be believed, he did not miss acting. Well fixed for money, he lived in a large Beverly Hills home. He only took a role in *The Spanish Main* (1945), he said, because his old friend Frank Borzage "said he had a good role for me ... I told him I had to be back in Mexico City by a certain date ... You see, I hate acting." Nonetheless, Antonio didn't retire until 1958, and even that was never official. He suffered a stroke in 1965 and was in failing health for two years before his death on February 15, 1967. The first of the Latin Lovers was survived by his "students" in the art: Ramon Novarro, Rod La Roque, Gilbert Roland, and Ricardo Cortez.

Nita Naldi

When Nita Naldi came on the scene, the day of the serious vampire was ending. Theda Bara had retired in 1919, and her fellow vamps Valeska Suratt, Virginia Pearson, and Louise Glaum were also fading away. Nita was one of the new wave: those women who bridged the gap between the vamp and the jazzy little flapper. She, Pola Negri, Barbara La Marr, and Dagmar Godowsky were neither one thing nor the other, and their careers ultimately suffered as a result. Nita Naldi was not the greatest actress of her day, but she enjoyed a respectable run in the 1920s (including three films with Rudolph Valentino), and she was a very funny woman with a keen sense of her own talents and liabilities. "The fans just assumed that I was in real life as I appeared on the screen," Nita later said with some amazement. " ... Everywhere I went people used to look upon me as something unreal—like griffins or unicorns."

The last of the heavy-breathing temptresses was born Donna Dooley on New York's East Side, on April 1, 1897. "I went to an Italian convent in Hoboken, a charitable school, and so did my sister," she told a reporter in 1924. Her great-aunt was the Mother Superior, and friends remembered Donna as a "good-natured bully," always cutting up and doing imitations. Stage struck, the tall, dark teenager left school and started a modeling career. "I didn't know ham from eggs," she laughed. "I had just brains enough to be a cloak model." She eventually began appearing onstage, beginning with *The Passing Show of 1918* and the scandalous hit *Aphrodite* (1919). In 1920 she appeared in *The Bonehead* and *Opportunity*, then got her first film role in a Johnny Dooley comedy. Though *Dr. Jekyll and Mr. Hyde* is always mentioned as her feature film debut, she actually appeared in Selznick's *A Divorce of Conscience* early in 1921, filmed in Fort Lee, New Jersey. "No bridges then," she joked. "We had to migrate across the river in canoes."

She was already renamed "Nita Naldi" when discovered by John Barrymore and cast as a Spanish vamp in his 1921 *Dr. Jekyll and Mr. Hyde*. It was filmed in the old Famous Players Studio

Nita Naldi in the Art Deco classic *What Price Beauty?* (Donna Hill).

in New York, so Nita was able to continue pursuing stage work ("When I couldn't get a job in a play I'd be a showgirl"). She went on to film *Experience* later in 1921, with Richard Barthelmess.

The mid–1920s were good to Nita. Someone at Jesse Lasky's Paramount Studios spotted Nita and cast her as Doña Sol in her first film with Rudolph Valentino, *Blood and Sand*, in 1922. Nita shocked censors in this role, luring Rudy away from Lila Lee with a combination of drugs and sadism. She was shipped out to the West Coast with a five-year contract. "This came so fast I didn't have time to figure it out until I saw the Rocky Mountains on my way to the coast," she recalled. "When I went out to the coast, some of the people on the Lasky lot tried to Ritz me. I heard a group of people say, 'Oh, she is only a showgirl.' Do you know what I said? 'God made showgirls, and Paramount made actresses.'" Obviously she was no dimwitted chorine. "They always hated me in Hollywood because I speak English correctly," the well-educated actress groused.

By 1923 she was appearing in film after film for Paramount, such as *Lawful Larceny*, *Glimpses of the Moon* (with Bebe Daniels), *You Can't Fool Your Wife*, and *Hollywood*. Her biggest hit that year was Cecil B. De Mille's *The Ten Commandments*, in which she played Sally Lung, an evil half-caste vamp who lures Rod La Roque away from sweet Leatrice Joy. She played it to the hilt, and her highly dramatic death scene is never to be forgotten once viewed. She made her second appearance with Valentino in 1924, vamping him in *A Sainted Devil*. "He was a charming man," she recalled, "brilliantly educated, and with a beautiful speaking voice. People forget his father was a doctor and his grandfather worked with Pasteur." Other films that year included *Don't Call It Love* and *The Breaking Point*.

Paramount's PR department went into overdrive. In interviews, Nita tossed off the usual vamp quotes ("To charm a man, act dumb. Looks are more important than books"), but as early as 1924, she sighed, "I'd love to get away from vampire roles." Everything about Nita made headlines, from her 1923 appendectomy to her up-and-down weight (her diet of lamb chops and pineapple and her refusal to exercise had very limited success). She took the whole thing with a grain of salt. "They used to put me in boudoir scenes wearing ermine tails and paradises in my hair and a couple of snakes coiled around my shoulders," she later said. "A man would run twenty miles if he ever stumbled on a woman really looking like that ... Even in those days the whole thing was ridiculous. It was difficult to convince an audience that you were such a femme fatale that you could lure a man from his work and his woman merely by raising and lowering your eyelashes."

Nita took off for Europe in the summer of 1924 with Rudolph and Natasha Rambova Valentino to make *The Hooded Falcon*, a film that never came about. She was reported to be married to Cleveland banker Giacimel Sanges, much to the chagrin of Mrs. Sanges. A Siamese prince was also rumored to be in her clutches, but Nita showed up in Hollywood later in the year, single and ready to work. Valentino used her one last time in the delightful modern-dress *Cobra* (1925), where Nita once again lured him from a nice girl (this time, Gertrude Olmstead). From there she went into a rollicking comedy, *Clothes Make the Pirate*, costarring Leon Errol and Dorothy Gish, for First National. Later in 1925 Nita appeared in *The Lady Who Lied*, *The Marriage Whirl*, and *What Price Beauty?*, the latter produced by Natasha Rambova.

In November of that year she took off for Europe again, without so much as telling Paramount, which was readying a new film, *The Desert Sheik*, for her. The studio put out an all-points bulletin, even contacting the State Department.

Nita Naldi at her most vampish (Donna Hill).

Syndicated columnist Ted Cook sarcastically wrote, "Your dressing room is just as you left it. There is the mascara bucket on the shelf. The barrel of rouge is in the corner. And even that old Gordon gin bottle is still in the wastebasket." This time, Nita did snag a husband in Europe, a wealthy middle-aged businessman named J. Searle Barclay. She lost whatever interest she'd once had in her acting career, blowing off her Paramount contract. She made several films in Europe, including *Prater Mitzi* (Vienna, 1926) and *La Femme Nue*, made in France. One of her last was *The Unfair Sex* (1926, for Associated Exhibitors). Nita Naldi never again appeared onscreen, but her public life was far from over.

She and Barclay lived in Paris, Hungary, and Germany, returning to the United States some time after the stock market crash. Ensconced in New York's Plaza Hotel, the couple discovered much to their alarm that their fortune had vanished. By 1933 they declared bankruptcy. "All I have in the world are these three pawn tickets," Nita told the court. "Two are for diamond pins, one for a diamond ring which I pawned for $350 with the Provident Loan Company, and the ring belongs to my husband." Moving to less expensive quarters in New York, Nita resurfaced on Broadway from time to time. She had smallish roles in such shows as *Firebird* (1932, with Judith Anderson), *Party* (1933), *Julie* and *Queer People* (both 1934), *Worth a Million* (1940), and her last, *In Any Language* (1952). Billy Rose's nostalgic *Diamond Horseshoe Revue* also provided work in the 1940s. Nita was philosophical about her rise and fall. "I had a good career," she told reporter Sidney Fields. "No complaints, though I never could keep a nickel ... I became passé. I always seem to put my foot in it and say the wrong things. They began treating me like Typhoid Mary. Well, I'm not married to an agent or a producer, which would help."

Barclay died in 1945, and Nita's plight became more desperate. She moved into The Hotel Wentworth, a seedy establishment off Times Square. Her rent was partially paid by the Actor's Fund. "A wretched little hotel," she called her home in 1958, "and they're raising the rents to make more cubicles for the transients ... I'd like to turn Radio City into a Roman arena and throw all the avaricious landlords to the lions." She got a little work on television in the 1950s, including an appearance with Bert Lahr on the acclaimed *Omnibus* series. "I keep telling the television people I want to be a character actress," she bemoaned, "and they keep telling me, 'You don't look like a character actress.'"

After her death, a rumor was started that Nita had been a drug addict. There is not a shred of evidence to support this claim, but it's easy to see how it started. She frequently went faint because of a heart condition. Additionally, Nita was nearly blind for the last ten years of her life but continued to apply her own makeup, what she herself called her "cement face ... It's easy to put on, but takes years to get off." With her dead-white face, blackened eyes and brows, blood-red lips, and bizarrely drawn-on widow's peak, Nita certainly looked like a deranged junkie. But she maintained her wit and had many loyal friends (Diana Barrymore called her Mother Moonbeam). Nita Naldi died of a heart attack in her sleep on February 17, 1961, just shy of her sixty-fourth birthday. Not long before she died, Nita told a reporter wryly, "Living today is like trying to cross a New York street. It's a miracle if you make it."

Alla Nazimova

Of all the foreign imports to the silent screen—Garbo, Negri, Banky, Ronald Colman, Emil Jannings, Anna Q. Nilsson—Alla Nazimova came to the movies with the biggest reputation and, some feel, the most talent. Her film career—which stretched from 1916 through 1944—was spotty, but no one ever doubted that she was a great actress.

She was born in Yalta, in the Crimea, on June 4, 1879, one of three children of Yakov Leventon and his wife, Sonya Horowitz. According to her biographer, Gavin Lambert, Nazimova (she later chose the name herself) had a hellish childhood. Her parents separated, and she was bounced from boarding school to foster home to unwilling relatives. Like Marlene Dietrich years later, Nazimova trained to be a violinist rather than an actress. But violin soon gave way to the stage, and Nazimova (her first name was rarely used) joined the Academy of Acting in Moscow and Stanislavsky's Moscow Art Theater. She married Sergei Golovin in 1899, but the two separated almost immediately. By 1903 the twenty-four-year-old actress was St. Petersburg's star attraction. Now the companion of colorful actor/producer Pavel Orlenev, she went on to tour with his company in Berlin and London.

In 1905 Nazimova and Orlenev came to the United States, opening a Russian-language theater in New York's Lower East Side. Within a year, the company (and Orlenev) returned to Mother Russia. Only the leading lady stayed behind, having been signed by producer Henry Miller. Her English-speaking debut came with Ibsen's *Hedda Gabler* (1906). Nazimova bowled them over on Broadway and became an instant star. Her older sister, Nina, followed her to the United States (and had a son who grew up to be director Val Lewton). Nazimova's theatrical successes came in droves: Ibsen's *A Doll's House* and *The Master Builder* (both 1906), *Little Eyolf* (Ibsen again, 1910), *The Marionettes* (1911), *Bella Donna* (a huge 1912 hit), and *War Brides* (a melodramatic antiwar play of 1915).

It was at this point that the movies came calling, in the person of Herbert

Brenon, who bought the film rights to *War Brides* for Selznick. Her 1916 film debut was a smash hit—Nazimova's kindness is also displayed by the presence of fledgling actor Richard Barthelmess in the cast. Barthelmess's mother, Caroline Harris, had been Nazimova's English coach, and the actress insisted that her beloved "Dickey" be given a role in the film. Nazimova was thirty-seven when she made her film debut, an age when many screen stars are retiring (voluntarily or not). Nazimova wasn't so much beautiful as striking: She was only 5'3" but looked much taller because of her lithe build. She had enormous, expressive blue eyes, a large mouth and nose, and piles of black hair. She also had the attitude and overpowering personality of a true diva. Film critics spoke of Nazimova's "marvelously mobile face, capable of indicating various shades of emotion, especially those of sorrow," her "masterly control of the emotions and their expression." She was signed by Metro in 1918 (starting at $13,000 a week) and made eleven films for them in only three years, all but one heavy dramas.

She was an artist's model in *Revelation*, a gypsy in *Toys of Fate*, and a sheik's tragic daughter in *An Eye for an Eye* (all 1918). According to Dewitt Bodeen, Nazimova's two best Metro films were released in 1919: She played an unwed mother (and her own daughter) in *Out of the Fog* and half sisters in China in *The Red Lantern*. The finale of the latter film was called "one of the poignant moments in the history of cinema" by writer Herb Sterne. Her only comedic film came with *The Brat*, in 1919. Nazimova (at forty) played a young chorus girl who upsets the wealthy family taking her in; it was a huge hit. She made four films for Metro in 1920, all reasonable successes and adding to her reputation as a great dramatic actress: *Stronger Than Death* (practically a remake of Theda Bara's *The Soul of Buddha*), *The Heart of a Child* (as an innocent Limehouse girl), *Madame Peacock* (as a Margo Channing–like stage diva), and *Billions* (as a Russian patroness of the arts).

Through all this filming, Nazimova was also making friends in the Hollywood community. She lived as the common-law wife of frequent costar Charles Bryant from 1912 till the early 1920s, though the two never married (she and her Russian husband Golovin didn't officially divorce until 1923). Nazimova was also openly bisexual. This led to rumors that she only hired gay cast and crew for her films, especially *Salome*. While she certainly had a good number of gay friends, Nazimova was not that narrow minded, and she didn't discriminate professionally or personally (in fact, she was future First Lady Nancy Reagan's godmother). After Bryant, Nazimova's last long-term relationship was with actress Glesca Marshall, from 1928 until her death.

By 1921 Nazimova was demanding more and more autonomous control over her films, and the results were astounding (certainly to Metro). Her 1921 *Camille* was certainly the most beautiful production ever of that film, thanks to costume and set designer Natasha Rambova. The former dancer was discovered by Nazimova and proved a genius at creating elaborate, film-friendly designs of flowing Arts Deco and Nouveau. With Rudolph Valentino as her Armand, Nazimova created a popular but still very artsy Camille. Costar Valentino and designer Rambova went on to marry in 1922.

A casual Nazimova, caught off-screen.

At this point, Nazimova left Metro for United Artists. Her first film for them was one of her pet projects, Ibsen's *A Doll's House* (1922). It was a critical hit, but the movie-going public cannot be relied upon to flock to theaters for Ibsen. Returns were disappointing. Nazimova's next film was to be her great achievement: Oscar Wilde's *Salome*, patterned visually after Aubrey Beardsley's 1890s ink drawings. She poured every cent she had into the project, which was released through United Artists. Seen today, the film is a stunner, even considering the poor quality and shortened prints available. Rambova's bizarre sets and costumes (including what must be the screen's first micro-mini) and Nazimova's petulant, seething performance result in an erotic, almost hallucinogenic drama. As both high art and high camp, it's hard to beat. But 1922 audiences weren't so much stunned as annoyed and confused by the artsy, pretentious film. *Salome* was a resounding financial disaster and lost a fortune for both Nazimova and the studio.

Her attempts to recoup financially also came to naught. She had purchased a large, rambling Sunset Boulevard estate in 1918 for $55,000. Complete with large pool and landscaping, "The Garden of Alla" served as her home until 1923, when she and some real estate sharpies added thirty self-contained bungalows (and an "h" to "Alla") and turned it into a hotel. It soon became Hollywood's most notorious (and popular) nesting spot for such tenants as the Barrymores, Tallulah Bankhead, Ramon Novarro, Clara Bow, Garbo, Buster Keaton, and writers Noel Coward, Robert Benchley, Dorothy Parker, and Alexander Woollcott. But Nazimova wound up losing money on it, and toward the end of her life she boarded in one of the cottages on her own former estate.

She made only three more silent films. Two were for First National: she was a fallen woman in *Madonna of the Streets* (1924) and a self-sacrificing mother in *My Son* (with Jack Pickford and Constance Bennett, 1925). She also made one for the then-ailing Vitagraph (*The Redeeming Sin*, a 1925 French underworld film with the equally troubled Lou Tellegen). Then she dropped from sight—at least, for moviegoers.

Joe Franklin, in his book *Classics of the Silent Screen*, rebuked Nazimova for returning to films in later years and ruining her Garboesque mystery. But unlike Garbo, Nazimova had not been idle during her absence from Hollywood.

"Madame" Alla Nazimova in 1920.

Among her many latter-day theatrical successes were *The Cherry Orchard* (1928), *Mourning Becomes Electra* (1931), *The Good Earth* (1932), *Ghosts* (1935), and *The Mother* (1939). She stayed socially active and was known as a humorous and intelligent woman, loyal to her many friends. In his book *Great Stars of the American Theater*, Daniel Blum listed her likes as "buttercups, yellow field flowers, Dreiser, Hugh Walpole and Heine" and her dislikes as "being alone, food talk, reptiles and yawning in public."

In 1940 Nazimova broke her fifteen-year absence from the screen and appeared in 20th Century–Fox's war thriller *Escape*, with Norma Shearer and Robert Taylor (she played Taylor's mother). She looked worn and haggard at sixty-one, but still lovely, like a ruined European castle. Nazimova made another four films: She played Tyrone Power's mother in the remake of *Blood and Sand* (1941), one of the doomed voyagers over *The Bridge of San Luis Rey* (1944), and Paul Henried's mother in another good war drama, *In Our Time* (1944). Her final role was as a Polish war emigrée in *Since You Went Away* (1944), a very respectable swan song.

In the summer of 1945 Nazimova had to be hospitalized for a heart condition; she died at Good Samaritan Hospital on July 13 of that year, at the relatively young age of sixty-six. Her ashes were interred in Forest Lawn. Fourteen years later, in 1959, her beloved Garden of Allah was bulldozed. At the time of Nazimova's death, she was remembered and lauded as one of the century's great stage actresses. Her films were a mere afterthought, all but ignored in her tributes. But today, most who saw her onstage are gone; her most recent theatrical successes are more than fifty years in the past. It's her films that live on—particularly her greatest project and biggest failure, *Salome*.

Pola Negri

The career of Pola Negri is proof positive that publicity can be a two-edged sword. In the late 1910s and early 1920s, Pola was often compared to Duse and Bernhardt. She was Europe's most-praised young actress, working with the best directors and given the choicest assignments. But, by the late 1920s, she'd become somewhat of a joke. Pola's own hunger for the limelight and the wacky PR put out by her American studio, Paramount, had turned her into a parody of the heavy-breathing silent-screen vamp. Her loves, her clothes, and her diva fits all became the stuff of legend, but the fact that she was a dedicated and versatile actress somehow was forgotten.

She was born Apollonia Chalupec on the last day of 1897, in Lipno, then a Russian territory in Poland (her birth year is variously reported as 1894, 1897 and 1899; Billy Doyle, in *The Ultimate Directory of Silent Screen Performers*, cites 1897, and I have elected to use that date). Her father, Jerzy Mathias-Chalupec, was a Slovakian immigrant, while her mother, Eleanora de Kielczeska, was vaguely described as "impoverished nobility" and earned her living as a cook. In the uprising of 1905, Pola's father was (by her own account) imprisoned for anti-Czarist activities, and she and her mother relocated to a Warsaw ghetto.

Somehow, enough money was raised to send Pola to the Imperial Ballet School. A bout of tuberculosis supposedly ended her dancing career (Pola never would have admitted to a lack of talent), and she transferred to the Imperial Academy of Dramatic Arts, where she showed great promise and—already—an artistic temperament. It was around this time that Pola adopted her new stage name. In Warsaw she appeared onstage in *The Wild Duck* and *Hannele* (both 1913), *The End of Sodom* (1914), as well as several other shows. She made her film debut in the first year of World War I as a dancer in *Niewolnica Zmyslow/Love and Passion*. She signed with the Polish Sphinx Company and made another seven films in Poland through 1916, all directed by Aleksander Hertz.

Her big break came in Max Reinhardt's hit revival of the stage show

Sumurun (1916–17) in Berlin. In this glitzy Arabian fairy tale, Pola played a fiery harem girl, and she became the toast of Berlin. Wiggling out of her long-term contract with Sphinx, Pola stayed in Berlin to star in German films. Pola arrived in Germany at a time when its social, economic, and political structure was collapsing, but its film industry was booming. Fritz Lang called postwar Germany "a period of deepest despair, of hysteria, cynicism, unrestrained vice. The most dreadful poverty existed side by side with immense new wealth." The huge film conglomerate Universum Film Aktien Gesellschaft, better known as UFa, was formed in 1917 and loomed over the artistic landscape. Pola made three films for them in 1917 and another six in 1918. That year, she worked for the first time with fledgling director Ernst Lubitsch, in *Der Augen die Mumie Ma/The Eyes of the Mummy*. Costarring Emil Jannings, it was a successful Egyptian melodrama, which left Pola and Lubitsch eager to collaborate again.

Her first big film hit was *Carmen* (also released as *Gypsy Blood*, mid–1918), directed by Ernst Lubitsch. Hers was a red-blooded, passionate Carmen, as was her *Madame DuBarry* (or *Passion*, 1919), also directed by Lubitsch. This latter film was a big hit overseas, the first German film to be seen in the United States since the war's end. Meanwhile, Pola continued starring in German films for Ufa: five in 1919, eight in 1920. Her bigger hits of this period were *Sumurun/One Arabian Night, Arme Violetta/The Red Peacock*, and Lubitsch's *Die Flamme/Montmartre*. Pola also married the first of her two allegedly royal husbands at this time; she was wed to Count Eugene Dambski from 1920 through 1922.

Pola Negri at her most intense (The Metaluna Collection).

Pola Negri was one of the first German stars to be lured to America, and she left a country in the midst of great artistic excitement. Such imaginative directors as Lubitsch, Fritz Lang, F. W. Murnau, Paul Wegener, and G. W. Pabst were inspiring film makers the world over. But Paramount offered Pola a huge salary and star treatment, so she was willing to check her artistic expression at the door. She arrived in America in mid–1922, and her first United States role was as an exotic, murderous vamp in *Bella Donna* (1923). The film had romance, tragedy, and enough forbidden, hinted-at sex to fill three Elinor Glyn novels. Audiences flocked to see Pola, and Paramount star Gloria Swanson was not amused. There never was a real feud between the ladies, but Paramount's cunning PR staff invented one for the press to play up. Later in 1923 Pola appeared in a remake of *The Cheat*, which had been such a hit for Fannie Ward back in 1915, as well as in *The Spanish Dancer* (with Antonio Moreno).

Four more films followed in 1924, including the Lubitsch-directed *Forbidden Paradise,* the romantic melodramas *Lily of the Dust* (with a very young Ben Lyon), *Men,* and *Shadows of Paris*. Despite the similarity in her roles, Pola's films did well at the box office. She herself was not happy, though, sneering that "There was no more call on my abilities as an actress than there was on one of Ziegfeld's showgirls." Moviegoers didn't seem to care, and Paramount certainly didn't. Fan magazines clamored for interviews; Pola posed in the acts of writing, sculpting, and reading, much as Sarah Bernhardt had done forty years earlier. Pola ("La Negri" to her detractors) became as famous—more famous, really—for her offscreen life than for her film roles. She popularized red nail polish, turbans, and high "Russian" boots. She began romancing Charlie Chaplin the minute she got off the boat from Europe, though that seems to have been a romance for PR purposes only. Certainly, Pola was not Chaplin's type: He preferred pliable pre-teen nymphets and only married them to the accompaniment of a shotgun.

In 1925 she met a man more to her tastes. Rudolph Valentino was on the rebound from his second wife, Natasha Rambova. Valentino was right up Pola's alley: a genuinely nice, uncomplicated guy with a fixation for controlling, ambitious women. Pola latched on to him like Velcro. Meanwhile, her career continued apace, with four more films in 1925. Certainly the best of the lot was *A Woman of the World* (from a Carl Van Vechten novel), one of Pola's rare excursions into light comedy. Starring as a scandalous titled foreigner who descends on a small Midwestern town to visit relatives, she gave a witty, subtle performance. Mocking her own vamp image, Pola showed in this film that she was more than a kohl-eyed siren; like her paramour Valentino, she was delightfully adept at drawing-room comedy. She had little opportunity to show that in her other 1925 releases, though: Pola was a dancer in *The Charmer*, what was quaintly called a "half-caste" in *East of Suez*, and a gold-mine gal in the Paul Bern–directed *Flower of Night*. By 1926 she was down to only two releases, not a good sign: the run-of-the-mill Ruritarian romance *The Crown of Lies* and another comedy, *Good and Naughty* (which, sadly, was neither).

Then an event occurred which forever changed the way people looked at Pola Negri: the death, in the summer of 1926, of Rudolph Valentino. Valentino died in New York while Pola was working in California. She took the first train east and, heavily veiled, threw herself on Valentino's coffin. She accompanied the body back to California for the funeral, and—according to Ben Lyon—tried to have a blanket of flowers spelling "Pola" draped over the coffin. She fainted at the funeral and generally carried on like Act III of *Camille*. If Pola thought she understood the press or the American public, she was quite wrong. She became a laughingstock, and Hollywood insiders resented her co-opting Valentino's death for her own publicity purposes. To be fair, Pola was an emotional, demonstrative European. It's quite possible that her grief was sincere. "How should I have behaved?" she asked years later. "I simply reacted to despair in the only way of which I was capable—naturally and spontaneously." But she laid it on with a trowel, and overnight, people became fed up with her.

But Paramount had an iron-clad contract with Pola and tried to make the best of things: They put her into three films in 1927, and another four in 1928. *Barbed Wire* (1927) was one of the best, an antiwar drama directed by Mauritz Stiller. It proved that Pola's talent for real acting—as opposed to melodramatic posing—had not atrophied. *Hotel Imperial* (also 1927 and also with Stiller) was another superior war film, with Pola as a chambermaid who falls in love with a soldier. These were her last really top-notch assignments, however. No one (including their star) was much taken with *The Woman on Trial* (1927), *The Secret Hour*, *Three Sinners*, *Loves of an Actress*, or *The Woman from Moscow* (all 1928). After that last film, her contract ran out. There was no talk of renewing it, especially as her heavy accent did not lend itself to the new talking pictures. She had made twenty films for the studio, with not a single loan-out.

Pola's personal life had not stood still after Valentino's death. She was romanced by one of the "marrying Mdivanis," Serge, in 1927. Serge and his brothers David and Alexis, all dubious Russian "princes," cut a swath through 1920s and 1930s Hollywood, dating and marrying as many actresses and heiresses as they could. Serge and Pola wed in France, but she was soon disenchanted with his personality (just as fiery as hers). When Pola's fortune was wiped out in the 1929 stock market crash, her husband took off for the hills. They were soon divorced, and Pola had to think about restarting her acting career. After some false starts, she made *The Woman He Scorned* (filmed silent and dubbed, 1929) in England. Her heralded American "comeback" was *A Woman Commands* (RKO, 1932), in which she sang (quite creditably) "Paradise." But the film itself was another dated Ruritarian romance, and these had ceased to be popular years before. Pola sailed back to Europe, where she made *Fanatisme* (France, 1934).

Grand diva Pola Negri at the height of her mid–1920s fame.

With a talent for being in the wrong place at the wrong time, Pola returned to Germany in 1935, when the film industry was being co-opted by the Nazi party. She made the highly successful mother-love drama *Mazurka* that year, then signed a contract with her old studio, UFa, which was by now merely a government mouthpiece, a shadow of its former self. She made five films for UFa: *Moscow-Shanghai* (1936), *Madame Bovary* and *Tango Nocturno* (both 1937), another mother-love weeper, *Die Fromme*

Luge/The Secret Lie (1938, costarring Eva Braun's brother, Hermann, as her son), and *Die Nacht der Entscheidung/The Night of Decision* (1938). Between each film, Pola would vacation in France with her mother, leaving Germany "with an enormous sense of relief."

Pola's work in Germany at this time haunted her for the rest of her life. Why did she return to that country when everyone else was fleeing? Why did she wait until the outbreak of war to wise up and escape? In her autobiography, she tried, of course, to cover her tracks. Hitler was a big fan, she admitted, but she never met him and said that "I was no more responsible for the fact that I happened to be Hitler's favorite movie star than I was for the crimes committed by the inmates of Alcatraz, who had once voted me their favorite star." Pola successfully sued the French magazine *Pour Vous* after they printed that she was Hitler's mistress. And, Pola pointed out, Goebbels hated her and tried again and again to have her thrown out of the country as non-Aryan.

In retrospect, Pola must have known and seen more than she let on; no one could be a big enough idiot to miss the horrors of Nazi rule by 1939. While not a sympathizer or even a collaborator, Pola must take blame for shutting her eyes and taking an easy paycheck. When her home country, Poland, was invaded, she finally snapped to attention and joined the Red Cross in France. With her American re-entry visa, she managed to get back to the United States, through Spain and Portugal, in 1941 (Pola eventually became an American citizen, in 1951).

She made one more comeback attempt, the 1943 screwball *comedy Hi Diddle Diddle*. It is not at all a bad film: Pola played a temperamental opera singer married to Adolph Menjou in this backstage love story. It was even a bit postmodern, with one actress described as "the director's girlfriend" popping up in scene after scene playing different roles. But *Hi Diddle Diddle* made little impact at the box office, and Pola's comeback suffered the same fate as Gloria Swanson's *Father Takes a Wife* had in 1941.

But, in 1948, Pola's lucky star came through for her again. Washed up professionally and with her finances in disarray, she met wealthy, retired radio personality Margaret West and moved to Santa Monica with her. The ladies became social gadabouts in Hollywood, throwing parties and building up an impressive collection of artwork. They relocated to West's hometown, San Antonio, in 1957, and, when West died in 1963, she left Pola her considerable estate. The relationship with West has always been shrouded in mystery. Whether West was Pola's fan, friend, or wife was never elaborated upon by either woman.

Pola's last film was a cameo in Disney's kiddie adventure *The Moonspinners* (1964), starring Hayley Mills. Playing a mysterious and slightly sinister millionairess, Pola appeared decked out to the nines, leading a cheetah on a leash. The press went nuts, and she was briefly feted and interviewed. Then she retreated back to her San Antonio mansion. After years of rewrites and dozens of ghostwriters, Pola's long-awaited autobiography, modestly titled *Memoirs of a Star*, was published by Doubleday in 1970. The book became an instant classic of entertainingly overblown prose, and it makes for very enjoyable reading.

While not a recluse, Pola shied away from the press in later years, only occasionally appearing in public and talking to few reporters. Her eyesight failed, as did her general health. In the early 1980s, she posed for photographer Horst, decked out in a black wig, jeweled gown, and perfect makeup. When Pola Negri died on August 1, 1987, the lengthy obituaries recalled a sultry vamp of days gone by. But Pola herself had the last word, in her autobiography: "The past was wonderful; it was youth and exhilaration. I would not have missed it for worlds. The present is tranquil; it is age and a little wisdom ... I would relinquish neither inner scars nor external glories ... There is even a certain edge of triumph in the peacefulness of my present life." Like her fellow vamps Theda Bara and Gloria Swanson, Pola proved that bad girls sometimes had happy endings.

Mary Nolan

There are many performers who manage to destroy their careers, through errors of judgment, addictions, or just plain bad luck. But actress Mary Nolan has the dubious distinction of having torpedoed two promising careers within the space of ten years.

She was born Mary Imogene Robertson in the boondocks of Hickory Grove, Kentucky. The date was December 18, 1905, and life quickly turned sour for the girl. Her mother died in 1908, leaving Mary and her three siblings at the mercy of their mostly absentee father. Mary was shipped off to a convent in St. Joseph, Missouri, where she lived until she was thirteen. She was rushed home in 1918 just in time for the death of her sister Sally; after that, Mary and her brother Ray were hired out by their grandmother as farm laborers, until they were finally rescued by their sister Mabel. It was Mabel, a small-time actress, who introduced Mary to the stage.

Mary saved trainfare to New York, where she arrived, broke and beautiful, in 1919. She really was breathtaking, with her perfect bone structure, cloud of thick blonde hair, and china-blue eyes. It wasn't long before Mary got work as an artist's model for such big shots as James Montgomery Flagg and Arthur William Brown. Like so many models, she eventually found her way to New York's theatrical agents and producers. It was Oliver Morosco who launched her stage career, in the choruses of *Daffy Dill* and *Lady Butterfly*. It was then that she took on the first of her several stage names, Imogene "Bubbles" Wilson (for the sake of simplicity, we will refer to her herein as Mary Nolan, her best-known moniker).

It was also at this time that Mary met the man who was to become her bête noir, comedian Frank Tinney. Tinney, who had been born in 1885, was already middle aged when the two met, but they quickly became an item. It is impossible to judge Tinney's work today, but his contemporaries called him a genius at both blackface comedy and emceeing (Frank Fay began his career as a second-string Tinney). Tinney was married and the father of a son, and he was not about to get divorced. But he

Follies **star Mary Nolan, circa 1924.**

and Mary were so drawn to each other that she was willing to become his mistress.

For the next several years, the two had a violent love/hate relationship. Tinney set Mary up in a West 72nd Street apartment and showered her with expensive gifts—but he also showered her with bruises, both physical and emotional. In a day when wife beating was lightly joked about, Mary's black eyes and bruises did not set off any alarms, as long as they could be covered by stage makeup. She was even written off as a masochist who no doubt enjoyed the battles. In a syndicated autobiographical newspaper series of 1941, Mary recalled that "My life with Frank Tinney was a nonsensical mixture of fights and laughs, and half and half." One brawl occurred when Tinney phoned to say he was bringing an important friend for dinner and came home leading a donkey. "I began throwing ashtrays, table lamps, anything I could get my hands on," Mary recalled, after which she went on a shopping spree on Tinney's credit.

But all this time, her own career was skyrocketing, and the chorine became a star showgirl in the *Ziegfeld Follies*, still billed as Imogene "Bubbles" Wilson. She first appeared in the 1923 edition (which starred Eddie Cantor, Fanny Brice, jazz dancer Ann Pennington, and Paul Whiteman's Band); Mary's fellow showgirls that year included Lina Basquette and the ill-fated Hilda Ferguson. Mary was back in the *Follies* in 1924, a slightly less stellar edition which mainly starred Will Rogers. But she didn't stay with the *Follies* for the entire 1924-25 season.

Scandal had first hit in the spring of 1924, when Tinney found Mary with another man (a reporter, she later said) and beat her so badly that she called the police, fearing for her life. Tinney was arrested and brought to trial—which finally ended his marriage—but Mary refused to testify against her lover, and charges were eventually dropped. So, unfortunately, was Mary. In the fall of 1924, Ziegfeld said that the scandal had made her unsuitable for the new *Follies*, and he unceremoniously fired her. Tinney fled to London, and the still-obsessed Mary was at the dock to tearfully beg him to stay. "As long as I live I will love Frank Tinney," she was quoted. "He is mine. I am his. We will be together so long as we live." Broke and in ill health, Mary was admitted to an Actor's Fund Home; she was still only nineteen years old, but her career as "Bubbles" Wilson was over. She soon sailed for London, where Tinney set her up in a flat, and the circus began all over again: the beatings, fights, and reconciliations.

But, while in London, Mary attracted the notice of the German film company UFa and was offered a role in *Die Feuertanzerin*, at the equivalent of $1,000 a week. Tinney was livid, but Mary somewhat gratefully fled from his influence to begin anew. She arrived in Berlin early in 1925 and made six films there over the next two years, for a number of production companies—billed now as Imogene Robertson, her birth name. "Fortune was kind to me there," Mary later wrote. "The people showed me every consideration. I was given every courtesy at the studios. The public was kind enough to like my pictures." While she didn't rise to the top of the German film industry, Mary did prove herself an able and photogenic actress, and she began to get offers from United States producers. She made preparations to return to her homeland. First, though, she had one last unpleasant encounter with Frank Tinney.

He came to Berlin and talked his way on to the set of one of her last German films. "He watched me go through a love scene," she recalled. "That seemed to make him bitter." His career and marriage in tatters, Tinney had to beg Mary for the fare back to England. "That moment on the train was the last time I ever saw Frank Tinney," Mary wrote. "It was a sad, heart-rending one." Tinney's freefall continued; he died impoverished in 1940.

Mary sailed, with fellow actor Nils Asther, on the Majestic, landing in New York in 1927. "The stain of scandal hadn't been erased by my success as a film star in Germany," she wrote. "I was not greeted as an actress home from exploits abroad, but as a notorious creature returning to the scene of her shame." She did not find Hollywood as companionable as Berlin: "I got more stares than smiles. Oh, there were some kindly friends and civil acquaintances, but for a long time I remained outside the barrier of Hollywood life, shunned by the elite of the film colony." To be fair, Hollywood had other reasons to shun Mary: There was always a snobbery about former showgirls, and a putative "German" actress coming to take U.S. roles would engender some hostility. With Clara Bow, Alma Rubens, and Juanita Hansen in town, Mary's scandals were relatively mild.

A contract with United Artists awaited her, but with one provision—she had to change her name. "Imogene Wilson" had too many bad associations; from now on she would be Mary Nolan. She was shown the morals clause in her contract and told that "I was on probation. One word of unfavorable publicity would ruin me."

Her American "screen test" was a small role in the Duncan sisters' *Topsy and Eva*, which also costarred Nils Asther (who went on to marry Vivian Duncan). Mary screened well enough—and behaved well enough—to qualify for leading roles. She starred for UA in the drama *Sorrel and Son* (1927), again with

Film star Mary Nolan, late 1920s.

Asther and alongside actresses Alice Joyce, Anna Q. Nilsson, and Carmel Myers.

Early in 1928 Mary signed a long-term contract with Universal, where she made seven films through 1930, along with another five on loan-out. At her home studio, she starred in *Foreign Legion* and *Good Morning, Judge* (both 1928), *Shanghai Lady* and *Silks and Saddles* (both 1929), *Undertow*, the circus drama *Young Desire*, and the reliable old melodrama *Outside the Law* (all 1930). None of these films were much better than programmers; Mary had much better luck with her loan-out assignments.

She traveled back to Germany to make the episodic *Uneasy Money* (1928) and the costume drama *Eleven Who Were Loyal* (1929), both for UFa. She also made *Charming Sinners* (1929) at Paramount, which featured a literate

Somerset Maugham script and costars Ruth Chatterton and William Powell. But her best loan-outs were two late silents at MGM, *West of Zanzibar* and *Desert Nights* (both 1929). Both were "A" films, and both show Mary to have been a superb actress and a lovely leading lady.

In *West of Zanzibar* she was menaced by Lon Chaney, who kidnaps her to his jungle hut, thinking her the daughter of an old enemy. Though she had little to do but look terrified, Mary came off quite well, showing fire and spirit in the role, also allowing herself to be photographed covered in mud and looking a wreck. She went from the jungle to the sands in *Desert Nights*, with John Gilbert (still at his prime). Playing a hard-boiled jewel thief, Mary gave a quiet, intelligent, and intense performance that boded well for her career. No mere *Follies* beauty, she obviously had talent and grit. When talkies came in, her voice "photographed" well enough to indicate a good future for the actress, still only in her mid-twenties.

But all was not rosy for Mary, who found herself in yet another abusive relationship, this time with MGM executive and notorious roughneck Eddie Mannix. The two met in 1927, and "In less than a week we were more than friends, we were in love," as Mary wrote. But by 1929, Mannix tired of Mary and returned to his wife. Mary threatened to raise a fuss, but Mannix was no Frank Tinney. Not only did he allegedly beat her so badly that she was hospitalized, but he put the word out around town that she was trouble. When she sued him for damages, her career was as good as over; in 1930, she was fired from Universal.

In 1929 Mary wed wealthy young stockbroker Wallace T. Macreary, Jr., who helped to set her up in a dress shop. But her luck had finally run out: A week after their marriage, the stock market crashed, and Macreary lost his entire fortune. In October 1931 Mary and her husband jointly filed for bankruptcy, and soon after, divorce. "The strain and sudden shock of poverty was too much for Wallace," said Mary. "We just didn't stay happy."

Still beautiful and still talented, Mary managed to get a few low-budget assignments despite Mannix's blacklisting. In 1931 and 1932 she made six films at last-ditch poverty-row studios, costarring with other desperate silent film refugees. She worked at Tiffany (*X Marks the Spot*, with Lew Cody), Regal (*Enemies of the Law*, with Lou Tellegen), Hollywood Pictures (*File 113*, with Clara Kimball Young), and Monogram (*Midnight Patrol*, with Betty Bronson and Mack Swain).

In 1932, at the age of twenty-seven, Mary Nolan's film career was over. By 1932 she was also a drug addict; she later claimed to have gotten hooked on morphine during her Mannix-induced hospital stay. She was reduced to singing in cheap nightclubs ("The only places that would permit me to appear were the dives that harbored the underworld"). The Actor's Fund set her up in an apartment and enrolled her in various rehab programs. In May 1937 she was arrested for failing to pay a dressmaker's bill and was hauled off to the prison ward of Bellevue Hospital in New York. Later that year, she was committed to a state hospital and was sent off, "cured," in October 1938.

"I wanted to return to Los Angeles, even though I had been told I could never go there again," Mary later wrote.

"My sister lived there. I had no one else, no other place to go." She made the rounds of the agencies. But not only did Mary have a bad reputation—by the late 1930s her looks were gone: Haggard, drawn, and overly made-up, she looked a wreck. There was no show business work for her. She got a job managing a bungalow court apartment, changing her name once again (to Mary Wilson) and keeping a low profile. "I was working for room and board, and gladly," she said. In 1941 Mary was induced to sell her story to *The American Weekly* for syndication; of course, it was written to sound as sordid as possible.

At the end of her newspaper autobiography, Mary wrote, "I don't believe anything bad will ever happen to me again. I hope the rest of my life will be normal and nice. I don't know what the future holds for me, but whatever it is I will face it with faith and courage. I owe that to those who had faith in me." The future had only seven years to hold for Mary, and not good ones. She moved back in with her sister Mabel, and she was in and out of Cedars of Lebanon Hospital for both malnutrition and morphine addiction; she also attempted suicide twice. When she died on November 12, 1948, of liver disease, she weighed only seventy pounds.

Hollywood excoriated itself at her Hollywood Cemetery funeral for ignoring the actress, just as it had ignored Marie Prevost, Florence Lawrence, and others before her. After it was too late, newspapers printed editorials about how drugs and two abusive men had helped send the talented actress to ruin and how she might have been saved. But there was a certain lurid, lingering quality to the obituaries; after all, everyone loved a good tragedy.

ANITA PAGE

When MGM released *Our Dancing Daughters*—the landmark tribute to flappers and jazz babies—in mid–1928, one star stood out from the crowd. It wasn't Joan Crawford who received the critical acclaim and word of mouth; it was lovely blonde Anita Page, for her portrayal of the self-destructive, amoral Anne. Yet within a few years, Crawford was Queen of the Lot, and Page was being loaned out for trash like *Jungle Bride*. Today, though, Anita Page has no regrets, no bitterness. She's bright, funny, and more than happy to talk about her career.

Page was born Anita Pomares on August 4, 1910, in Queens, New York. "Grandpa was consul from San Salvador when it was a beautiful place, many years ago. We have a family crest—we don't all come from Schwab's Drugstore, you know," Anita laughs. "My grandmother was a marvelous pianist, but she was a very strong Catholic. She just didn't believe in girls going into careers. I don't think she knew I had a career—her daughters went through the papers, cutting out my photos, saying they needed recipes. My mother was different, though." After a few school plays, dance lessons from Martha Graham, and bit parts in two films, Anita was ready to take on Hollywood.

Her entrance into films came courtesy of her friend, actress Betty Bronson. "Betty's mother put one of my photos up in her home. A gentleman who was handling Betty's fan mail saw it and said he was going into the business of handling stars. I didn't want to call him, but my mother said, 'Honey, if you want to go into the movies, then you'd better call him!' I called, and he told me to be at the front gate of Paramount at 9:00 the next morning and to bring the picture. The casting director took one look at the picture and gave me a test!"

MGM was also interested. "The phone rang, and someone said, 'This is Mal St. Clair from MGM.' I thought it was one of my boyfriends kidding me, so I said, 'Well, this is Gloria Swanson!' Well, it turns out Mal St. Clair had been looking for a new face." Anita showed up for her MGM test despite a cold and a red nose, not worried, because "When you're young it's all going to be great tomorrow. [Director] Sam Wood took one look at me and called up Bill Haines, who was one of my favorites. Well! Paul Bern was walking me up and down and telling me I'd be wonderful. Bill Haines walked in in his riding clothes—I took one look at him and decided I had to do it, red nose and all. It was the easiest test I ever had to do."

Anita was put through the delicious dilemma of having to choose between MGM and Paramount contracts. "I would have liked Paramount, but Metro was so great for women stars. I told MGM, 'I will not sign one of those six-month contracts where you play hands and feet!' I wanted to get on the screen, because I had such confidence in myself—and you have to have confidence, you just *have* to." She decided to take the MGM contract. "I don't think I realized how lucky I was! Of course, I was only 17, and, well, you can imagine, I was in seventh heaven!"

That first MGM film, with William Haines, was *Telling the World* (1927). "Bill Haines was very cheery, well-liked," recalls Anita. "I had a big crush on him, but after awhile he was like a brother. He used to say I had the longest eyelashes he'd ever seen, and I always thought he had the most perfect teeth—when he laughed it looked just like a horseshoe! When I came on the set, he used to sing, 'Nothing could be sweeter than to be with my Anita in the morning,' and I would say, 'Bill, I am *not* your Anita!'"

Among a star's duties was photo sittings, and Anita's favorite photographer was George Hurrell. "We worked beautifully together—he'd say something funny, and I'd start laughing and he'd snap me. One time I had tears in my eyes thinking of a scene; he knew just when to take you. He took some of me where I looked just like Barbara La Marr—though I think her mouth was prettier than mine. Another actress I loved was Madge Bellamy—wasn't she gorgeous? I met her at a party, and she thought we looked a little alike—and I loved that!"

Anita Page in *Broadway Melody*, 1929 (Randal Malone).

Anita's height—5'5"—nearly lost her a role opposite Ramon Novarro in *The Flying Fleet* (1928). "The producer wanted another girl, Josephine Dunn, because she was much shorter, but Novarro saved the day," says Anita. "He said, 'I've worked with Joan Crawford, and she was taller than Miss Page.' I was so crushed when that man was killed. That man was..." She searches for words. "He didn't just go around with anyone, he went around with the highest people in society. He bought land, put up seminaries, churches ... he didn't belong in this kind of business." Another early role was as Lon Chaney's love object in *While the City Sleeps* (1928). "Lon Chaney was a dear man," Anita recalls. "This was one of the few films he made without makeup, he played a policeman. He was not a handsome man, but without all the weird makeup he had a rugged appeal. On seeing him now, I think, he's not a bad-looking man at all! One thing we had in common is that we knew that a lot of the work was done through the eyes—we used to talk that over and over. He had a very good heart, I loved working with him. I was so sad to hear he'd passed away—I couldn't believe it, because he was so strong and virile."

Anita Page's biggest break was *Our Dancing Daughters*. Director Harry Beaumont was "scared to death to take me. He went to L. B. Mayer and said, 'I can't take this girl, I need a consummate actress. The whole story will rise and fall on her performance.'" Beaumont didn't know that Anita had recently thrown a diva fit in Mayer's office over a publicity still she considered scandalous: "I was ordering Mayer around like an office boy," she recalls in amazement. When Beaumont voiced doubts, Mayer smiled, "She's a Bernhardt." Her role in *Our Dancing Daughters* was "terribly naughty," Anita laughs, "but as long as I died, that was all right. But Joan Crawford was getting scared to death. She came up to me just before I was going to do the heavy work [a dramatic scene with Johnny Mack Brown] and said, 'Anita, you'd better be careful, you have to kick Johnny Mack Brown and fight him—don't be too harsh.' Hoping I'd hold back! Johnny was a football player, as if he couldn't protect himself! I told him, 'Joan is worried I was going to hurt you,' and he told me, 'Give it everything you've got.' So her little ploy didn't work."

Anita made two more films with Joan Crawford, *Our Modern Maidens* (1929) and *Our Blushing Brides* (1930). "We thought they'd put us in *Our Galloping Grandmas* eventually," she laughs. Although Anita is no Crawford fan, she also has no kind words for Christina Crawford's book *Mommie Dearest*. "What's fair is fair," Anita chooses her words carefully. "That girl would have had a terrible life if it weren't for Joan—maybe Joan was a little hard to get along with, but her career was it. But you can't blame her; she was fighting for her life, her career. This girl should have shut her big fat mouth. I don't want to criticize, but I feel that was very unkind, to put it mildly."

Talkies and Anita Page met head-on in 1929 when she appeared in MGM's all-star *Hollywood Revue* and the Academy Award-winning *Broadway Melody*. In the former, she was billed above her idol William Haines, Marion Davies, John Gilbert, and Laurel and Hardy, though she only appeared in one brief sketch. *Broadway Melody*, she admits, "was not my favorite, because I hated saying things like, 'Gee, ain't it elegant?' I thought *Our Dancing Daughters* was my picture, but *Broadway Melody* was Bessie Love's. Bessie had hopes that she would make quite a bit out of it, spent a lot of time taking dancing lessons, and she gave a beautiful performance. At first I didn't like it at all," Anita says, "but I do like it now."

Making those early talkies was literally like learning a new trade. "It was very hot," she recalls; "They had to use a lot of things like cheesecloth on the set because of the sound. One day I was sitting down in this scene, and everytime we'd start, there would be this rat-tat-tat. We'd look all over the set wondering what on earth it was—and it was me, filing my nails! Once we heard a rustle and they found it was my petticoat—I had to take it off. And, of course, you couldn't have your mood music while you were working. I loved working with the music." "There were a lot of things we had to worry about in talkies," Anita adds. "If someone opened a door, it stopped the whole scene. I was working with one of Garbo's directors, and he wanted me to have one tear—just one—falling down my cheek. Well, try it some time! I was laying in bed thinking, 'How am I going to get one tear?' Polly Moran told me, 'Oh, just turn your profile,' but that was not what they wanted. Finally, we got the one tear—and somebody opened a door! We had to do the whole thing over again."

Then, in the early 1930s, things began to go wrong. "I was getting so much publicity, my agent did a very dreadful thing: He said, 'You've got to demand more money'—he didn't ask for better parts, darn it! But you're not supposed to ask for more money after one year, and he made it all sound like it must be done! We won our point, they paid the money, but we didn't get that I would get starring roles, and that was the most important thing. Mayer said to me, 'I can make you the biggest star with three pictures—and I can kill Garbo in three pictures—and I'll never lift another finger to help you.' He snapped his fingers. The power was there," Anita maintains. "He was one of the most powerful men in the world for about seven years. But I loved him for what he did for me in the beginning."

From about 1930 on, MGM began to lose interest in Anita's career; a personal clash with one of the studio's PR men didn't help matters. "They'd never loaned me out before, but now they gave me to Universal, put my name as number two, and people began to wonder. There was nothing I could do. They finally wound up giving me a part in a Chesterfield film [the 1933 programmer *Jungle Bride*]. And I had been the belle of the ball for a year or more," she sighs. "I was getting the second highest fan mail on the lot, after Greta Garbo. The whole thing was my agent, who wanted the extra money. If only he'd left me alone … That's what happened to me." One of Anita's problems was that she was just too pretty. With her classic baby-doll looks, she was rarely given much to do beyond looking lovingly at her leading man. But when called upon to act, Anita was capable of brilliant performances. One of her best was in the underworld drama *Night Court* (1932), playing the wife of Phillips Holmes.

But her career still had another few good years to run. Among her leading men was John Gilbert, in the 1931 gangster drama *Gentleman's Fate*. "I loved John Gilbert," Anita says. "He was a great actor. Once he was lying on a couch playing a death scene, and he cried like a baby—and I thought, gosh, how can you do this? Little girls are allowed to cry, but little boys aren't supposed to! He said, 'If the scene plays true, I can do it every time. If there's one false moment and I don't believe it, I can't.' After the Garbo thing, he used to invite me to his bungalow to have lunch—I trusted him, he was a gentleman. I knew the people I could trust. I felt so sad for him, but I think he was happy with Virginia Bruce; he loved to tell me about how happy John Barrymore was with Dolores Costello."

Anita was Clark Gable's first leading lady, in *The Easiest Way* (1931, with Constance Bennett). "I thought he was charming, but there was never in my mind any romantic feeling. People can't understand that, but he just wasn't my type. He asked to drive me home one night, but I had my car with me. People said, 'The girl who said no to Clark Gable!' But he just wanted to give me a lift home, not marry me! Many years later he wrote an article where he said, 'Grace Kelly reminds me of my first leading lady, Anita Page.' And of course I loved Grace Kelly, so that didn't hurt my feelings at all!"

Both Marion Davies and Jean Harlow proved good friends to Anita. "Marion invited me to the Hearst Castle, and I wound up staying for five months—they wouldn't let me go! One day we were going up to Wyntoon, with all her friends from the *Follies*, and Marion said, 'You have the most beautiful bone structure.' I almost fell off my chair—here she was so beautiful herself!" She also recalls trying to smuggle a drink up to Marion's quarters and being caught by Hearst's security. Finding her way to Marion's room, she was asked, "Well, do you have it?" and pointing to her tummy, moaning, "Yes, it's in here!"

Anita and Jean Harlow only met a few times, but they got along like sisters. "The first time I met Jean was when I was a Wampus Baby Star [1929]. They brought her along to see what was going on. I was standing across this pool from her, all I could see was that hair and that figure, and I thought, 'This girl is gorgeous.' She made a big impression on me—and she wasn't even one of the Baby Stars! Then I saw her again when she invited me to her wedding party with Paul Bern [1932]. She told me, 'Anita, if I have a little girl, I want her to be just like you.' To show you how sensitive that girl really was, once she told me, 'I walked past you once on the lot and you never said hello, and I put my head in my hands and cried, I felt so terrible. And I looked up at myself in my red wig [for *Red-Headed Woman*, 1932] and I burst out laughing—of course, you didn't recognize me with red hair!' She was starved for women friends because women were jealous of her."

Anita and Jean didn't meet again until a 1936 vacation at Hearst's ranch, when Jean brought along fiancé William Powell. "We were sitting on a couch in the ladies' room talking, and she said, 'Have you ever given thirteen months of your life to a man?' And I said, 'I should say not, I wouldn't give thirteen days!' She said, 'You know, Bill has been very good to me. He's teaching me to save—I didn't want that big house on the hill, but [Jean's stepfather] Marino wanted it, my mother wanted it...' She was crazy about Bill, but I don't think there was any chance. I have the funniest feeling that after he'd lost her he would have married her in a minute."

In the early 1930s Anita took a leave of absence to appear onstage in Billy Rose's *Crazy Quilt* on Broadway. "I wanted to learn timing, one-liners. I asked Bob Montgomery, and he told me to do summer stock. Then I got this offer from Billy Rose." The one downside was that "Roosevelt—one of my great heroes—was starting the March of Dimes and requested my presence in his box, and Billy Rose wouldn't let me go. They sent Eleanor Powell instead—I was so upset about that!" In 1934 Anita

Anita Page as photographed by George Hurrell (Randal Malone).

wed songwriter Nacio Herb Brown, who had dedicated the song "You Were Meant for Me" to her. But she patiently explains today that "He was not really my husband—I was not in love with this man. He was a dear man, but I am a Roman Catholic, and we were not married in the church."

In 1937 she did marry in church, to a tall, handsome naval officer named

Herschel House. "He was the handsomest man I ever saw," Anita sighs. "He had the most chiseled nose. We loved each other so, and we were married fifty-four years." The two travelled all over the world and invested wisely, finally settling down in California. House, who eventually made Admiral, died in 1992, but Anita takes comfort in her friends and her daughters, Sandra and Linda. She continues to socialize and keeps up to date on current films (one of her favorite actresses is Whoopi Goldberg), and she is delighted that cable and video have given her a whole new audience.

In September of 1992, the Screen Actor's Guild asked Anita to attend a showing of *While the City Sleeps*, and she was treated to public acclaim reminiscent of a 1930s premiere. "I must have signed five hundred autographs," she delightedly recalls. "They were screaming and yelling for me. There were four standing ovations!" The Guild told Anita that her presence made the night into an old-time Hollywood Event. Anita finally had the last laugh on Garbo and Crawford.

Marie Prevost

Some performers are unlucky enough to be remembered chiefly for their death rather than their life. Thelma Todd, Sharon Tate, and Carole Landis all had talents and respectable careers, but they have been reduced to the lowest common denominator by their grisly endings. So, too, Marie Prevost. A bright star of the silent screen and one of the most delightful comediennes of the early talkies, she is best known today for the postmortem photo in *Hollywood Babylon*. But there was a lot more to Marie Prevost.

She was born Mary Bickford Dunn on November 8, 1898, in a small fishing town outside Ontario. Her family moved to Denver shortly after the turn of the century; when she and her sister Margaret were teenagers, their father, a champion athlete, died. Mrs. Dunn and the girls moved to Los Angeles, where both daughters drifted into the film business (Margaret, as Peggy Prevost, had a brief career and survived her sister). The newly named Marie Prevost became one of Mack Sennett's first Bathing Beauties, in 1917. Her natural athletic skills and acting talents were enhanced by her perky good looks. Marie was round and tiny, with big blue eyes and a mop of curly dark hair. She looked a lot like the Boop-a-Doop girls who were to gain popularity in another decade.

Marie and her lifelong friend Phyllis Haver became two of Sennett's biggest female stars in the late 1910s; Marie appeared in twenty-six Mack Sennett short comedies between 1917 and 1924, costarring with such Sennett reliables as Chester Conklin, Ben Turpin, James Finlayson, and Ford Sterling. The titles tell it all: *Her Nature Dance* (Marie's first film, 1917), *East Lynne with Variations* (1919), *Why Beaches Are Popular* (1919), and *She Sighed by the Seaside* (1921). But Marie interspersed her short comedies with features as early as the 1919 *Yankee Doodle in Berlin*, probably the most bizarre war film of the period. Costarring female impersonator Bothwell Browne, *Yankee Doodle* had Browne in female drag and Marie (as a French peasant girl) in male drag behind the lines. She appeared in three more Sennett

A soulful Marie Prevost, toward the end of her silent-film career.

features (*Down on the Farm* and *Love, Honor and Behave*, both 1920, and *A Small Town Idol*, 1921) before beginning to moonlight at Universal. In 1918 Marie married one H. C. Gerke; the marriage lasted until 1923. The following year she wed actor Kenneth Harlan, who had costarred with her in two films. The marriage didn't last, and the two soon separated, though they didn't divorce until 1929.

"Soon," Marie wrote in the late 1920s, "I began to regard motion pictures as a serious career in which I was determined to succeed, rather than as the lark it had seemed to me at first. After a couple of years in comedy work I decided it was time for me to look for dramatic roles." Marie made eight films at Universal in 1921 and 1922. They were pleasant, forgettable comedies with classic Flaming Youth titles like *Moonlight Follies* and *A Parisian Scandal* (both 1921) and *The Married Flapper* (1922). Things looked up when Marie began studio hopping. For the rest of her career, Warner Brothers would be her home base, but she made films for everyone from MGM and Paramount to Invincible Pictures. Her first Warner Brothers film was a well-received version of Fitzgerald's *The Beautiful and the Damned* (1922). She was to appear in another four indifferent films before her big break came.

In 1924 German director Ernst Lubitsch chose Marie to appear in *The Marriage Circle*, his sophisticated bedroom comedy. Marie played Mizzi, the discontented flapper wife of Adolphe Menjou (the sterling cast also included Florence Vidor, Creighton Hale, and Esther Ralston). Marie had been working up to this, getting her comedy training from Mack Sennett and working her way through the dramatic ranks at Warner's. She was very proud of her work with Lubitsch, and he cast her in two more films, as a gold-digging flapper in *Three Women* (1924; the other two being Pauline Frederick and May McAvoy) and the now-lost *Kiss Me Again* (1925, with Clara Bow). Lubitsch taught her things she never could have learned from Mack Sennett. "He made me do simple scenes, just coming in and out of rooms 15 or 20 times," she recalled. "At first it seemed as though there wasn't any sense to it at all. Then it began to dawn upon me what the art of acting was all about, and it seemed intolerably and impossibly difficult. Then I began to see it as he saw it ... He deals in subtleties that I never dreamed of before."

Marie continued appearing in film after film through the 1920s. There were nine in 1924 (including a little-known version of *Camille*, entitled *The Lover of Camille*); four in 1925 (including *Bobbed Hair*, with husband Kenneth Harlan); and seven in 1926 (all romantic comedies, the most successful being *Up in Mabel's Room*, with Harrison Ford and old pal Phyllis Haver). Marie's personal favorite film was *Cornered* (1924), a gangster drama in which she played a dual role. Her reputation as a comic actress had worked against her, she recalled. "I almost had to break into the movies all over again to get the leading role."

Tragedy struck in 1926, when Marie's mother was killed in an automobile accident. More than the breakup of her marriages, the death of her mother shattered Marie; it was at this time that she took to drink. By 1927 Marie was well established in the second tier of stardom. She never became an "A" star like Clara Bow or Colleen Moore, but she had thousands of loyal fans, appeared in fan magazines and newspapers, and was applauded by critics for her ability to skitter between drama and comedy. Her biggest hit came with 1927's *Getting Gertie's Garter*, a classic Jazz-Age comedy with Charles Ray and future fan dancer Sally Rand.

Marie's success continued unabated up to the time of the sound revolution, with *The Girl in the Pullman* (1927, one of several films with Harrison Ford), *The Racket* (a 1928 crime drama), and Cecil B. De Mille's ill-fated *The Godless Girl.* This last film, costarring Lina Basquette, was released as a silent and part-talkie in 1929 and died at the box office. The fact that Marie was a freelancer didn't help matters; in 1929, studios were hiring New York stage-trained actors, and anyone without a long-term contract was in trouble. Marie's voice didn't help matters, either. For someone from Canada, she had an oddly Bronx-like twang—great for taxi dancers and molls, but very limiting for other roles. Her drinking didn't interfere with her professionalism but, more importantly, Marie had been putting on weight. She no longer looked like the chipper flapper Ernst Lubitsch had hired back in 1924.

Marie Prevost at her comic apex, mid–1920s (The Metaluna Collection).

Suddenly—almost overnight, it seemed—she was relegated to second leads and character roles. The stars of her films were Barbara Stanwyck (*Ladies of Leisure*), Anita Page (*War Nurse*), and Joan Crawford (*Paid*, all 1930). Marie found herself playing heroines' friends and wisecracking second bananas. It's usually written that Marie Prevost's talkie career didn't amount to much, but this can be disproved by looking at her films (many are turning up on television). Marie steals every film—every scene—she's in. Just watch her as Stanwyck's hard-boiled but heroic friend in *Ladies of Leisure*; her final scene is amazing in its drama and passion. *Paid* was Joan Crawford's breakthrough drama, but Marie blows her off the screen as her devil-may-care convict pal.

Marie Prevost was not frequently out of work, as her obituaries later implied; she appeared in twenty-three films from 1930 till 1936. Sadly, the roles didn't pay much, and there was no paycheck between films. Freelancing had its drawbacks. But she worked as hard as she could: The high points were *Sporting Blood* (1931, with Clark Gable), *The Sin of Madelon Claudet* (1931, with Helen Hayes), *Three Wise Girls* (1932, with Jean Harlow), and *Only Yesterday* (1933, with Margaret Sullivan).

By 1934 the work had slowed down; there were no films that year. Every few months, a sad little notice would appear in the newspapers about how much weight Marie had lost, how she was trim and healthy and available for work again. But her dieting methods were slowly killing her: All booze and no food does not make for "trim and healthy." She had to sell her home in Malibu and moved into a small apartment at 6230 Afton Place, not far from Sunset Boulevard in Central Hollywood. There were small roles in four final films, including Carole Lombard's *Hands Across the Table* (1935), *Tango* (1936, for a small production company), and *13 Hours by Air* (as a waitress in a flying film with Fred MacMurray and Joan Bennett). The 1935 short *Keystone Hotel*, was a funny yet sad reminder of her glorious past: She played Ford Sterling's wife and received a pie in the face. Marie's last role was as a gum-chewing receptionist in the Clark Gable/Marion Davies comedy *Cain and Mabel* (1936); her screen time amounted to all of two minutes. Her friends knew she was in bad shape, but Marie was too proud to take help: Joan Crawford gave her an IOU for $100, but Marie was too embarrassed to collect on it.

Marie Prevost died of "acute alcoholism" on January 21, 1937, at the age of thirty-eight. Her body was discovered on January 23 by a bellboy, kept away for two days by the rather peremptory note on her door reading, "Please don't knock on my door more than once because it makes my dog bark. I can hear—I'm not deaf." The dog, a dachshund named Maxie, was howling so piteously that the door was forced. Marie was lying face-down in bed, dressed in polka-dotted silk pajamas. Tiny bite marks covered her legs. Her death was made even more horrible in retrospect by Kenneth Anger's contention in *Hollywood Babylon* that Marie's dog had partially devoured her. But anyone who owns a cat or dog will recognize what really happened: Maxie, annoyed that Marie would not feed him and play with him, simply tried to nip at his mistress to awaken her. Even more sadly, poor Maxie was destroyed right after Marie's death. Marie herself was cremated and her ashes mingled with those of her mother. They were re-interred together.

Friends and fans were taken by surprise by the untimely death of the former bathing beauty, still shy of forty. "Marie Prevost's Tragic Fate Shocks Hollywood Stars," read a typical headline. "Her death strikes sharply at the very heart of Hollywood," wrote Louella Parsons. The mid–1930s saw the deaths of several once-famous stars reduced to poverty: Roscoe Arbuckle died in his sleep in 1933, Lou Tellegen stabbed himself to death in 1934, Karl Dane shot himself the same year, John Bowers drowned himself in 1936, and Florence Lawrence took poison in 1938. These deaths began to wear on the consciences of those in Hollywood who had one. In 1940 the Motion Picture Country House was erected in Woodland Hills, to care for those film professionals without funds. The home has cared for thousands in the years since—but, ironically, Marie Prevost probably would have been too proud to go there.

Esther Ralston

At the time of this 1992 interview, Esther Ralston was living modestly in Ventura, California. Ralston, dubbed The American Venus, had a career and a life as brilliant as Norma Desmond, but she was no bitter, deranged recluse—at the age of eighty-nine, Esther was charming, funny, and minced no words.

Esther Ralston was born Esther North in Bar Harbor, Maine, on September 17, 1902. Her family can be traced back to the *Mayflower*: "My mother was a Howard of England," she proudly noted, "Catherine Howard having been one of the wives of Henry VIII; one of mother's grandfathers had been secretary to Queen Victoria. And Jane Carleton of Ireland was one of my ancestors. When I was doing *The Spy Ring* [1938] the director said I would play a murderess. I said, 'Oh, my fans would never forgive me—I'll do it on one condition: you let me change my name.' I did it under the name Jane Carleton. And, by golly, I got letters from fans saying, 'Dear Miss Ralston, what is this Jane Carleton business?'"

Around 1904 the Norths changed their name to Ralston and took to the stage. By the mid–1910s, Esther, her four brothers, and her parents were touring the United States, appearing in everything from large theaters to high schools to insane asylums. Esther also appeared as an extra in East Coast films occasionally, beginning with Clara Kimball Young's *Deep Purple* (1916). Some might complain about the constant traveling and lack of schooling, but Esther said, "I had a wonderful, wonderful, close family. I didn't miss a thing. I had a lot more than most kids have—I got the applause of an audience. Of course, we couldn't carry any toys with us, but my brothers more than made up for that. The only thing I missed was friends—we didn't stay in any one place for more than a week, so I would no sooner make friends than I would lose them again."

The Ralstons arrived in California in 1917; Esther spent the next few years playing bit parts in films. Her first major role was in William Desmond Taylor's *Huckleberry Finn* (1920). Taylor, whose 1922 murder has never been solved, "was wonderful to work with, it meant a lot to me that he was so understanding. I was playing Mary Jane, and he came up to mother and said, 'Esther is supposed to be fourteen, but she's starting to develop a little bit—is there anything you can do about it?' So mother took me to the dressing room and bound me so my approaching womanhood wasn't too obvious."

"I did almost all my own stunts: anything that was part of the work," Esther recalled. "They practically dragged me by my hair from the mountaintops! Almost set me on fire a couple of times." Not all of her early films met with her approval. "The worst was *$50,000 Reward* [1924], with Ken Maynard," she laughed. "It was so horrible I tried to sneak out of the preview. The press was there, and they said, 'Wait a minute! You made this movie. If we have to sit through it, so do you!' Any time anyone mentions that movie I want to vomit; it had all the verve of wet bread."

Esther appeared in twenty-four films before being signed to a contract at Paramount to play Mrs. Darling in *Peter Pan* (1924). She was twenty-two years old and costarred with Betty Bronson and Mary Brian. "My dearest friend was Mary Brian. She is a dear lamb. I discovered her, you know. I was a judge in a beauty contest and said, 'What about that little dark girl?' Her name was Louise Dantzler and she was only fourteen, too young to be Miss Los Angeles. But she was so charming I suggested they name her Miss Personality, which they did. About two days later I went to Paramount to start rehearsals for *Peter Pan*, and who's playing Wendy but Louise Dantzler? She'd changed her name to Mary Brian. I named my first child after her—we're still very close."

During the next six years, Esther rose in the Paramount ranks, starring or costarring in another twenty-five films. Among the better known were *The Best People* (1925, with Warner Baxter), *The American Venus,* as a beauty contestant, (1926, with Louise Brooks); *Old Ironsides* (1926, with Wallace Beery and Charles Farrell, one of her favorite films); the touching fantasy *A Kiss for Cinderella* (1926, again with Betty Bronson); *Children of Divorce* (1927, with Gary Cooper and Clara Bow); *Betrayal* (1929, with Emil Jannings); and her first talkie, *The Wheel of Life* (1929).

Esther felt that her *Children of Divorce* costar Clara Bow was a brilliant actress but found her behavior somewhat off-putting. "She was pretty loose, and I suppose that's why I didn't make a friend of her," she recalled. "I didn't dislike her or anything, but she'd pull up her dress and show us she had nothing on in front of men, and I'd been brought up differently. Around the set, her casualness was offensive, I thought." She regretted inadvertently hurting Bow's feelings, however. "Clara's dressing room was next door to mine, and I was on my way home, where I was giving a party. She was sitting on the front porch and said, 'Are you having a party?' and when I said yes, did she want to come, she looked very sad and said, 'That's all right, you didn't want me.' I feel just awful about that."

When she later heard the 1920s and 1930s referred to as The Golden Age of Hollywood, Esther Ralston was "surprised. It was just ordinary work for me at the time, we didn't know it was going to be any more important than it was at the time." She noted that the fan magazines were surprisingly accurate. "I was on so many covers, interviews one after the other. I enjoyed them, and they

Esther Ralston toward the end of the silent era.

pretty much followed the truth. I don't remember them writing anything about me that was imaginative."

Possibly her greatest performance was in Josef von Sternberg's *The Case of Lena Smith* (1929). "That was the only time they let me act. When I was mentioned for the part, they said, 'Esther Ralston? She's a comedienne!' But Josef von Sternberg said, 'I think she can act.' Well, from that time on I was so thrilled to be called an actress that I did my best. If I ever looked for an Academy Award, that film would be the one. But it came out the same time the talkies did, and it was a silent, which is why it never got the showing it might have."

Esther held no grudge against talkies. "I was sure they would catch on. I was brought up in the theater, and I need my voice," she said. "To think directors would say to me, 'You can't open your mouth, you can't use your voice'—I was frantic, it was so difficult for me." In her first talking film, *The Wheel of Life*, "they were still experimenting. It was the most stilted, cold thing, it had no life in it at all." Although she was one of Paramount's top stars, Esther was let go in 1929, at the dawn of the talkie era. "My husband [George Webb] was very money-conscious, you know, and sent me in—if you please!—to ask for $100,000 to sign a talkie contract. They said, 'Look, Esther, we'd love to have you, but we can't take the chance to pay that much money without knowing if talkies will catch on.' So I refused to sign the talkie contract, and they didn't take up my option." Her last Paramount picture was *The Mighty*, that same year.

Esther's luck in marriage wasn't much better. Actor/manager Webb, her first husband (1925–33), was an emotionally unstable gambler; her second husband, singer Will Morgan (1934–38), was an alcoholic; and her third, journalist Ted Lloyd (1939–54), was unfaithful. She did, however, come out of these marriages with three children, Mary Esther (born 1931), Judy (1942), and Ted (1943).

Esther retained happy memories of her career and most of her costars, including those with reputations for being difficult, such as Wallace Beery ("he was a dinner guest several times"), Joan Crawford ("a damn good actress"), and future Nazi Emil Jannings. "He was very nice to me," she said of him. "He always wanted me to have a glass of beer, and I didn't drink; but I enjoyed working with him very much." Among her best friends was Gary Cooper. "I loved Gary. My fondest memories are of him and Randy Scott. Warner Baxter was very good; he was more reserved

A mid-1920s candid of Esther Ralston (The Metaluna Collection).

than Gable. Gable was a showman; Warner was more sincere and quiet. We were neighbors and very good friends. Thelma Todd was lovely, charming. I was at a party one night with her and we were all going in to see a fortune teller. She came out looking pale and quiet, and the next night she was killed."

Being beautiful and innocent had its pitfalls, especially in Hollywood.

Esther got it from both men and women. Dorothy Arzner was one of the few successful female directors of the 1920s, as well as being one of the few open about her homosexuality. "She was very open with *me* about it," recalled Esther, "and I resented it. I went to the authorities at Paramount and asked them not to put me with her again." When signed to MGM in 1934, Esther claimed to have refused the favors of Louis B. Mayer several times, although she never reported it to the press. "Not at that time. He threatened to blackball me, and I'd never get another job. He sold me to Universal for five or six pictures instead of paying me the MGM salary. The only major studio that would take me was Paramount, thanks to Randy Scott. All the rest of my films after that were at the independents."

Few of Esther's talking films are classics, although several are quite enjoyable. She was hardly inactive, appearing in an impressive twenty-seven films from 1931 through 1941: from the drawing room comedy *Lonely Wives* (1931) to her last film ten years later, *San Francisco Docks*. Esther spent those years bouncing from studio to studio, at a time when freelancing wasn't as respectable as it became later. She worked at the majors (MGM, Universal, Paramount) and Poverty Row units (Monogram, Republic, Mascot). Among her more memorable talkies are *Sadie McKee* (1934, with Joan Crawford), *The Marines Are Coming* (1934, William Haines's last film), the docudrama *Reunion* (1936, with the Dionne quintuplets), and as Nora Bayes in the delightful *Tin Pan Alley* (1941, with Alice Faye, Betty Grable, John Payne, and Jack Oakie). *Sadie McKee* was one of her favorite films, "the first time they let me sing." Although she got along fine with Joan Crawford, costar Gene Raymond was another story entirely.

Joan Crawford once strongly hinted that Jeanette MacDonald and Gene Raymond were gay and that their 1937 marriage was an arranged one. But Esther's experiences with Raymond tell quite another story. "Most of my scenes were with him. He came up to my dressing room after our first love scene and made a pass at me," she recalled, still annoyed after nearly sixty years. "I put a stop to that. He said, 'You'll fall—they all do.' And from that time on we fought through the whole picture. The prop boys put up a black screen on the set with 'Gene' on one side and 'Esther' on the other, and every time we insulted each other they'd chalk off a '1.'"

Esther never gave up acting. While supporting herself working at B. Altman's and an electrical supply store, she managed to stay active in show business. She went into vaudeville in the 1930s, appearing twice at the Palace Theater on Broadway and at the London Palladium. She felt that the Palace was "the greatest thing that ever happened to me: that I headlined at the Palace in New York," and expressed shock and dismay that the theater's exterior had been demolished in 1988. Esther also did TV commercials, soap operas, radio, and theater (including *Arsenic and Old Lace* in 1975). She wrote a bright and funny autobiography, *Someday We'll Laugh*, in 1985.

Esther eventually gave up filmgoing, although she continued to enjoy television till the end of her life, particularly the older films on cable, "with people I know." She was not familiar with the new generation of stars: "I look at them and go, Susie Fewclothes? who?

I went to see *Sophie's Choice* and I wanted to throw up—that brilliant girl, that wonderful actress Meryl Streep working in such filth." Esther noted proudly that "I have fifteen grandchildren and three great-grandchildren. They're all over the world, so I can't see them now, but I write to them and talk to them. I lost my dearly beloved brother Howard last week [Howard Ralston died on June 1, 1992]. He played opposite Mary Pickford in *Pollyanna*. He and I were the only ones in pictures. Three of my brothers are gone now, young Carlton is the only one left of the Ralstons. You have to get over it sometime," she sighed uncertainly. "You get used to it."

"I'll be ninety in September, if I'm still here. I have had a very long and brilliant life. I've been very, very grateful—and grateful to be as well as I am." Indeed, Esther Ralston has to think hard to come up with any regrets. "It's hard for me to walk," she admits, "and I can't dance and kick the back of my head..." Esther Ralston did indeed make it to ninety; she died on January 14, 1994, in her ninety-second year.

WALLACE REID

Imagine Tom Hanks or Mel Gibson, rather than River Phoenix, dying of a drug overdose. When Wallace Reid—as wholesome a star in his day as Hanks or Gibson—died while in rehab for morphine addiction in 1923, a shock wave ran through the film community and the world at large. Reid, second only to Douglas Fairbanks as the epitome of the All-American Boy, was the last person anyone would associate with drugs. But as his story became public, Reid was recognized not as a thrill seeker or jaded Hollywood playboy, but a genuine victim.

William Wallace Reid came of such good theatrical stock that it would be surprising if he hadn't become a star. He was born on April 15, 1891, in St. Louis, Missouri. Father Hal Reid was a well-known playwright and, later, a director and actor in films. His mother, Bertha Belle Westbrooke, was a successful leading lady. Wallace began acting as a child, but he was treated to a well-rounded education as well. A dedicated bookworm and talented painter, Wallace was also an all-around athlete. But it was music and cars which he really loved. Wallace was a professional singer and an ace sax and violin player, and he'd no sooner discovered the automobile than he was racing and repairing his own models.

After pre-med school, Wallace became the motor-car reporter for the *Newark Morning Star*, then worked out west as a government surveyor. But acting was in his genes and in his future. With the help of his father, he began appearing onstage. By 1910 his father was working at Selig's Chicago studio, and that year Wallace got his first job—as a stuntman—in *The Phoenix*. For the next year, the young actor—not yet out of his teens—worked as a character actor, Tom Mix's stuntman, and behind the scenes as writer. Soon he'd ruled out race driver and musician as career choices and concentrated on acting.

In 1911 Wallace was hired as cameraman, writer, and actor at Vitagraph, where he appeared in ten films (with John Bunny, Florence Turner, and Helen Gardner) before moving with his father to Reliance Studios, again as a

The jaunty all-American Wallace Reid in 1920.

jack-of-all trades. The 1912 western *His Only Son* (for Reliance), changed Wallace's life. His leading lady was Dorothy Davenport. The seventeen-year old actress, while not particularly pretty, was a sparkling, intelligent woman, fully Wallace's intellectual equal. The two married on October 13, 1913. Their son William Wallace, Jr., was born in 1918, and in 1922 they adopted a daughter, Betty Ann (there was much gossip that Betty Ann was the offspring of Wallace and an unnamed actress). This marriage was a very happy one, but it put a wedge between Wallace and his mother. Bertha Reid was a very controlling woman whose ideas of child rearing come off as rather horrifying in her 1923 book about her son. She and Dorothy Davenport took an instant dislike to each other, and Wallace rarely visited home after his marriage.

By the time he became a newlywed, Wallace had starred in another forty or so films, hopping from studio to studio, finally settling down at Universal's offshoots Bison and Nestor and, in 1914, Mutual. By late 1915 Wallace Reid had starred in well over one hundred films, including *The Picture of Dorian Grey* (1913), *The Deerslayer* (also 1913, with his father and Florence Turner), *Down the Road to Creditville* (1914, with Dorothy Gish), as a bit player in *The Birth of a Nation* (1915), *Enoch Arden* (1915, with Lillian Gish), and as "The Student Prince" in *Old Heidelberg* (1915, again with Dorothy Gish). But it took opera singer Geraldine Farrar and producer Jesse Lasky to make Wallace Reid a star. Lasky signed Wallace to a Paramount contract in mid–1915; he stayed with the company for the rest of his brief life. That same year, Farrar chose him as her Don José in *Carmen*, and his fame was made. Slim, handsome, and intelligent, Wallace became the dreamboat of the year. Farrar liked him, too—he made three more films with her, the most popular being *Joan, the Woman* (1917).

But Wallace Reid was possibly most popular as a racing star, in motorcar adventure films, beginning with

1919's *The Roaring Road.* "Audiences couldn't get enough of him behind a steering wheel," said Lasky, and of course Wallace insisted on doing his own stunt driving. The films—with titles like *Double Speed*, *Excuse My Dust*, and *What's Your Hurry?*—were enormous hits, especially with male teenagers (today, still, a studio's dream audience). The women loved him, too. Wallace Reid was one of the most popular leading men of the time, costarring with such lucky actresses as Ann Little (in a series of films from 1917 through 1920), Anna Q. Nilsson (*The Love Burglar*, 1919), Bebe Daniels (*The Dancin' Fool* and *Sick Abed*, 1920, and *Nice People*, 1922), Agnes Ayres (*Too Much Speed* and *The Love Special*, 1921), and with Paramount's other major star, Gloria Swanson (in the sophisticated bedroom comedies, *The Affairs of Anatol* and *Don't Tell Everything*, both 1921).

But by the time he was making those comedies with Swanson, Wallace Reid was a marked man. All of Hollywood knew it, though the press kept it quiet: By the beginning of the 1920s, Wallace Reid was a morphine addict. It began on the set of the 1919 lumbercamp adventure *The Valley of the Giants*, when a train wreck left Wallace in such pain that the studio doctor prescribed morphine to get him through filming. Wallace made another twenty-three films, some of them his most popular, though everyone in Hollywood was whispering of his problem. In 1922 alone he made nine films, including *The World's Champion* (as a boxer), *Forever* (an adaptation of *Peter Ibbetson* with Elsie Ferguson), *The Dictator* (with Lila Lee), and *Nice People* (with Bebe Daniels). But it was obvious his health was failing.

Wallace Reid, shortly before his death.

How responsible was Paramount for Wallace's condition? Stories vary. While Dewitt Bodeen said in a 1966 *Films in Review* article that Lasky begged Wallace to go for treatment, director Karl Brown had a different story. "Normally," Brown told Kevin Brownlow in the TV documentary *Hollywood*, "he could have been sent to a sanitarium, a cure, or something—but he was altogether too good box office. There was too much more to be gotten out of

Wallace Reid. So in order to keep the services of this most popular of popular leading men alive, they kept him supplied with more and more and more morphine." Dorothy Davenport Reid said that "Wally could charm any doctor into giving him the tablets he wanted. He knew just enough about medicine to convince doctors that he knew exactly how many grams he could safely take every day ... And when he found that he couldn't put a stop or even a check to the morphine, he began to use liquor as a cover-up for what he was really doing."

It soon became obvious even to fans that something was wrong: Wallace was gaunt and haggard, his hair thinning rapidly, and at thirty he looked twenty years older. Henry Hathaway, who worked on *Thirty Days* (1922), Wallace's last film, recalled that "He sort of fumbled around the set and bumped into a chair and then he just sat down on the floor and started to cry." When filming was finished, he checked into the Banksia Place Sanitarium, telling his wife, "I'll either come out cured or I won't come out." He didn't come out. Wallace Reid developed pneumonia and died of hypostatic congestion of the lungs and renal suppression on January 18, 1923. He was thirty-one years old.

After Wallace Reid's death, his widow became an outspoken antidrug crusader. Never mincing words about her husband's problem, Dorothy Davenport Reid went on to produce the antidrug film *Human Wreckage* (1923), as well as other social-problem films (*Broken Laws*, *The Red Kimono*). She continued as a social reformer and film producer, writer, and director for decades. Before her death on October 12, 1977, she told a reporter why she never remarried. "No one came around. [Wallace] was the kind of man that men tried to be like and I guess they didn't feel up to following him."

Alma Rubens

There was no indication in the 1910s of Alma Rubens's fate. She was a slim, dark actress, capable in both action and dramatic roles. She was quiet, unassuming, and modest. "I'm not a good interview subject," she laughingly told *Motion Picture Magazine* in 1919. "I can't talk of my art and all that. I guess I'm plain uninteresting." Her friends and fans would never have believed that Alma Rubens would die a drug addict at the end of the silent era, after spending months in jails, mental homes, and rehab clinics. There seemed to be no warning signals.

She started out well: she was born Genevieve Driscoll in San Francisco, on February 19, 1897. Her French father and American mother sent Genevieve to the Convent of the Sacred Heart, but she already had her life mapped out. "As a little girl, I didn't just want to be an actress," she later told a reporter, "I was quite certain that I was *going* to be one. I acted all the time." Some time in the early 1910s, she changed her name to Alma Rubens and took to the stage as chorus girl. Her parents couldn't have been overly horrified, as Alma lived with them until her first marriage (Alma's older sister Hazel married young and stayed out of the spotlight).

Alma met actor Franklyn Farnum in one of her shows, and he introduced her to director Rollin Sturgeon. He, in turn, helped her get the female lead, as a dance-hall girl, in Douglas Fairbanks's *The Half-Breed* (1916). It wasn't her first film: Alma had already appeared in *Reggie Mixes In* (also with Fairbanks) and *The Lorelei Madonna* (both 1915), but *The Half-Breed* was her big break. Nearly everyone at Triangle appeared in D. W. Griffith's *Intolerance* (1916); Alma can be spotted as a slave girl in the Babylonian auction sequence. Next came another teaming with Douglas Fairbanks, in *The Americano* (1917), then her first full-fledged starring part, in *Truthful Tulliver* (also 1917). That same year the busy—and increasingly popular—young actress appeared in Triangle's *Master of His Home*, played the title role in *The Firefly of Tough Luck*, starred in *The Gown of Destiny* (which featured a $1,000 gown of brocade and beading), and costarred with Western hero William S. Hart in *The Cold Deck*.

Alma's sponsor Franklyn Farnum himself enjoyed some success in westerns. On June 14, 1918, Alma and Farnum married; the couple separated within a month, and Alma returned to her parents' home. The former Mrs. Farnum had legally changed her name to "Alma Rubens" early in 1918. The spelling had varied alarmingly early in her career: Reuben, Reubens, Ruben, Rubens. She once saw herself referred to as "Alma Boobins," which prompted the legal revision. She continued to work hard and gain popularity. "I just want to be a human being on the screen," Alma told one interviewer. When asked in 1918 if she believed in Fate, she answered that "Well, yes, in a way I do. What I really believe in, however, is the theory that, if anything is really essential to you, somehow, sometime, you are going to get it. For instance, it was absolutely essential to me that I should act, and so the chance to act came to me quite easily."

Her workload at Triangle was impressive: in 1918, Alma appeared in *The Painted Lily*, *Another Foolish Virgin*, *False Ambitions*, *The Answer*, *Madame Sphinx*, *The Love Brokers*, *I Love You*, and *The Ghost Flower*. The following year, she starred in two westerns, *A Good Bad Woman* and *A Man's Country*, as well as *Restless Souls* and *Diane of the Green Van*. In 1919 a reporter noted that "In private life Miss Rubens is just a normal, healthy girl, interested in everything from pretty clothes of strictly conservative models to fluffy dogs." Alma loved dogs in particular and was heartbroken when her poodle, Trixie, was killed by a bulldog while being walked in 1917.

Alma Rubens in 1920, before her troubles descended.

Nineteen-nineteen was an important year for Alma, and a dizzying one. Her studio, Triangle—which had been a major force in the industry since 1915—folded. Alma moved to the brand-new Cole-Robertson Company in April, then on to Pathé. In August that same year, she was signed by Paramount-Artcraft to make films under their Cosmopolitan branch. She was also arrested for the first time in 1919 for drug possession. She was sentenced to dry out at a state hospital and was paroled fairly quickly. But she was not cured.

Alma took her work seriously, and poor reviews upset her. In 1920 she chided *Variety* for what she thought were unwontedly cruel notices, writing to the editor, "All men and women in pictures are giving their best efforts ... Don't you think you ought to consider this fact a little more?" But bad reviews were, happily, rare. The 1920s started out promisingly for Alma, with leading roles in *The World and His Wife* and *Humoresque* (both 1920), *Find the Woman* (1921), and *The Price She Paid* (1924). Alma had met her second husband, screenwriter Daniel Carson Goodman, when he wrote the screenplay *Juneo* for her. Goodman had previously been engaged to actress Florence LaBadie and had been in the car with LaBadie when she suffered a fatal accident in 1917. Goodman wrote several of Alma's screenplays (including *Thoughtless Women*, 1921), and the two wed in 1923. They separated within a few months and were divorced—Alma charged cruelty—in early 1925.

Nineteen-twenty-five was a big year for Alma career-wise, perhaps the pinnacle of her career. She starred in *The Dancers* (which had been a scandalous stage hit for Tallulah Bankhead), the umpteenth remake of *East Lynne*, *She Wolves*, *The Winding Stair*, *A Woman's Faith*, and *Fine Clothes*. But when Alma married for the third time, her career was beginning to slow down somewhat. Her 1926 releases, all for Fox, included *The Gilded Butterfly*, *Siberia*, and *Marriage License*. That same year, on January 30, she married actor Ricardo Cortez. Cortez, a "Latin Lover" (actually a New Yorker named Jacob Krantz), was a popular and talented actor whose career was just getting off the ground when he and Alma wed. Cortez had to know of Alma's past drug problems when they married; he probably didn't suspect that she was still using. But she was becoming increasingly unable to work: In 1927 she made only one film, *The Heart of Salome* (Fox). In 1928 she appeared in one more, *Masks of the Devil* (MGM).

By then, her life was coming apart. Her drug habit was destroying her marriage; she and Cortez briefly separated in mid–1928, then got back together. Alma was arrested on disorderly conduct charges in late 1928 and early 1929. Then, in January 1929, Alma collapsed of a drug overdose and was rushed to the Hollywood Hospital. Her doctor, L. Jesse Citron, was cited for supplying the drugs, and Alma herself was committed for six months to the California State Insane Asylum to dry out. Amazingly, she was still able to get work when she checked out of the asylum. "I am feeling wonderful again after my rest," she told reporters.

Universal took her at her word and hired Alma to play the good-hearted, tragic Julie—the role originated by Helen Morgan—in the first screen version of *Show Boat*. The film (which has been recently restored) was a part-talkie, costarring Laura LaPlante as Magnolia and Joseph Schildkraut as Gaylord Ravenal. Later in 1929 Alma made her last film appearance, in a World War I drama called *She Goes to War* (United Artists). This part-talkie—which also still exists and is available on video—costarred Al St. John and Eleanor Boardman. A comedy/adventure about soldiers and their girls, it featured Alma in a supporting role as Rosie Cohen, the ukulele-playing comic relief.

But Alma was still using drugs, and a completely discouraged Cortez filed for divorce. She went to the East Coast in late 1930 to star in a stage show, *With Privileges*, which closed after a one-week tryout. Alma headed back west in early January 1931 to pick up her film career and to try to reconcile with her husband. In San Diego, she appeared at a police station to charge her maid with theft; when police searched Alma's room, they found morphine cubes sewn into the

Alma Rubens posing for *Motion Picture Classic* magazine.

Alma Rubens

hem of one of her gowns and arrested her. She was released on $5,000 bail to await trial.

She never made it. Tired and ill, she gave a heartbreaking last interview. Usually portrayed as a hardened good-time girl, Alma comes across as a sad and exhausted woman. "I have been miserable for so long," she told *The Los Angeles Examiner*. "I was afraid to tell my mother, my best friends. My only desire has been to get drugs and take them in secrecy. If only I could go on my knees before the police or before a judge and beg them to make stiffer laws so that men will refuse to take dirty dollars from murderers who sell this poison and who escape punishment when caught by lying their way out."

Alma collapsed at her doctor's house in late January. The doctor, Charles Pfleuger, decided she was too ill to be transferred to a hospital. After three days in a coma, Alma died of pneumonia on January 21, 1931, with her mother and sister at her bedside. She was interred in a mausoleum in Fresno. Today she is lumped together with other unfortunate, ill-starred scandal victims. Wallace Reid, Juanita Hansen, Virginia Rappe, and Olive Thomas are all brushed off with barely a glance at the careers and talents which brought them to public notice in the first place. But even if Alma Rubens had not fallen prey to drugs, she would deserve notice as an important and hard-working actress.

Clarine Seymour

No one can call the 1920s a boring decade for film fans. The actresses flashed brighter than ever before: dazzling flappers and jazz babies like Joan Crawford, Clara Bow, Colleen Moore, Mae Murray. But the girl who might have been the brightest of them all died at the dawn of the decade.

Frustratingly little is known of Clarine Seymour's youth. She was born into a close, supportive family on December 9, 1898. While she was still young, her father, Albert V. Seymour, moved the family from Brooklyn to then-bucolic New Rochelle, New York. While still in high school, Clarine got her first acting job, at the nearby Thanhouser Studios. She hung around hopefully for weeks with no luck, until finally a few small roles were thrown her way. After another few roles at Pathé's New Jersey branch, Clarine was given a long-term contract by the Rolin Company.

Clarine was shipped out to the West Coast to costar with clown actor Toto in his knockabout comedies. But Clarine was not destined to become Rolin's star comedienne—within months she was back in New York, suing the company for a broken contract. She claimed they'd wanted her to engage in dangerous stunts; Rolin countered that she was fired for incompetence. The judge found in Clarine's favor; by that time, she had been engaged by D. W. Griffith, so she obviously did not lack talent.

She'd been job hunting since she returned from her ill-fated trip west and had applied for work with Griffith. Not getting any response, she was packed and ready to leave on a trip with friends to San Diego when summoned to Griffith's studio. "To my amazement, he signed me on the spot and had me get into makeup for my first scene," she later recalled. That first film for Griffith was *The Girl Who Stayed at Home*, released early in 1919. She played the title role: a showgirl in love with soldier Robert Harron. Richard Barthelmess and Carol Dempster had larger roles, but Clarine had Harron (and the delightful screen name "Cutie Beautiful"). She and Harron were terrific together: both slim,

One of Clarine Seymour's last portraits.

dark, and intensely youthful. They looked to become the first great love team of the twenties.

Clarine Seymour was an unusual choice for Griffith. Most of his actresses were Edwardian flowers: serene dramatic stars like Lillian Gish, Blanche Sweet, Mae Marsh. Clarine was small, jittery, with huge rolling eyes and a mop of unruly hair. She was something altogether new on the screen. Her next film was *True Heart Susie* (released in the summer of 1919), again paired with Harron. Clarine played a baby vamp, a milliner named Bettina Hopkins who steals Harron away from country sweetheart Lillian Gish. Ominously, Clarine's character dies from pneumonia after being caught in a blizzard, leaving Harron and Gish free to wed. A change of pace was *Scarlet Days* (released in the fall of 1919). Clarine played a role that in later years might have been taken by Lupe Velez: Chiquita, a high-spirited Mexican girl during the California gold-rush days. Clarine told an interviewer that the role had been written especially for her; she was hanging around the set looking bored, when Griffith wrote in a comedy bit for her which proved so successful it was expanded into a supporting role.

Griffith decided it was time to star Clarine in her own film; she'd been second banana for Gish and Dempster long enough. She sat idle while he filmed *Broken Blossoms* and *The Greatest Question*. Then, on a trip to Florida in late 1919, Griffith made two tropical-locale films: *The Idol Dancer* and *The Love Flower*. The latter starred Dempster, with whom Griffith was falling in love. The former was Clarine's bid for stardom. *The Idol Dancer* was something of a throw-away film for Griffith, not a work of art like *Intolerance* or *Broken Blossoms*. It was an adventure romance about a South Seas girl named White Almond Flower, who has to choose between a seedy beachcomber (Richard Barthelmess) and an uptight missionary (Creighton Hale). Seen today, *The Idol Dancer* is a rather silly programmer, but Clarine and Barthelmess give vivid, funny, and intelligent performances. One is particularly struck with Clarine's resemblance to Clara Bow in her earlier films: the same large expressive eyes, the same vivacity, mingled with a slightly self-conscious coyness.

In the early months of 1920, Clarine joined the rest of the Griffith company in White River Junction, Vermont, to film the melodrama *Way Down East*. *The Idol Dancer* had not yet been released, and Clarine was cast in a rather small supporting role: Kate Brewster, a country girl who falls in love with a professor played by her recent costar

Clarine Seymour sporting with her kid brother for *Motion Picture Classic* magazine, 1920.

Creighton Hale. Robert Harron was being replaced by Richard Barthelmess as Griffith's leading man, so Hale was being teamed with Clarine to see how they worked together. She was still on location when *The Idol Dancer* opened on March 21, 1920. The film got the lukewarm reception it deserved, but there was distinct interest in its leading lady. Indeed, audiences were much warmer to her than to Carol Dempster, whose career Griffith was trying to push. "I want to go on working and learning for a long time yet," Clarine told *Motion Picture Classic*'s Harrison Haskins at this time. "Then if I am worth it, I hope for stardom—like all the rest."

In mid-April, less than halfway through filming *Way Down East*, Clarine took ill. She was taken to Misericordia Hospital in New York, where an intestinal ailment did not respond to treatment. An unspecified operation was performed, but Clarine died on Sunday evening, April 25, 1920. She was twenty-one years old. The cause was released as "strangulated intestines." Because she was filming in a blizzard, pneumonia was also suggested as a contributing cause. To modern ears, Clarine's death sounds suspicious. But it must be remembered that 1920 was a different world, one without antibiotics. Reading obituary notices of the time, one is struck by how terribly easy and common it was to die young then. Pneumonia, flu, any minor infection could easily turn fatal, and any invasive surgery in 1920 was fraught with danger. Clarine's early death, while lamentable, was all too familiar to her contemporaries.

She was replaced in *Way Down East* by Mary Hay, who later married Richard Barthelmess. Clarine can still be seen in some long shots—one of the reasons Hay was chosen was their resemblance from a distance. Clarine's former costar Robert Harron had only a few months to live himself, dying of a self-inflicted gunshot wound on September 4, 1920. Just as suddenly as she'd appeared, Clarine Seymour sadly vanished from the public's mind. The Jazz Age got along quite well without her—yet it's fascinating to consider what contributions she might have made: Just imagine Clarine Seymour starring in *Our Dancing Daughters*, *It*, *Flaming Youth*, *Show People*....

Milton Sills

The silent screen was not an industry brimming with intellectualism. Most performers were itinerant stage veterans or children barely out of their teens. Behind the camera, cutthroat businessmen predominated, with perhaps a news hack writing titles or scenarios. So Milton Sills stood out like a beacon: Fluent in French, German, Italian, and Russian (the last "in order to read Turgieneff and Tolstoy in the original"), this matinee idol of the late 1910s and 1920s started his professional life as a student of calculus, psychology, and philosophy at the University of Chicago.

He was born in Chicago on January 12, 1882, the son of Milton Henry Sills, a mineral dealer, and Josephine Antoinette Troost Sills, of a wealthy banking family. According to film historian Louis Devon, Milton's one sibling was Clarence, who became vice president at Halsey Stuart Corporation. Milton told *Motion Picture Magazine* in 1918 that his youth had consisted of "the usual seasons of top-spinning, marbles, baseball and later football. I was not punished for bringing home poor class reports..." Milton modestly referred to himself as a lazy student, but in 1999 his daughter (by his first wife), Dorothy Sills Lindsley, proudly noted that her father "graduated from the University of Chicago on scholarships and won a Fellowship in Philosophy ... He studied calculus before bedtime so he could discuss astronomy with his friend, Edwin Hubbell." Dorothy added that her father did not hold Mary Pickford or Theda Bara up as role models: "He said he hoped I would be like Mme. Curie."

Studying psychology and philosophy, Milton was offered a job as a researcher upon graduation, writing for local newspapers and magazines to supplement his income. All this came to an end in 1905 when actor Donald Robertson visited the school, lecturing on Ibsen. "You can imagine my surprise," Milton later said, when Robertson suggested the handsome young student try the stage for a living. Amazingly, Sills took up his suggestion and took to the stage, eventually joining Robertson's stock company and playing the classics in Chicago and New Orleans. His roles ranged, he said, "from leading man to 'a crash without.'"

He hit New York in 1908 and had the kind of instant success generally seen only in Busby Berkeley musicals. He admitted that he "was given splendid parts right from the very start ... I think I must have been a rotten actor, but they were all very kind and taught and encouraged me continually, until I gained a little self-confidence. I was endeavoring to find my personality, a thing without which no actor can be a success." Milton Sills must have had quite a personality, as top-rank producers Henry Miller, Charles Frohman, William A. Brady, and David Belasco all vied for his services. He starred in *This Woman and This Man* (his Broadway debut, 1908), *The Man on the Box*, *The Rack*, *The Fighting Hope*, *Diplomacy* (1910), *The Governor's Lady* (1912), *The Law of the Land* and *Panthea* (both 1914), and also starred in the touring company of the mystical melodrama, *The Servant in the House* (1910). In all, Milton Sills appeared in about a score of Broadway shows and major touring companies between 1908 and 1914.

Milton Sills at the dawn of his career.

He married for the first time in England in 1910. His bride was actress (and sometimes costar) Gladys Edith Wynne. A native of London, she took Milton home to get her father's permission. By 1914 Milton Sills was well established as a leading man on Broadway and in stock, but his career had reached a plateau. He wasn't becoming a huge star like John Barrymore or William Collier. The 1910s were a slow time for men onstage; most good roles were written for star actresses. So Milton was not at all adverse when the opportunity came to move into films. He was thirty-two when theatrical and film producer William A. Brady (who was also actress Alice Brady's father) offered him a role in the big-budget Frank Norris drama *The Pit* (1914). He had the same immediate success he'd enjoyed onstage (and which must have proven so annoying to less fortunate actors). Milton made another three features for Brady's World company, including *The Deep Purple* (1916, costarring Clara Kimball Young) and *The Rack* (also 1916, with Alice Brady).

"Then, for my many sins," he said at the time, "I did penance for nine months of my life in *Patria*." That fifteen-part adventure serial costarred the popular dancer Irene Castle and was one of many patterned after hits such as *The Perils of Pauline* and *The Million Dollar Mystery*. "Mrs. Vernon Castle is

A more mature Milton Sills in the late 1920s.

delightful, droll, original, a splendid vis-à-vis on the screen," Milton said diplomatically. "But the play itself! Brr! To me it was most uncongenial." By this time, he was an established hit with moviegoers. Tall, handsome, and athletic in an Arrow Collar way, Milton possessed a dazzling smile and the kind of unruly, wavy hair that was so popular at the time (à la Francis X. Bushman and Crane Wilbur). After the horror of *Patria*, Milton left World and spent the next seven years as a very successful freelancer, working for nearly every studio in the industry, large and small alike.

He made some fifty films during this period, working his way into the hearts of his fans. While Milton Sills never became a top-flight star, like Valentino or Fairbanks, his fame was not to be sneezed at. Always placing high in popularity polls, Milton graced the covers of fan magazines, his postcards sold well, and most importantly, theater owners found that his films (for no matter which company) always drew a loyal, steady crowd. He played a convict in *The Honor System* (1917, costarring Gladys Brockwell, at Fox), a prohibitionist in *The Fringe of Society* (1917, with Ruth Roland), costarred with Clara Kimball Young in the Elinor Glyn-based bodice-ripper *The Reason Why* (Select, 1918), and was a newspaperman in the Fannie Ward drama *The Yellow Ticket* (Pathé, 1918). He costarred several times with opera diva Geraldine Farrar at Goldwyn (*The Hell Cat*, 1918, *Shadows* and *The Stronger Vow*, both 1919), and with Clara Kimball Young (most notably *The Eyes of Youth*, 1919, which was all but stolen by bit player Rudolph Valentino).

In the early 1920s Milton Sills appeared in an average of five or six films a year, bouncing from one company and leading lady to another. The major studios were more than happy to work with him: He starred for Metro (*Dangerous to Men*, a sex comedy with Viola Dana, 1920), and Paramount (*The Great Moment*, the first film actually scripted by Elinor Glyn, opposite Gloria Swanson in 1920, and *Adam's Rib*, with Anna Q. Nilsson, 1923). For Famous Players-Lasky, he appeared in the popular *Miss Lulu Bett* (1921) with Lois Wilson, the desert drama *Burning Sands* (1922), and *Adam's Rib* (1923), among others. For Goldwyn, he was in one of umpteen versions of Rex Beach's *The Spoilers* (1923). But Milton also worked for smaller studios throughout this period: Realart (*Sweet Lavender*, 1920, with Mary Miles Minter), Robertson-Cole (*Salvage*, 1921, with Pauline Frederick), Principal (*The Marriage Chance*, 1922), Mastodon (*The

Last Hour, 1923), and Associated (*Why Women Remarry*, 1923).

If anyone had the right to be snobbish about "photo-plays," it was Milton Sills. But he showed such a genuine enthusiasm for the medium that he became just as popular within the professional community as he did with fans. He stayed in New York as much as possible, renting a book-lined apartment on Riverside Drive, not far from Columbia University. But unlike some former stage stars, he professed no desire to return to the boards. The screen, Milton said, "removes the stiffness from actors long accustomed to doing one part for perhaps two years." He added that "I find the best directors suggest, but allow the details to be worked out by the actor, provided he is at all intelligent."

Milton had worked as a freelancer for First National several times, including one of his most successful films, the classic flapper comedy *Flaming Youth* (1923, as Colleen Moore's steady older boyfriend). He finally settled down and signed a long-term studio contract with First National in 1924, staying with that studio until the advent of talkies. He made twenty-three films with First National without a single loan-out. In the late 1920s—an age of sheiks and parlor snakes—Milton Sills provided a more dignified, almost stolid, leading man for older women to daydream about. Among his more popular First National films were *Flowing Gold* (1924, the first under his new contract), *Madonna of the Streets* (1923, costarring Alla Nazimova as his vampire wife), the rousing and brilliantly produced *The Sea Hawk* (1924, later remade by Errol Flynn) as the swashbuckling hero, *Paradise* (1926, with Betty Bronson), *Valley of the Giants* (a 1927 remake of the lumberjack film which nearly killed poor Wallace Reid in 1919), and *The Barker* (a 1928 carnival tale, as Douglas Fairbanks, Jr.'s father).

In 1925 Milton's wife Gladys divorced him, charging desertion. A year later, he wed his occasional costar, twenty-nine-year-old Doris Kenyon, in a small ceremony overlooking an Adirondack lake. The two had a son, Kenyon Clarence Sills, in 1927. Milton's health broke in 1929, and there is some mystery behind this period. A "breakdown" is sometimes mentioned in the press, though whether it was physical or emotional is unclear. A combination of tax and stock-market troubles were named as possible causes, but—as was later made clear—Milton's heart was not all it could have been.

His last First National film was his first part-talkie, the South Seas drama *His Captive Woman* (1929). It was silly stuff, but Milton had nothing to fear from talking pictures. He was still young (forty-seven in 1929), good looking, and had a stage-trained voice. He moved to Fox, where he starred as a gangster in the musical *Man Trouble* (1930, with Dorothy Mackaill). He next starred in *The Sea Wolf* (1930, not to be confused with his earlier films, *The Sea Tiger* or *The Sea Hawk*). In this, a Jack London adventure, Milton played a tough sea captain with unruly passengers aboard. It was a respectable hit, and his future looked assured.

But death came suddenly and unexpectedly to Milton Sills on September 15, 1930. He was playing tennis at his Santa Barbara home with his wife, daughter, and screenwriter John Goodrich when he was stricken with an instantly fatal heart attack. He was only forty-eight and still a major, marketable star. Doris Kenyon went on to marry twice more and continued acting until her 1939 retirement (she died in 1979). Milton Sills's last work turned out not to be *The Sea Wolf*, but rather a book published in 1932. Co-edited with Ernest Holmes, *Values: A Philosophy of Human Needs* consisted of "six dialogues on subjects ranging from reality to immortality." It was an odd but fitting finale to Sills's career.

Constance Talmadge

The silent screen produced many great comics, and not a few of them were women: Mabel Normand, Dorothy Gish, Colleen Moore, Billie Rhodes, Louise Fazenda; the list goes on and on. One of the brightest was (like her friend Dorothy Gish) somewhat dimmed by being the sister of a great dramatic star. But the few available films of Constance Talmadge reveal her to be one of the cleverest and most unaffected comic actresses of her time.

Constance was the youngest of three acting sisters: To the best of our knowledge, Norma Talmadge was born in 1895, Natalie in 1898, and Constance on April 19, 1899, in Jersey City, New Jersey. The family moved to Brooklyn, where the girls attended P.S. 9 and Erasmus High School. All the time, their formidable stage mother, Margaret "Peg" Talmadge, was nudging her daughters into acting careers. Their father, Fred Talmadge, soon vanished from the scene and wound up broke—the sisters took him in shortly before his death in 1925.

Of the three Talmadge sisters, two became stars: not a bad average. Norma began acting in 1910, and by the late 1910s she was one of the country's most popular dramatic actresses. After a brilliant career, she retired in 1930. Natalie had an indifferent career and an unhappy marriage to Buster Keaton. Nicknamed "Dutch," Constance was a hell-raiser from an early age, "one of the few genuine femme fatales I have ever known," according to Anita Loos. "Naughty Constance!" wrote Peg in a 1924 book about her daughters. "Her childhood days were a series of tiny mischiefs and small spanked fingers!" A risk-taking tomboy from childhood, Constance also developed an enthusiastic interest in the opposite sex.

When Norma began acting at Vitagraph in Brooklyn, little Constance begged to come to work with her. Norma relented, and soon Constance was the pet of the studio. The cute kid was used as an extra in a few films, but her first documented role didn't come until 1914, as the female lead in the knockabout comedy *Buddy's First Call.* Constance continued at Vitagraph through mid-1915, performing in a score of comedies

Eternal flapper Constance Talmadge.

(as well as a few dramas) as The Vitagraph Tomboy. Not a stunner like Norma, Constance looked rather like an egg with a face painted on it: cute and pert, just short of real beauty. Her costars at Vitagraph included such early greats as Billy Quirk (in several comedies), Maurice Costello, Antonio Moreno, Anita Stewart, Flora Finch, and sister Norma (in *The Peacemaker*, 1914, and *Captivating Mary Carstairs*, 1915).

In the summer of 1915 the Talmadges decamped to California, where they eventually landed at D. W. Griffith's West Coast studio, Fine Arts-Triangle. Constance remained there only two years, appearing in six films and learning a lot about her art (as well as making a lifelong friend of Dorothy Gish). The film that changed Constance Talmadge's career was *Intolerance* (1916). It's often been called the greatest film ever made, and Constance—along with Mae Marsh—gave one of the greatest performances of the year. As the feisty Mountain Girl, Constance all but stole the Babylonian sequence away from Griffith's stunning sets and costumes. She refused a double for her chariot-driving scene and rehearsed it for three weeks, coming home bruised and exhausted each night. So impactful was she that her other role in the film, as Marguerite de Valois, was cut to a cameo, and Griffith shot a happy ending for her in a separate release.

Lillian Gish later recalled that the flat-as-a-pancake Constance would remove and lose her Mountain Girl padding, and "We would all go in search of Constance's figure ... Constance's carefree, fun-loving nature made her the pet of the studio." A friend compared Dorothy Gish and Constance to "two young puppies, standing on their hind legs, wagging their front paws at each other." Peg Talmadge recalled Constance enthusing, "I suppose a studio is the funniest place in the world, and screen actors are the funniest people I have ever seen! I adore them."

When Norma Talmadge married influential producer Joseph Schenck in late 1916, it proved a boon to both sisters. Schenck and Lewis J. Selznick bought up Constance's contract and distributed her films through Select, First National, and United Artists for the rest of her career—and quite a career it was. She finished the 1910s with such bright little comedies as *The Studio Girl* and *Sauce for the Goose* (1918), and *Who Cares?* and *A Virtuous Vamp* (1919). By the time the 1920s dawned, she and her pal Dorothy Gish were two of the screen's most popular comediennes.

On December 26, 1920, Constance eloped with businessman John Pialo-

Constance Talmadge

glou; Dorothy Gish and James Rennie also eloped, "to keep them company." Neither marriage worked out; Constance and Pialoglou divorced within a year. Gish told film historian Dewitt Bodeen, "Constance was always getting engaged—but never to less than two men at the same time ... She could go from a thé dansant at the Ritz to a dancing party at the Plaza and end up getting engaged at least twice." Bodeen listed among her more serious beaux actors Jack Pickford, Buster Collier, Jr., and Richard Barthelmess, composer Irving Berlin, and author Michael Arlen. All this romance didn't slow down Constance's workload, however. She starred in twenty-four films during the 1920s, the majority of them jazzy, light-hearted comedies. She played the same sort of roles Colleen Moore did: good-hearted flappers, ambitious small-town girls, discontented wives. Her two most frequent leading men were Harrison Ford (twelve films) and Kenneth Harlan (seven films).

Nearly everything she touched turned to gold: "Constance Talmadge" on a theater marquee was a guarantee of box-office success. She played a merry widow in *In Search of a Sinner* (1920), a trouble-making heiress in *Lessons in Love,* a lovesick, repressed daughter in *Mama's Affair* (both 1921), a Ziegfeld Girl in *Polly of the Follies* (1922), a dizzy wife in *Dulcy* (1923), a millionairess after Ronald Colman in *Her Night of Romance* (1924), twins in *Her Sister from Paris* (1925, remade less successfully by Greta Garbo as *Two Faced Woman*), and an American in Russia in *The Duchess from Buffalo* (1926). One of her few dramas, and quite a successful one, was 1922's *East Is West.* Based on the stage play, it featured Constance as Ming Toy, a Chinese girl who escapes her evil guardian and who—in an unconvincing plot twist—turns out to be Caucasian.

Although she thought Norma the more talented sister, Constance took a workmanlike and intelligent approach to her comedy. "I try to handle a comedy role in much the same way a cartoonist handles his pencils," she told a fan magazine. "If he is drawing a picture of the late Theodore Roosevelt, he emphasizes Teddy's eyeglasses and teeth, and leaves the ears and nostrils and the lines of the face barely suggested. One must leave a great deal to the imagination of the audience."

Constance nearly became Mrs. Irving Thalberg in the late 1920s, which certainly wouldn't have hurt her career. From 1924 to 1926 a smitten Thalberg paid court to Constance, who was not seriously interested. According to Norma Shearer biographer Gavin Lambert, Constance spent more time with the gay couple William Haines and Jimmie Shields than with Thalberg, much to his despair. When Constance married in 1926, to a Scotsman named Alistair MacIntoch, Thalberg finally went looking elsewhere and married Shearer, in 1928. The Talmadge-MacIntoch marriage lasted about a year. In 1929 Constance wed Chicago businessman Townsend Netcher; this also did not last long. By now Constance, immensely wealthy, was beginning to tire of acting. Her last film was released in 1929: In *Venus*, filmed on the Riviera, she played a lovestruck princess. It was one of the last silents released by UA. Norma went on to make two indifferent talkies, even though Constance reportedly wired her, "Leave them while you're looking good and thank God for the trust funds Momma set up."

Constance Talmadge in *Polly of the Follies*, 1922.

Like fellow flapper Colleen Moore, Constance Talmadge was a smart woman with her money, and retirement did not mean poverty. Constance's story has a happy ending. Her fourth marriage was the lucky one: In 1939 she wed New York stockbroker Walter Giblin, and their combined fortunes allowed them to own homes on Park Avenue and in California. Constance worked as a Red Cross nurse during World War II, enjoying it so much that she continued volunteering at hospitals after the war ended. When asked if she planned a comeback, she gasped, "Why on earth would I ever do a thing like that?" Giblin died in 1964; her sisters Norma and Natalie died in 1957 and 1969. The last survivor, Constance Talmadge, lived the life of a wealthy society matron until her death on November 23, 1973.

Norma Talmadge

In her time, Norma Talmadge enjoyed the same reputation as Bette Davis and Meryl Streep later did: quite adept at comedy, but more popular as a moist-eyed, star-crossed victim of circumstances. Talmadge's career began in the early 1910s and continued unabated through the silent era. She never succeeded in talkies, however, so her reputation today rests solely with a few dedicated silent film scholars.

Norma Talmadge was born on May 26, in Jersey City, New Jersey (not Niagara Falls, as was sometimes reported). The year has been estimated as everything from 1892 to 1897, but 1895 seems the likeliest bet. She was the eldest daughter of ad salesman Fred Talmadge and overbearing stage mother Peg. The Talmadges moved Norma and her two younger sisters Constance and Natalie to Brooklyn, where they spent their childhoods. The girls attended P.S. 9 and Erasmus High School, participating in amateur theatricals. By the time she'd entered her teens, Norma was commuting to New York City to pose for music slides and magazine covers.

In 1910 Norma played hooky from school and began showing up at Brooklyn's Vitagraph Studios, and where she was, miraculously, given a featured role (at $2.50 a day) in her first film, *A Four-Footed Pest*—but she never forgot one of the actresses remarking, "Pretty child, but absolutely no talent!" She dropped out of school and, over the next year or so, appeared in such one-reelers as *Mrs. 'enry 'awkins* (with Maurice Costello), *In Neighboring Kingdoms* (with John Bunny), and *The Dixie Mother* (with her idol, "Vitagraph Girl" Florence Turner). Norma made her first big impression as the tragic little seamstress in *A Tale of Two Cities* (1911).

Her first starring role didn't come until *The Battle Cry of Peace* (1915). By this time she was earning an impressive $250 a week, and her two younger sisters had followed her into the profession. Norma was certainly the prettiest of the three, with her large dark eyes and full lips. Her swan-like throat and rounded nose gave her the most beautiful profile on the screen until Garbo showed up in the mid–1920s. The success

Norma Talmadge's classic profile, circa 1924.

of *The Battle Cry of Peace* brought an offer from the West Coast National Pictures. Norma moved to California with a $400-a-week contract and sister Constance in tow. She'd made only one film for National (*Captivating Mary Carstairs*) when the studio folded. Norma freelanced for Griffith's Triangle and Fine Arts, making such films as *Missing Links*, *The Children in the House*, *Going Straight* (in which she played an ex-gun moll), and *The Devil's Needle*.

In October 1916 Norma made a very smart career move, marrying producer Joseph Schenck. Under his guidance, her career took off; she starred opposite Eugene O'Brien in a popular series of films and, in 1919, formed The Norma Talmadge Film Company, which released through First National. She made four pictures a year, resting in her Bayside, Long Island, estate between films. Although she and Schenck had no children, Norma surrounded herself with pets: dogs, cats, birds; she even expressed a fondness for angle worms.

Norma Talmadge was known as a good-natured, tireless worker, but impatient with unprofessionalism. Once, a group of extras balked at standing in a pool of slimy water during the filming of *The Branded Woman* (1919). Norma snapped, "I don't ask you to do what I won't do myself," and strode—costume and all—into the pool. She didn't take herself too seriously as an actress, though, and didn't profess to fret over her parts (she was often heard to exclaim, "I was rotten in that picture!"). Though Norma was a smart businesswoman and knew her forte, she described herself as a frustrated feminist and balked at all her clinging-vine roles.

In 1924 Norma wrote about her screen successes in her mother's book, *The Talmadge Sisters*. The most important thing for screen success, she said, "is to have a camera face ... a face that photographs both beautifully and expressively." It was impossible to tell in person how someone would register on film, and Norma recalled seeing "plain, ineffective" types who photographed beautifully. She also denied any ambitions to act in the legitimate theater: "I find the films entirely to my liking. I am essentially a film actress and prefer to remain so. The desire of the actor to hear the spectators' plaudits ringing in his ears, to feel the personal gratification of swaying the crowd across the footlights does not tempt me." True to her word, Norma never appeared onstage.

Her popularity continued rising through the 1920s. She made scores of films, and a year didn't pass without a highly successful Norma Talmadge movie: *The Passion Flower* (1921), *Smilin' Through* (1922, a popular hearts-and-

Norma Talmadge

flowers tearjerker), *Within the Law* (1923, based on a Broadway hit), *Secrets* (1924), *Graustark* (1925), *Kiki* (1926, an unusually high-kicking role and one of her biggest hits), *Camille* (1927, with young Gilbert Roland as her Armand), and *The Dove* (1928). Most of her films were elaborate costume dramas, earning Norma the title of "The Lady of the Great Indoors." Although she herself dismissed many of her films as "sobs and smiles," her public loved her—and in 1927 Norma became the third star to place her footprints in the forecourt of Grauman's Chinese Theater (Mary Pickford and Douglas Fairbanks had preceded her by two weeks). Her salary rocketed to $7,500 a week, and her weekly fan mail averaged three thousand letters. "Making pictures is a colossal game," Norma told one reporter at the height of her fame. "To me it is life. It gives me what I want, and I try to give it the best that is in me."

When sound arrived, Norma took a break to have her Brooklyn-bred voice trained. An infamous photo of her gazing hopefully up at a microphone became a symbol of the era (the number 13 was ominously painted onto the mike in later reproductions of the photo). Norma made only two talkies, neither of them terribly successful. She played a gangster's wife in *New York Nights* (1930, featuring teenaged Jean Harlow as an extra), and she played Madame DuBarry in *DuBarry, Woman of Passion* later that year. Constance supposedly wired her, "Leave them while you're looking good and thank God for the trust funds Momma set up." Norma took the advice and retired. Incidentally, she *was* looking good: She was a stunning woman of thirty-five (or thereabouts) with a deep, melodious voice. With luck and perseverance, her career might have continued indefinitely.

But Norma's life did not end with retirement. Her marriage to Schenck deteriorated in 1932 during her vaudeville tour with comic George Jessel. The headlines dragged on for two years; Norma and Jessel wed promptly after her 1934 divorce from Schenck (who reportedly settled one million dollars on Norma—extremely surprising, considering how the marriage ended). Norma's marriage to Jessel lasted a scant three years. By 1946 Norma Talmadge was fifty-one years old, enormously wealthy, and still very attractive (in later years she took on a marked resemblance to Paulette Goddard). She married for the third time, to Dr. Carvel James. That marriage lasted for life.

The Jameses traveled between Palm Springs, Tucson, and a large home in

Norma Talmadge at the end of her film career, in the late 1920s.

Las Vegas. Norma remained close to her sisters (mother Peg had died in 1934). Norma's wealth and happiness were, sadly, not complemented by good health; crippling arthritis confined her to a wheelchair by the early 1950s. In 1957 she suffered a series of strokes, and pneumonia finally ended her life on December 24, 1957. Norma left her estate—valued at more than $1 million—to sisters Connie and Natalie; her widower didn't lack for money.

When Norma Talmadge died, silent films were still considered embarrassingly quaint. Scholars were not yet interviewing retired stars; silents were only shown in rare revival houses or on TV as vandalized *Fractured Flickers*. Had she lived another ten years, Norma Talmadge might have been venerated and feted as were fellow pioneers Mary Pickford, Lillian Gish, and Blanche Sweet. Instead, she has drifted into an undeserved obscurity.

"Those Talmadge Girls," ***left to right:*** **Natalie, Norma, Constance.**

LILYAN TASHMAN

There have always been certain actresses known more for their chic style than for their talent. Kay Francis, Ina Claire, and Constance Bennett were all talented and versatile actresses, yet they turned up more often in Best-Dressed lists than Best-Performance lists. Thus it was with Lilyan Tashman, whose film career took in an impressive sixty-six films from 1921 through her death in 1934. She never became an "A" star, but her supporting performances are sharp, clever, and have aged little over the decades. Blonde and very tall, with sly cat-like features, Lilyan began her career playing vamps and "other women," and when talkies came in, she segued into grifters and the heroine's best pal. Producers had a hard time typing her: She was more acidic than Joan Blondell, sexier than Aline MacMahon, classier than Una Merkel. She might have aged into a superb character actress, but she didn't have the time.

She was born in Brooklyn, New York, the tenth and youngest child of clothing manufacturer Maurice Tashman and his wife Rose. Lilyan's birthdate is always listed as October 23, 1899, but this is highly unlikely, as her first marriage took place in 1914. She was probably born closer to 1895. She attended the Girl's High School in Brooklyn, during which time she freelanced as an artist's and fashion model. After this point, her "official" biography takes leave of all reality. According to studio press releases and her obituaries, Lilyan went to either Hunter College or "finishing school," and 1917 found her dining with friends at Martin's Restaurant on Broadway. There, Florenz Ziegfeld picked her from the crowd, offered her a job in that year's *Follies*, and the teenaged schoolgirl was rocketed to stardom. This was, of course, utter nonsense.

In actuality, Lilyan Tashman was a seasoned vaudeville trouper by 1914. That year, she was playing in the *Song Revue* in Milwaukee, on the same bill as the rising team of Eddie Cantor and Al Lee. Late that year, Lilyan married Lee. Cantor went on to fame, and Lee left acting to become stage manager for George White's *Scandals*. As for Lilyan,

Lilyan Tashman, circa 1930 (The Metaluna Collection).

she stayed with Lee until 1920, when the two separated (they divorced the following year). By that time, she had been in the *Follies*, though Ziegfeld probably did not spot her in a restaurant. More likely, she showed up at a casting call like most of his showgirls. Her first *Follies* was actually the 1916 edition. Lilyan played Viola in a Shakespeare number, and cavorted on- and offstage with fellow showgirls Marion Davies, Ina Claire, Allyn King, and Ann Pennington. She also feuded with fellow showgirl Peggy Hopkins Joyce, who recalled in her amusing memoirs that "I have had a quarrel with Lilyan, one of the girls; in fact almost a fight but we were stopped and the stage manager said he would fire us if we did it again."

Lilyan stayed with the *Follies* for the legendary 1917 and 1918 editions, which starred Fanny Brice, W. C. Fields, Bert Williams, old friend Eddie Cantor, Marilyn Miller, and Will Rogers. But no showgirl stayed with the *Follies* forever, and by 1919, Lilyan had joined the Winter Garden chorus. Later that year, producer David Belasco gave Lilyan her first chance at a "book" show, Avery Hopwood's hard-boiled comedy *The Gold Diggers* (based partly on the exploits of Kay Laurell). Starring fellow *Follies* refugee Ina Claire, the show featured Lilyan in a supporting role as the mercenary Trixie. It ran for two years and gave Lilyan her first real acting lessons. "I learned from oversureness how to ruin a performance by anticipating when the laughs were coming and waiting for them," she wrote in 1931. "That is the fascination of stage work—its unexpectedness. One must anticipate nothing, as no two audiences are alike." Lilyan also filled in from time to time for star Ina Claire, as her understudy.

It was an exciting two years for Lilyan: She also made her film debut. She and fellow showgirl Nita Naldi played Pleasure and Temptation in an allegorical segment of the Richard Barthelmess film, *Experience* (1921). Among Lilyan's many fans was the actor Edmund Lowe, currently playing in another Belasco show, *The Son-Daughter*. The two began keeping steady company. When *The Gold Diggers* closed, Lilyan had a rough period, professionally. Her first starring show, *The Garden of Weeds*, was critically panned, she was fired from the show *Madame Pierre,* and Edmund Lowe headed west to make films, leaving her lonely and depressed. Films were an option she now more seriously considered. Her second appearance, a small role in the Mabel Normand film, *Head Over Heels* (1922), convinced Lilyan to abandon the stage and follow Lowe to Los Angeles.

She promptly found work in Hollywood, appearing in five films in 1924: among them a filmed version of her stage flop, *The Garden of Weeds* (not, however, in the starring part, which was taken by Betty Compson), and the Gloria Swanson comedy *Manhandled* (filmed mostly in New York). She began getting good notices, too. *Variety* said of Lilyan in *Nellie, the Beautiful Cloak Model* that she "does a loose lady vamp in a manner that registers as to the manner born," and that she "does well in a thankless role" in the Buck Jones western *Winner Take All.*

It was a good start, and Lilyan found herself in demand as a freelancer. Throughout the 1920s she hopped from studio to studio, both large and small, making perhaps more films with First National than any other. Not until 1931 did she sign a long-term contract, with Paramount, where she made nine films. She appeared in another ten films in 1925, including the part-color *Pretty Ladies* (with MGM neophytes Joan Crawford and Myrna Loy), the Charles Ray comedy *Bright Lights,* and *Ports of Call.* In that last film, she played a Sadie Thompson-like tramp on the lam, with boyfriend Edmund Lowe costarring. *Variety* noted that "She is acquiring poise and seems more at ease in this picture than previously." There was good reason for that; she and Lowe married on September 1, 1925.

"We were two people who had reached the years of mental discretion," she later wrote, "who knew exactly what we were doing with our lives and why." The two quickly became one of the most popular and socially active couples in filmdom. More fun than Doug and Mary, more sane than Mae Murray and Bob Leonard, Lilyan and Edmund gave pool parties, beach parties, and cocktail parties that were famous for their chic and wit. Their ultra-modern, red-and-white Beverly Hills home (coyly dubbed "Lilowe") became known to fans throughout the world via magazine layouts. It was also about this time that Lilyan began appearing on "best-dressed" lists, much to her chagrin. The title, she said, "was forced upon me. I wear only what I like." She later added that "It's more boring for a woman to talk about clothes than for a man to talk of his golf score." Besides her clothes, Lilyan became known for her acid wit, not always appreciated by its targets (she referred to Jack Pickford, accurately if indelicately, as "Mr. Syphilis").

From 1926 through the end of the silent era, Lilyan appeared in twenty-one films, working her way up to become one of the most reliable and sharpest supporting players in the industry. She even starred in a handful of films, including the independent *Rocking Moon* (1926) and the gold-digging saga *The Woman Who Did Not Care* (1927). But her forte was in stealing films from their nominal stars. She was a naughty French dancer in the Ernst Lubitsch farce *So This Is Paris* (1926), a mercenary wife in *For Alimony Only* (also 1926), Olympe to Norma Talmadge's *Camille* (1927), vamped Will Rogers in *A Texas Steer* (1927), and was a showgirl in *Hardboiled* (1929). Her reviews proved her growing talent. *Variety* said that she "makes the most of the vamp role and looks great in her silk trick pajamas" in *Don't Tell the Wife* (1927), that she "comes pretty close to stealing" *Take Me Home* (1928) from star Bebe Daniels, and "gives an excellent account of herself" in Dorothy Arzner's *Manhattan Cocktail* (1928). She also got a chance to costar with her

Lilyan Tashman earning her "best-dressed" title, early 1930s.

husband in *Siberia* (1926) and *Happiness Ahead* (1928).

When sound arrived, the stage-trained Lilyan had little to worry about: Her crisp contralto voice recorded perfectly. She appeared in some of the very first feature talkies, including United Artists's slick, entertaining *Bulldog Drummond* (1929), and she was a showgirl testifying at *The Trial of Mary Dugan* (also 1929). She was an "upstage show dame" in the all-color, high-budget (and, sadly, lost) musical *Gold Diggers of Broadway* (1929) and played Norma Talmadge's cynical, seen-it-all pal in *New York Nights* (1930). As Lilyan aged into her thirties, the parts remained small in size but sharp and eye catching. Even if the film itself bombed, she stood out: In the unbearable Harry Richman vehicle *Puttin' on the Ritz* (1930), she and James Gleason were delightful as Richman's wise-cracking vaudeville chums, and in the equally dreadful *The Matrimonial Bed* (1930, starring Frank Fay), she was the only performer to emerge unscathed.

She made twenty-eight talking films, again nabbing a starring role from time to time. Two atypical roles were as a murderess in the effective and amusing melodrama *Murder by the Clock* and as Peggy Shannon's self-sacrificing mother in *The Road to Reno* (both 1931). Lilyan also starred as a chorus girl and mother in *Wine, Women and Song* (1933), but she mostly supported other stars in shorter, snappier parts. She was the comic relief in the Helen Twelvetrees mystery *The Cat Creeps* (1930), a trollop in *One Heavenly Night* (1931, played "to the last inch with a nice sense of judgement in swagger," according to *Variety*), was a tough sob sister in *Up Pops the Devil* (1931), a hard-drinking soldier in the fascinating all-female war film *The Mad Parade* (1931), and a warm-hearted gold digger in the melodramatic *Millie* (1931). In that last, pre–Code, film, she notably shared a bed—in lingerie—with Joan Blondell.

There was some talk in Hollywood about Lilyan's private sexual proclivities as well, and rumors were rife that she and her husband had a "friendly arrangement." It might be put off to idle gossip, but Greta Garbo biographer Barry Paris quotes both Lina Basquette and Irene Mayer Selznick as claiming that Lilyan made passes at them. Maybe, maybe not; at this late date there is no way to either confirm or deny the rumors. The only public rift in the Tashman/Lowe marriage came in 1931, when Lilyan apparently beat the tar out of actress June Marlowe after catching her in Lowe's dressing room (assault charges were later dropped).

Lilyan only made three films in 1932: Claudette Colbert's crime drama *The Wiser Sex*, the Mary Astor mother-love saga *Those We Love* (*Variety* noted that one of Lilyan's dresses "is about the ugliest thing she has ever worn in a picture"), and as a grifter in the odd, unsatisfying Russian Revolution film *Scarlet Dawn*. After that last film was shot, she entered a New York hospital for what was described as an appendectomy, emerging pale and thin. She was never really well from that point on. "She was worried about her health," said Lilyan's friend, reporter Virginia Maxwell. "If the physicians knew that she had a tumor, I don't believe they ever told her so."

But she did indeed have a tumor: The appendectomy story was probably just a cover for the discovery of some form of abdominal cancer. Lilyan made another five films after that surgery, her strength slowly ebbing from month to month. She vamped Charlie Ruggles in the comedy *Mama Loves Papa* (1933), traded quips with expert scene stealers Bing Crosby, Jack Oakie, and Skeets Gallagher in the musical *Too Much Harmony* (1933), and played Norma Shearer's wise older sister in the slick tea-cup drama *Riptide* (1934). Lilyan still looked wonderful and seemed to have all her snap, but in actuality, her role in that last film had to be shortened to accommodate her weakening condition.

In February 1934 Lilyan traveled to New York to appear as Nellie Bly in Republic's *Frankie and Johnny*, starring Helen Morgan and Chester Morris. She stayed with a friend on East 70th Street, and she was so weak that she took time off to rest in Connecticut with her husband. She returned to work in March, finished her role on the 8th, appeared at a benefit for the Israel Orphan's Home on the 10th, and checked into The Doctor's Hospital for surgery on the 16th. By that time, there was nothing more to be done, and her friends and family gathered at her bedside. Lilyan never lost consciousness and was even reading a script shortly before her death on the afternoon of March 21.

Her death came as a shock to the public, although her coworkers had known she was quite ill. She had an Orthodox Jewish funeral the following day, and it turned into a near riot. Crowds jammed the Temple Emmanu-El on Fifth Avenue, and her family mingled with celebrities such as Mary Pickford, Sophie Tucker, Clifton Webb, Jack Benny, Cecil Beaton, Mae Murray, Fanny Brice, and Carl Van Vechten. In his eulogy, Eddie Cantor said that Lilyan had been "one of the few people in the film world who had a sense of proportion and to whom success made no difference." He added that "I never heard her speak ill of anyone," a statement which must have raised many an eyebrow. At the Washington Cemetery in Brooklyn, the crowds were so thick (about ten thousand) and unruly that the tombstone of Lilyan's sister Annie was knocked over and several onlookers injured.

Lilyan left some $31,000, along with $121,000 in furs and jewels, and no will, which resulted in some nasty squabbling between Lowe and Lilyan's sisters Hattie and Jennie. Lilyan's last film, *Frankie and Johnny*, wasn't released until May 1936, with her part cut to a brief cameo. As for Edmund Lowe, his best work was behind him. He briefly remarried and continued acting until 1960, dying in 1971 at the age of seventy-nine.

Olive Thomas

Of all the *Ziegfeld Follies* Girls who entered films—the long list includes Mae Murray, Marion Davies, Billie Dove, Lilyan Tashman, Louise Brooks, and Paulette Goddard—the one with the most going for her seemed to be Olive Thomas. Olive had incredible beauty, was well liked by her coworkers, and had an enormous amount of pluck. Yet five years after her *Follies* debut, Olive lay dead in France under very mysterious circumstances.

She was born Oliveretta Elaine Duffy ("than which there is no better Irish name," she bragged); the date was October 20, 1894; the place, Charleroi, a small mining town in Western Pennsylvania. Olive's father died when she was young and her mother remarried, but the family (by now living in Pittsburgh) was still dirt poor. Olive left school at an early age to seek work. In 1911 she married a local salesman, Bernard Thomas, but left him in 1915 to move to New York (the two soon divorced, though she kept his name). She worked as a salesgirl in a Harlem department store, but she soon became a photographer's and artist's model, appearing in such magazines as *Vogue* and *Vanity Fair*.

Olive Thomas had one of those faces which would be considered beautiful in any era. Her large eyes and thin, delicate features, topped by thick brown curls, look remarkably modern to us today. Artist Harrison Fisher later called her "the prettiest girl on the New York stage." Olive had been in New York only a few months before success came calling. Her first *Ziegfeld Follies* was the 1915 edition, at $75 a week; her fellow "girls" included Mae Murray, Kay Laurell, and Ann Pennington. She also appeared in the 1915 *Midnight Frolics*, and in 1916 she was named Ziegfeld's "*Midnight Frolics* Girl" (the *Frolics* taking place atop the New Amsterdam's Roof Garden). Ziegfeld seems to have developed feelings for Olive (this was not an unusual situation for *Follies* Girls) and was reportedly crushed when she married Mary Pickford's brother Jack in 1917. But Ziegfeld—who was married to Billie Burke at the time—got over it.

Olive couldn't have picked a worse

Olive Thomas sporting curls à la sister-in-law Mary Pickford.

husband than twenty-one-year old Jack Pickford. Like many alcoholics and drug addicts, he was breezy and charming on the surface. His good looks and connections to sister Mary may have swept Olive off her feet. Jack (who later wed musical comedy star Marilyn Miller) died of hard living at the age of thirty-seven. By the time she became Mrs. Pickford, Olive was also a film star. In October 1916 she was signed for films by Triangle and moved west. With her beauty, she became a popular star—the fact that she was a quick learner and a hard worker assured her success. Among Olive's early films were *Beatrice Fairfax* (1916), *Indiscreet Corinne*, A *Girl Like That*, *Broadway Arizona*, *An Even Break* (all 1917), *Betty Takes a Hand* (her first real big hit), *Heiress for a Day*, *Limousine Life*, *The Follies Girl,* and *Madcap Madge* (all 1918).

Olive became one of the film community's most well-liked residents; people also liked Jack's company, though many viewed his antics with alarm. *Photoplay*, visiting Olive in 1917, wrote that "Her dressing room is more popular than a Town Hall." Her nickname around the Triangle lot was Miss Encyclopedia, for her constant reading and inquiring mind. Any time a question came up, Olive was appealed to—if she didn't know the answer, she couldn't rest till she'd looked it up. Her interviews reveal a level-headed girl with an utter lack of pretension. "Life's too short and fate's too funny to get upstage," Olive said in 1919, brushing herself off as "only a *Follies* girl." She went into films, she said, for "plenty of clothes and fun." One director said of her, "That girl has a business woman's head. I believe she will be capable of directing someday. Olive is a joy-of-living optimist—but an intelligent one."

By 1919 her career's pace was pick-

Olive Thomas in her Ziegfeld days.

ing up: She was signed by Selznick that year, at an impressive $2,500 a week. Among her 1919 films were *Upstairs and Down*, *The Glorious Lady*, *Love's Prisoner* (her only known surviving film), *Prudence on Broadway*, *Out Yonder*, *Tonton*, and *The Spiteful Bride*. The dawn of the 1920s brought another spate of smash-hit Olive Thomas vehicles—*Youthful Folly*, *Darling Mine*, *Footlights* and *Shadows*, *The Flapper* (one of her biggest hits), and *Everybody's Sweetheart*.

But all was not well in Olive's life; her marriage to Jack Pickford was proving insupportable, and there were signs that she may have been using drugs as well. On August 12, 1920, Jack and Olive sailed for London, then to France, to mend their troubled marriage and relax from their film work. The star-studded passenger list included the Talmadge sisters and Dorothy Gish. The weeks in London and then Paris did not go well. Things came to a tragic end on the night of September 6 when, after a night on the town, Olive was found writhing on the bathroom floor in her Hotel Crillon suite. Jack summoned help, and she was rushed to the American Hospital at Neuilly, where one Dr. Choate told reporters, "The situation is serious, but recovery is hopeful." But Olive died on September 9 from bichloride of mercury poisoning, after several agonizing days of blindness, paralysis, and convulsions.

Olive Thomas's death has long been one of Hollywood's darkest mysteries. The official story was told by Jack (and reportedly by Olive herself, from her deathbed). This has Olive getting up with a midnight headache and searching for aspirin powder in the darkened bathroom. There, she accidentally drank a mixture of twelve grams of

The lovely Olive Thomas (The Metaluna Collection).

bichloride of mercury in alcohol. The fact that the mixture was used to treat syphilis hardly reflected well on Pickford. But it was better than the other scenarios being spread: Olive had committed suicide after Jack gave her syphilis; Olive committed suicide because of her husband's drug addiction; Olive herself was a drug addict; Jack killed her for the insurance money—the theories went on and on. No one will ever know. But drinking a large dose of bichloride of mercury by mistake seems unlikely; it is a harsh corrosive which burns horribly (any deathbed statement also seems out of the question, as Olive's vocal cords would have been destroyed).

A requiem mass was held for Olive in Paris. In New York, Olive's brothers James and William collected her remains. Her cars, jewels, and clothing brought $36,000 at auction after her

Screen Impressions

By LOUISE FAZENDA

ALMA RUBENS—A red lily—Messages d'amour in an old prayer book—Rubies—Moonbeams on the Alhambra

MAY ALLISON—Corn-flowers and daffodils—Turquoise—Sunshine after rain—White rabbits

MARY MILES MINTER—Dickens' Little Nell—Daisies—Lavender and old lace—Valentines

VIOLA DANA—Johnny Jump-Ups—Peter Pan—A baby-cloud against a purple mountain—Wisteria

OLIVE THOMAS—Forty-second Street and Broadway—"Lalla Rookh"—Pink satin and pearls—Mignonette

ENID BENNETT—Easter lilies—Mendelssohn's "Spring Song"—White moths—St. Cecilia

EUGENE O'BRIEN—Sir Walter Raleigh—The Barcarolle from "Tales of Hoffman"—Old-rose drawing-room

TOM MEIGHAN—Gorse-covered moors—A shepherd on a lonely hill—Shamrocks in Central Park

CLARINE SEYMOUR—Fireflies—Night, the scent of orange-blossoms and thrumming ukuleles—Bloom of apricot

Photograph by Monroe

Photograph © by Evans

Photograph by Charlotte Fairchild

Photograph by Evans

Photograph by Evans

Photograph by Hartsook

Photograph by Northland Studio

death—and that's not including the significant insurance policy Pickford had taken out on his wife. The beautiful New Amsterdam Theater, where Olive first found fame in New York, has recently been remodeled as one of Times Square's architectural gems. Every so often, a workman or stagehand reportedly sees the ghost of Olive Thomas on the empty stage, wandering sadly around the scene of her early success.

Opposite: **From the July 1920 *Motion Picture Classic, closewise from upper right:* May Allison, Viola Dana, Enid Bennett, Thomas Meighan, Clarine Seymour, Eugene O'Brien, Olive Thomas, Mary Miles Minter, Alma Rubens.**

Rudolph Valentino

Asking "Who was the most popular leading lady of the silent screen?" is a great way to get into a fistfight, as proponents of Gish, Pickford, Garbo, et al. jump into the fray. But as far as male stars go, it's hard to dispute Rudolph Valentino's title as the greatest leading man of all. More than seventy years after his death, the name Valentino is still familiar to even non-film buffs. Sadly, his talents and his bright personality are less well appreciated.

The most successful of the so-called "Latin Lovers" hailed from Castellaneta, on the heel of Italy's boot. Rodolpho Alfonzo Raffaelo Pierre Filibert di Valentina d'Antonguollo was born on May 6, 1895—but not to a dirt-poor peasant family, as is often assumed. "We were middle class," said his brother Alberto, "but in a quite comfortable position—my father was a veterinarian, health officer and a biologist." Why then did Rudolph emigrate to the United States in 1913, at the age of eighteen? "In his life he was always guided and pushed by the spirit of adventure," Alberto explained. "He used to say, 'Italy is too small for me.'"

Valentino needed that spirit of adventure: Between jobs as a taxi dancer and gardener in New York, he sometimes had to sleep in Central Park. His dancing (he was self-taught) was his key to fame—he and his pal Mae Murray began gaining reputations as up-and-coming ballroom dancers. In 1917 the twenty-one-year-old Rudolph decamped for Hollywood. Things were not easy for him there; Valentino did not look like the popular all-American boy. His first documented screen role was as a bit player in *Alimony* (1918). After that—slowly—came small parts in *A Married Virgin* (made in 1918, released 1920), *A Society Sensation* and *All Night* (both 1918), *A Rogue's Romance*, *The Homebreaker*, and *Out of Luck* (all 1919, the latter with Dorothy Gish). Dorothy Gish tried to convince D. W. Griffith to sign Rudolph, but Griffith felt him too foreign looking. Rudolph went horseback riding with the Gish sisters, who tried to cheer him up, but they couldn't help him find much work. New York friend Mae Murray, her own star on the ascendant, got Rudolph roles in *The*

Delicious Little Devil and *The Big Little Person* (both 1919).

Then came the most mysterious chapter in Rudolph's life: his marriage to Jean Acker, a minor actress through the 1920s. She and Rudolph hastily wed in November 1919, and—according to their divorce papers—she walked out on him on their wedding night. Many writers since have said that both Acker and Rudolph were gay, but this fails to explain an awful lot. If she knowingly married Rudolph to hide her sexual orientation, why would she immediately walk out? Did he throw her out on discovering her orientation? No one will ever know, and the Acker/Valentino marriage remains a frustrating question mark.

Rudolph Valentino, shortly before his death.

The winter of 1919 was obviously a gloomy one for Rudolph. Actress Viola Dana recalled that he had no place to go for Christmas. "I said, you're gonna come home with me... So we made him Santa Claus ... and he handed out the presents." His first real break came with *Eyes of Youth* (1919), a Clara Kimball Young melodrama. Rudolph played a hired gigolo who locks Clara in a hotel room and threatens her with A Fate Worse Than Death. Female audience members sat up and—rather than cringing for the heroine—envied her. Still, another year of small roles followed. In 1920 Rudolph appeared in six films, none very impressive credits. There was *An Adventuress* (this role was played by famed female impersonator Julian Eltinge), *The Cheater*, the delightfully-titled *Passion's Playground*, *Once to Every Woman*, *Stolen Moments,* and *The Wonderful Chance*.

Rudolph's own wonderful chance came in 1921. Many people today think that *The Sheik* made him a star, but his breakthrough role was actually in *The Four Horsemen of the Apocalypse* (1921). He got the job through screenwriter June Mathis, who became a friend and sponsor of Rudolph's. After seeing *Eyes of Youth*, she arranged a Metro contract for him. Playing a ne'er-do-well playboy who is caught up in the horrors of World War I, he turned in a delicate, intelligent performance, as well as electrifying the screen in a sensuous tango scene. Suddenly, audiences and executives alike sat up and took notice. His follow up, *Uncharted Seas* (1921), was fairly unremarkable except for his appearance.

Rudolph's next Metro film, *Camille* (1921), not only provided him with more public exposure but introduced him to the love of his life. Brilliant set and costume designer Natasha Rambova helped put *Camille* over the top. Rambova was born Winifred Hudnut, heiress to a cosmetics fortune. Ambitious, beautiful, and talented, she was as catnip to a cat for Rudolph. Throughout his life, he

Rudolph Valentino in *The Conquering Power* (1921).

showed a preference for dominant, successful women. As for the film itself, it was the most beautiful production of the play ever filmed, thanks to Rambova's sets and costumes. Leading lady Alla Nazimova made a wonderful Marguerite Gautier, but the male ingenue role of Armand Duval is notoriously thankless. Rudolph looked concerned, love stricken, and heartbroken as required. Trying to recapture the success of *Four Horsemen*, Metro reteamed costars Rudolph and Alice Terry with writer June Mathis and director Rex Ingram (Terry's husband) for *The Conquering Power* (1921). Based loosely on a Balzac tale, the film was a dreadful experience for all concerned, but it remains a riveting, dramatic experience for audiences. After the difficult and unpleasant shoot, Rudolph and Mathis decamped for Paramount, at a starting salary of $500 a week.

Then came the role that was forever after identified with Rudolph Valentino. *The Sheik* was based on a best-selling trashy novel by Edith M. Hull. Rudolph portrayed Ahmed Ben Hassan, a handsome young Arabian sheik who kidnaps and eventually wins over a headstrong English girl (Agnes Ayres). It was a fairly awful film, and Rudolph overacted much of the stilted script. But his appeal came across like a thunderbolt, and Rudolph Valentino became the first full-fledged male sex symbol of the screen. Songs were written about him (and about Ahmed), he was suddenly mobbed each time he went outside, and the entire country went Rudy-mad.

It's hard to overestimate the effect that Rudolph and *The Sheik* had on the nation—for decades, the term "sheik" was used to describe a desirable man. To this day—some eighty years after the film was released—it's still an icon of its time, the quintessential daring 1920s film. As for Rudolph, his appeal is still obvious. Ignoring the overly made-up lips and the too-enthusiastic eye work, you can still see his magnetic eroticism in the love scenes. These are scenes that obviously lead to the bed, not ending in the drawing room. Though he just couldn't make his eyes behave, Valentino was a man who knew how to use his hands.

As is usual, the studio found it difficult to quickly come up with a follow up to such an unexpected hit. His first 1922 films, *Moran of the Lady Letty* (a sea adventure) and *Beyond the Rocks* (a heavy-breathing romance with Gloria Swanson), pleased audiences but not critics—and certainly not Rudolph or Natasha. By this time, the two were an item. She took more and more control of his life—he posed for erotic photos and searched out artsy film properties, all at her behest. To be fair, Rudolph was more than willing to be wrapped around her little finger. The two married on May 13, 1922. Then all hell broke loose.

It seems his divorce from Jean Acker wasn't finalized, and Rudolph was hauled into jail for bigamy. The case was eventually decided in his favor, but the whole incident embarrassed Rudolph and Natasha; the fact that Paramount had let him go to jail—however briefly—made them wary of the studio. But Rudolph was back in top form as a cocky bullfighter in *Blood and Sand* (1922). Filmed in Los Angeles—rather than in Spain, as Rudolph wished—it was one of the year's biggest hits and his first unqualified success since *The Sheik*. This gave Rudolph and Natasha—by now his unofficial manager—leverage to demand more control over his projects. It was a move that nearly wrecked his career.

The first film to be demanded by the Valentinos was *The Young Rajah* (1922). It was a notorious flop. Nonetheless, *The Young Rajah* is an eagerly sought-after missing film. The story line—deposed Rudolph tries to regain his throne—isn't up to much, but the sight of the star wearing nothing but a few strands of pearls or a very revealing swimsuit make this a great loss to Valentino fans. Paramount took all artistic control away from Rudolph and Natasha, and the two walked out on his contract (and his salary, by now $7,000 a week).

The couple went on a cross-country personal appearance tour to pay the bills. A few months were all the level-headed, middle-class Rudolph could take of this, and he went back to Paramount, hat in hand. The studio allowed him and his wife to take a European vacation in late 1923 before resuming work. With typical down-to-earth cynicism, he told Bebe Daniels, "In Italy, I was just another wop." But back in the United States he was the biggest star in Hollywood. He also made his only two recordings that year. They reveal that Rudolph had a deep, slightly accented voice, but that he did not possess Ramon Novarro's talent as a singer.

All of his coworkers seemed fond of Rudolph, who was known around town as a gracious host, good cook, and a simple, friendly man. "He was a very serious worker," recalled costar Lois Wilson. "Rudolph didn't kid on the set. A very generous actor to work with, charming, with a terrific sense of humor." He needed that sense of humor on the set of *Monsieur Beaucaire* (1924), an overstuffed and pretentious costume romance, set in the court of Louis XIV. To Paramount's embarrassment, it was as big a flop as *The Young Rajah* had been. Rudolph's audience did not want to see him dolled up in laces and powdered wigs, so his next film—*A Sainted Devil*—had Rudolph butching it up as a macho Argentinean. It seemed to work; Rudolph's popularity was back on the rise and *A Sainted Devil* did well at the box office.

That year—1924—he spent $175,000 on a Spanish-style mansion he dubbed Falcon Lair. It was, perhaps, an effort to save his marriage. The Paramount debacle and Rudolph's buckling under did not sit well with Natasha. Many writers find other problems with the marriage, claiming that either Natasha or Rudolph (or both) were gay. One cannot write about Rudolph Valentino without discussing his sexuality. But—so many years after his death—it is impossible to say with any authority if he was straight, gay or bisexual. In an age when male homosexuality was still equated with effeminacy, Rudolph's wristwatches and slave bracelets made some people suspicious (he had a violent feud with the *Chicago Tribune*, which called him a "pink powder puff"). Rudolph went on the warpath, claiming himself to be 100 percent man, having himself photographed boxing and working out. But there is no hard evidence that Rudolph Valentino was gay or straight; it's too late in the day to pretend authority on the subject. Ironically, fans of Ramon Novarro and William Haines never suspected their homosexuality, the whole time Rudolph was screaming from the rooftops about how straight he was.

Cobra, one of Rudolph's best, though unjustly neglected, films, was released early in 1925. A quiet, unassuming love triangle, it shows Rudolph at his best—a sort of silent Cary Grant. Playing a good-natured scamp who is pursued by his best friend's wife, he turns in a bright, modern performance. Nothing is overdone; Rudolph shows a wonderfully light touch which might have given him a whole new career in talkies. It's a 180-degree turn from his Ahmed and shows the true versatility of the actor.

Perhaps the death blow to Rudolph's marriage was the failure of *The Hooded Falcon*, a pet project of his and

Natasha's. Rudolph grew a very becoming goatee and did piles of research for this medieval tale. When Paramount refused to produce it, everything seemed to crumble. Rudolph left Paramount and signed (at $10,000 a week) with United Artists. He and Natasha separated quietly in mid–1925. They were legally divorced shortly thereafter, and Rudolph bitterly said that he'd never marry again.

But if his personal life was in shambles, Rudolph's career was still on the upswing. With the enjoyable *The Eagle* (1925), he was back to that mixture of romance, open-air adventure, and light comedy at which he excelled. In *The Eagle*, Rudolph played a Russian Robin Hood, with Vilma Banky as his love interest. Their appearances—his dark and Italian, hers blonde and Nordic—meshed perfectly, and the studio planned to team them again.

In 1925 Rudolph met perhaps the only woman in Hollywood with more drive and self-importance than Natasha Rambova. Pola Negri had been a star for nearly a decade when she and Rudolph began their affair. They seemed genuinely fond of each other, but Pola was not above using him for publicity purposes. "He was a like a little boy believing implicitly in some romantic image of himself," wrote Negri in her extremely overwrought memoirs, "afraid to show weakness out of the misguided notion that a he-man must rise above all malaise." "He was a fascinating kaleidoscope of a man," Negri went on, "carefree schoolboy taking delight in his athletic agility, dashing Beau Brummel and sophisticated lover, brooding ascetic torturing himself with bitter memories and dire forebodings." He was also deeply in debt—the divorce from Natasha and the building of Falcon Lair had cost a fortune.

Both UA and Rudolph hoped that *The Son of the Sheik* (1926) would solve his financial problems (Rudolph received a percentage of his films' take). *The Son of the Sheik* mixed sex, adventure, and self-conscious camp to great effect. Rudolph played the role with tongue in cheek; it was a much lighter—and better—film than the original had been five years earlier. He and Vilma Banky proved as hot as they'd been in *The Eagle*, and when the film opened on July 9, audiences lined up around the block. It was a silly little film, but many a silly little film has become a huge success. Critics as well as fans had been won over, and Rudolph's career seemed assured.

Rudolph was in New York to promote his new film (which was becoming one of the summer's biggest successes) when he collapsed on August 15 and was rushed to the Polyclinic Hospital with a ruptured appendix and perforated ulcer. "They didn't want to take the responsibility of making an operation on Rudolph Valentino," his brother Alberto recalled. "So they were waiting for some ... big, well-known surgeon to come along." The surgeon came too late—peritonitis (an abdominal infection) set in. These were the days before antibiotics, and any infection could swiftly lead to death.

Rudolph was a strong, athletic, and otherwise healthy young man, and he put up a brave fight. He nearly pulled through. All through late August, the nation hung on every word as radios and newspapers reported on the star's condition. He seemed to be recovering—he was sitting up, eating and joking with his doctor about a fishing trip. Then the infection spread to his heart, and Rudolph Valentino died shortly after noon on August 23, 1926. He was thirty-one years old.

The hysteria following his death became nearly as legendary as his career. Thousands of normally blasé New Yorkers rioted outside Campbell's Funeral Church, breaking windows, fighting police, fainting, and generally carrying on like lunatics. The rumored mass suicides of his fans were probably apocryphal, but the country was indeed shocked as it never had been by the death of a film star. Up to 1926 only a handful of movie favorites had died, certainly no one as popular as Rudolph had been.

Alberto remembered the cross-country train ride, taking Rudolph from New York back to California for interment. "The people, they came and were trying to show their shock and their affection for Rudolph. I was awakened early in the morning… The train stopped and I was informed that there was a group of people from Erie [who] had came with guitars, mandolins; the great majority were Italian, living here in this country. And they just asked me permission if they could sing and play some of the Italian songs for the memory of Rudy." He was buried in June Mathis's vault. Mathis—perhaps the one truly selfless woman in his life—joined him a year later, dying of a heart attack at the age of thirty-five.

Death was an excellent career move for Valentino. Had he lived one more year, talkies would have crippled his career: Not that he had a bad voice, but the era of the Romantic Lover ended with the dawn of the 1930s. Like Ramon Novarro and John Gilbert, Valentino would have drifted into character roles. He might have still had a long distinguished career, but the legend would have ended. Instead, it took off like a shot—the unruly, hysterical crowds at his viewing and funeral; the Ladies in Black at his grave each year; the keepers of the flame, from Pola to Natasha to every showgirl who ever met him. There have been three film biographies of him and countless revivals of his movies. Sadly, there has not yet been a biography published worthy of his talent and fame (the best being Alexander Walker's short but intelligent 1976 book).

Fannie Ward

Some stars "get the joke," others don't. Fannie Ward not only got the joke, she wrote it and played it up for all the years of her considerable career. She was a light comic star on Broadway and vaudeville as well as a movie star, but Fannie Ward went down in history as The Youth Girl, The Eternal Flapper, America's Peter Pan. Her ever-youthful appearance became more and more of a joke as the years went on, and Fannie increased interest by coyly hinting that she might well be even older than anyone suspected: "Just put down that I danced with Lincoln," she once winked when asked her age.

No one knows exactly when Fannie Ward was born, but reliable film historian Billy Doyle's estimate of June 22, 1872, in St. Louis, Missouri, is as good a guess as any. According to Fannie herself, her parents, Mr. and Mrs. John Buchanan, were very religious, shocked when their daughter went on the stage. Her version of events becomes somewhat suspicious when it's revealed that Fannie's mother was acting alongside her by the early 1890s. "I made my stage debut as Cupid in *Peppino* in 1890 at the age of fifteen," Fannie said in 1917 (settling for a birthdate of 1875). A photo of Fannie in that role, dressed (barely) as Cupid, posed with a bow and arrow, sold briskly as postcards and was reproduced in every newspaper and magazine in the land, becoming as famous as the later pin-up poses of Betty Grable and Farrah Fawcett.

She joined Henry Dixey's company and became one of the premiere ingenues of the early 1890s. Her beauty was astonishing: reddish hair, a round face, turned-up nose, and baby-blue eyes. Fannie herself was hardly babylike, though. In 1894 she became embroiled in a scandal with New York stockbroker "Duke" Brown. Newspapers delighted in covering her tearful stories of broken hearts and confiscated jewels, even following Fannie and her mother as they laid siege to Brown's Fifth Avenue home.

Shortly thereafter, Fannie sailed for London, "for a pleasure trip, as well as to round out my education" (though it would seem that Fannie's education was

The eternally youthful Fannie Ward in the mid–1910s.

already sufficiently rounded out by this time). She played in *The Gaiety Girl* in London in 1895 and made a hit in music halls. But her crowning glory was her 1900 marriage to diamond broker Joe Lewis, who was worth an estimated $50 million. Lewis moved her into a Berkeley Square mansion, and she gave birth to their daughter, Dorothy (who would go on to become Lady Plunkett before dying in a plane crash in 1938). But a few years of wealthy leisure were all Fannie could take. She appeared on the British stage in *A Night Off* and *The Climbers*, among others. "I thought I could give up the stage. But I couldn't," she told *The Chicago Tribune* in 1909. "Each of the six years I was away from it I grew more and more restless ... For six weeks my husband would not speak to me, so angry was he."

Fannie Ward in *Tennessee's Pardner*, 1916 (The Metaluna Collection).

In 1907 Fannie Ward Lewis sailed back to her native land to star in *A Marriage of Reason*. There was a lot of "money doesn't buy happiness" press about the wealthy society woman giving up her place in the British upper crust to return to the stage. Fannie went on to star in a series of fluffy drawing-room comedies: *The Three of Us* and *Fannie and the Servant Problem* (both 1908), *The Marriage of William Ashe* (1908–09), *The New Lady Bantock* (1909), and *Madame President* (1913–14). It was while playing in that last show that Fannie fell in love with her leading man, the thirty-eight-year-old Connecticut native John W. Dean. She divorced Lewis and wed Dean, who would eventually costar with her in several films.

It was at this time that Cecil B. De Mille asked Fannie to make her film debut in his production of *The Cheat* (1915). When Fannie countered that she was a comedienne, not a dramatic actress, DeMille told her that she could play it and play it well. "That put me on my mettle," she said in 1918, "and I was determined to do that role better than anything I had ever done before." She did just that. *The Cheat* told the story of Edith Hardy, a frivolous, selfish society woman who becomes indebted to a "Burmese ivory trader" (Sessue Hayakawa). Playing him mercilessly, Edith is finally branded by him and shoots him in hysteria, letting her husband (played by Jack Dean) take the fall. In an ending which strikes modern audiences as more than a little unfair, Edith gains the jury's sympathy when she reveals her brand and the shooting is seen as justified.

Fannie was forty-three when she made her film debut but was admitting to forty. This was frankly middle-aged in 1915, but Fannie's youthful appearance and impressive dramatic performance—making Edith a horrifying character who still managed to capture audiences' sympathy—earned her a long-term contract with Paramount. She appeared in a dozen or so films over the next few years, many costarring Jack Dean. *Tennessee's Pardner* (1916) was based on Bret Harte, and *The Crystal Gazer* (1917) had Fannie playing three roles. Her other Paramount films included *The Marriage of Kitty* (1915), *A Gutter Magdalene* (1916), *On the Level, School for Husbands,* and *Unconquered* (all 1917). "The pictures are lots of fun," Fannie told a movie magazine. "They give one wider scope for work, and incidentally I have discovered that I am a dramatic actress."

Director George Fitzmaurice coaxed Fannie to signed with Pathé in 1918, where her first film was *Innocent*. She went on to make *A Japanese Nightingale*, *The Narrow Path,* and *The Yellow Ticket* (all 1918), as well as four Pathé films in 1919: *Common Clay* (as a servant girl in society), *The Cry of the Weak*, *Our Better Selves,* and *The Profiteers* (all but *The Yellow Ticket* were directed by Fitzmaurice). In 1919 she and Dean built a huge Italianate mansion in Hollywood, to the delight of the press and fans. After one more film, *The Hardest Way* (1921), Fannie found that vaudeville was more remunerative, and she toured on the Keith/Albee circuit for a few years.

With her daughter's marriage into British society, Fannie took off for Europe and made her home there for much of the 1920s and 1930s. She also kept an apartment at 421 Park Avenue, which, according to one reporter, "was a mélange of antiques and souvenirs from both [European] establishments, including rare Aubusson carpets three to five deep on every floor." She befriended Elizabeth (the current Queen Mum), who admired her pearls—"a double string ... and probably as good as anything she owned herself," Fannie later mused. By 1926 Fannie had opened a Paris beauty shop, coyly called *The Fountain of Youth*. Her status as The Eternal Flapper had become a worldwide joke by now: In a tune about the new model Ford cars, The Happiness Boys sang, "I'll bet my socks that this Miss Ford/Will live as long as Fannie Ward." In her delightful 1925 novel, *Gentlemen Prefer Blondes*, Anita Loos had Lorelei Lee encounter Fannie in London. "I mean, Fanny [sic] is almost historical," Lorelei bubbles, "because when a girl is cute for 50 years it really begins to get historical."

An article from 1923 called her "the medical sensation of the continent," stating that Fannie had undergone a procedure (mysteriously referred to as The Steinach Method) and that "Her body has been rejuvenated to the same strength and freshness that she possessed when twenty years of age." In 1934 Fannie was approximately sixty-two and occasionally touring in vaudeville, while interviewers continued going on about her flawless complexion and youthful demeanor. "She writes friends that young blades still make passes at her when she trips through various hotel foyers to afternoon teas," wrote one reporter. "Only her hands are a give-away, but they are always daintily gloved." In looking at mid-life photos of her today, Fannie looks like nothing so much as a middle-aged woman being kittenish, so a lot of the effect had to have been in her personality.

She barely slowed down, though her daughter's death put an end to Fannie's acting career. She was widowed by

Jack Dean in 1950, but her social life remained active, despite contracting diabetes. A friend who was planning to accompany Fannie to Palm Beach found her unconscious in her Park Avenue apartment on January 25, 1952. Doctors said she'd suffered a stroke; Fannie never regained consciousness and died on January 27. She left some $40,000 in cash and belongings, which went to her three grandsons, the eldest of whom was by then Lord Patrick Plunkett. The obituaries, of course, dwelled on the age question, rather cruelly printing photos of Fannie as a merry matron, overly made up and looking rather silly. The breathtaking ingenue of the 1890s, the stunning comedienne of the 1900s, and the dramatic actress of the 1910s had been forgotten; all anyone wanted to know was, was Fannie seventy-five, eighty, or eight-five at the time of her death?

Pearl White

Pity the poor Pearl White biographer! When it comes to throwing smoke screens and oil slicks behind her to put pursuers off the trail, James Bond had nothing on Pearl. Throughout her career, she gleefully lied her head off to interviewers about her past, her family, and her career, even signing off on a highly dubious autobiography. Since her death, only one book has been published on her, but the 1969 *The Fearless, Peerless Girl* is not so much a biography as a collection of musings and questionable dialogues. If there is an afterlife, no doubt Pearl White laughs shamelessly every time someone tries to research her life.

The most famous of the silent serial queens was probably born on March 4, 1889, in Greenridge, Missouri. After her death, Pearl's father threw another monkey wrench into the works by announcing that she'd really been born in 1897 but had added the years on "to keep ahead of Mary Pickford." But this posthumous youth treatment has been generally disregarded. According to Pearl herself, she came from the poorest family in town and was one of eight siblings born to an Irish father and an Italian mother. In one of her biggest whoppers, when discussing her fatalistic attitude toward stunt work in 1918, she told a reporter that "in the last three generations of our family there hasn't been one natural death. There were eight of us children, born in the Ozark mountains. Today there only remain my mother, my sister and myself. The rest all died in various accidents. So you see my fate will get me sooner or later." Pearl's father and brother were still alive and well at the time, and how they reacted to their reported demise can only be imagined.

According to film historian Wallace Davies in a *Films in Review* article, Pearl was actually descended from early Massachusetts colonialists, and her mother died when Pearl was three (sadly, Davies does not list his source for that information). Her father, Edward G. White, does turn up as a farmer in an 1880 census and later worked as a deputy assessor in Missouri. At her death, Pearl was survived by her father (whom she helped support) and at least two siblings, Fred and Grace, as well as a number of nieces and nephews.

Some of Pearl's childhood reminiscences may be true: She recalled picking berries, working in stores, and delivering newspapers for extra money, not out of the norm even today. She also insisted that she played in *Uncle Tom's Cabin* at the age of five, with a traveling "*Tom*" troupe. "Of course the other children wanted to do it; and because I got the chance and they didn't, they were jealous. So they picked on me all the more." This episode is generally dismissed as fabrication, though traveling theater groups did frequently pick locals to play roles, to attract good will and larger audiences.

At this point, Pearl's life becomes a complete mystery. She told a very convincing and detailed story of running away to join the circus in her early teens, becoming a bareback rider and trapeze artist. She spoke of this time in her life with such conviction that it is tempting to believe her. "Once when I was hanging by my right hand," she told *The American Magazine*, "the ligaments in my wrist pulled out, and I dropped. I fell on the edge of the net, rolled out of it, came down on my shoulder, and broke my collar bone." But researchers are equally insistent that Pearl attended high school in Missouri until joining a stock company—against her father's wishes—when she was in her late teens.

She acted in her hometown with the Diemer Stock Company, then toured through the Midwest in "some of the worst shows in the business." She married fellow actor Victor Sutherland in 1907 in Oklahoma City (this early marriage, which Pearl later shrugged off, ended in 1914). Pearl's stage career foundered, and she admitted herself that

A serene Pearl White at the height of her *Pauline* fame, circa 1914.

she was strictly amateur material at first. Most filmgoers were unaware of Pearl White before *The Perils of Pauline* rocketed her to stardom in mid–1914. But she had actually been a busy—if not terribly successful—screen actress for four years by then. She was doing stock work in Connecticut when she first entered films with The Powers Film Company in mid–1910. She later laughed about "Pat Powers' livery stable studio ... everything was worse than crude. Oh, if people only knew how this business has grown." Pearl made a handful of films at the Bronx-based Powers Company before decamping to Philadelphia early in 1911.

There, she joined the larger and more professional Lubin Film Company, presided over by the paternal Siegmund "Pop" Lubin. Pearl worked there with actor/director Arthur Johnson and

Florence Lawrence—but only briefly. She was fired from Lubin and back in New York, hat in hand, by the summer of 1911. Pearl later admitted she'd been a terrible actress at the dawn of her career, and she made no bones about her failure with Lubin. She wasn't out of work for long, as the Pathé Company of Jersey City signed her up soon after. She was only there for a few films before jumping ship for the Crystal Film Company, back in Manhattan, late in 1912. Finally, at Crystal, Pearl began her career in earnest and set about learning the fundamentals of film acting.

Over the next two years, Pearl made dozens of films at Crystal, including such star showcases as *Pearl as a Clairvoyant*, *Pearl's Admirers*, and *Pearl as a Detective* (all 1913), and *What Pearl's Pearls Did* (1914). Other Crystal titles include *The Girl in the Room* (her first, 1912), *The Chorus Girl* and *Her Visitor* (also 1912), *A Dip Into Society*, *Knights and Ladies*, and *The Hallroom Girls* (all 1913), *Oh! You Puppy*, *Lizzie and the Ice Man*, and *East Lynn in Bugville* (all 1914). By the time she left Crystal, *Moving Picture World* noted that "Pearl White has a large following among picture fans, and she deserves to have."

She also began saving her money. By 1913 she claimed she had saved $3,000 and had used it to visit Europe. Again, this trip has long been denounced as fiction, but as Pearl later did prove herself a financial wizard, it is not impossible. Early in 1914 Pearl returned to Pathé and stepped into film stardom. The twenty-episode *The Perils of Pauline*, which was distributed from March through December, 1914, was not the first serial. It was not even the first successful one: Kathlyn Williams's *The Adventures of Kathlyn* (1913–14) probably convinced Pathé to film their own entry. But *Pauline* became a national phenomenon. William Randolph Hearst helped matters by plugging it in his newspapers, but such assistance wasn't really necessary.

Seen today, it's easy to understand all the fuss: *The Perils of Pauline* is still exciting and involving, and it contains a lot of good-natured humor. Contrary to popular belief, Pearl was not left "cliff hanging" at the end of each chapter; her rescue was completed by the time the audience went home. She had great chemistry with her leading man, the wavy-haired and charming Crane Wilbur. Pearl portrayed an orphaned heiress who is pursued by the murderous Koerner (Paul Panzer), next in line to her fortune. Her boyfriend, Harry Marvin (Wilbur), stands guard over Pauline. What strikes audiences today is how modern Pearl White appears. She is no simpering baby doll, but an active, athletic, humorous woman. To Harry's dismay, she insists on flying airplanes, racing cars, and otherwise putting herself into danger's path. Far from relying on Harry's help, she refuses to marry him and views his paternalism with undisguised annoyance. Understandably, Pearl White became the idol to a generation of girls, just as their brothers worshipped William S. Hart and Tom Mix.

While *Pauline* cemented Pearl's fame and fortune, it also nearly killed her. Pearl later insisted that she performed all of her own stunts. Her studio backed her up on this: It was great publicity. "I've done a million stunts. I've been hurt over and over again. But it never happened when what I was doing looked really dangerous," she said. This is sheer nonsense—no stars did all their own stunts; even Douglas Fairbanks and Harold Lloyd had doubles (the only exception to this rule may have been Buster Keaton). To be fair, Pearl did do more stunts than many actresses: She gamely leaped, swam, and fought her way through many a scene. For PR purposes—and later to sell war bonds—she also dangled from several construction sites in Manhattan. "It is born to every Western girl to like outdoor life and to do all kinds of wild, daring things," she bragged.

But Pearl was terribly injured while filming *Pauline*, as was later confirmed by scenarist Charles Goddard. Paul Panzer was carrying an unconscious Pauline up a flight of stairs when Pearl shifted her weight, and the two went over backwards. "I struck on the top of my head, displacing several vertebrae," she recalled in 1920. "The pain was terrible. For two years I simply lived with osteopaths, and to this day I have some pretty bad times with my back." Indeed, Pearl's back injury—aggravated by years of active filming—eventually led to her retirement and early death.

With the unprecedented success of *Pauline*, Pathé put their new star into three more serials in 1915, changing her character's name to Elaine and her leading man to Creighton Hale. In *The Exploits of Elaine* (fourteen chapters) Pearl was menaced by a villain called The Clutching Hand; in *The New Exploits of Elaine* (ten chapters) she battled evil Chinese opium dealers, and in *The Romance of Elaine* (twelve chapters) she joined the war effort against Germany. That war plot was on target, as action-filled serials were very popular with troops at the front. Because Pathé had a strong overseas distribution unit, Pearl's films were seen in countries other companies could only dream about. By 1916 Pearl White had huge followings in Japan, Russia (where Czar Nicholas II was an admirer), and France (where Jean Cocteau also fell under her spell).

Pearl good-naturedly confessed to be amazed by her sudden popularity, pointing to a sack of fan mail and telling a reporter, "I get letters from every conceivable place. A bagful of stuff a week. I don't know why they keep up. You'd think all the people that intended to write would have written by this time and gotten over it. But the stuff keeps coming." But Pearl wasn't bothered on the street by stalkers. She always wore thick blonde wigs in her films and public appearances and went unrecognized in her own wispy auburn hair. In later years, she laughed that her hair had been dyed so often it was "plaid."

As is usual under these circumstances, Pathé got carried away with their success and rushed Pearl into one adventure serial after another, each more hurried and frenzied than the last. She made six (containing between fifteen and twenty chapters each) over the next four years. They made money, as serials (like Westerns) did not cost much and sold well to theater chains. Without a vacation, Pearl rushed from *The Iron Claw* (1916) to *Pearl of the Army* (1916–17) to *The Fatal Ring* (1917) to *The House of Hate* (1918, costarring young Antonio Moreno) to *The Lightning Raider* (1919) to, finally, *The Black Secret* (1919–20).

At the height of her serial career, in 1916, Pearl said to *Motion Picture Classic* that the action format "suits me perfectly, though it is very hard work, every day in the week, with long hours and a great deal of traveling. But you know, work that interests us and that we thoroughly enjoy, is never drudgery." She did add rather plaintively that "All the home I know is a hotel. Why, I don't even have a dog ... I don't know the first thing about cooking or taking care of a house." She learned about housekeeping in 1918, when she rented a twenty-room mansion situated on seventeen acres overlooking Long Island Sound. Always fond of children, she threw a party there in 1920 for the wards of the Ottile Orphan Asylum. The thrifty Pearl noted that "The thing you've got to watch for is going broke when you're old. Look at all the people that go down and out at the finish. The man who built my country place is blind now and penniless. That's terrible!" Pearl made quite sure she never suffered such a fate.

In 1919 Pearl signed off on *Just Me*, a highly imaginative autobiography (it's doubtful she even read the book, let alone wrote it). She also married for the second time, to actor and dancer Wallace McCutcheon, who had been injured in active service during the war. They divorced in 1921, and shortly thereafter McCutcheon vanished, suffering from mental and emotional trauma possibly brought on by his head injuries. He finally resurfaced in a sanitarium and died in 1928.

By 1919 Pearl had completely lost patience with serial acting. "There is no acting in a serial," she told *Motion Picture Classic*. "You simply race through the reels. Your dear old mother dies in a [feature-length] photoplay, and she takes 120 feet to do it. In a serial she gets 20 feet and has to step lively at that. I want to emote. Who doesn't?" Pearl did convince Pathé to star her in several feature-length films, *The King's Game* and *Hazel Kirke* (both 1916) and the hand-colored *May Blossom* (1917), but she later dismissed them as "rotten as they make 'em. They were the three most terrible plays ever done. Lord, but I was awful! One of them was hand-colored, but even the color didn't hide my acting." Pearl was also fed up with the nonstop pace of Pathé's filming. One day she called in sick, and "I got a sweet little telephone call from my director to the general effect that we can't fall behind in our schedule ... I had to go—and leave behind me all the pleasures of a snow white bed, and candy and flowers, and the other lovely things that make illness a positive privilege." Not surprisingly, when Pearl's Pathé contract ended in 1919, she left that studio, signing with Fox to do features.

Pearl made nine films for Fox between 1920 and 1922. They were mostly Norma Talmadge-like society dramas, with a few adventure films thrown in. None of the films, sadly, made much of an impression on the public. Pearl played a girl who infiltrates the mob as an undercover police agent in *The White Moll* and an ambitious society woman who turns to stealing in *The Thief* (both 1920). In her four 1921 releases, Pearl played a South Seas girl encountering New York society in *A Virgin Paradise*, a tough tomboy in *The Mountain Woman*, and dissatisfied society wives in *Know Your Men* and *Beyond Price*. Her first two 1922 films were yet more society love triangles: *Any Wife* (which had an unsatisfactory dream ending tacked on to brighten it up) and *Without Fear*. Finally, Pearl's U.S. feature career ended with *Broadway Peacock* (1922), in which she played a social-climbing cabaret hostess (based, possibly, on her friend Texas Guinan).

She reluctantly returned to serials and Pathé, one last time, with the fifteen-chapter *Plunder* (1923). In August

1922, while filming *Plunder*, a tragedy occurred which disproved once and for all the rumor that Pearl never used doubles. John Stevenson, dressed in Pearl's costume, was attempting a stunt wherein he tried to jump from atop a moving bus onto a Manhattan elevated track as it passed overhead. Stevenson's grip slipped from the rusty, grime-encrusted girder, and he fell backward onto the street. He died without regaining consciousness. Early in 1923, before *Plunder* was even released, Pearl took off for Europe under a cloud. The breakup of her marriage, her husband's subsequent troubles, Stevenson's death, and her increasing back trouble all ganged up on her. Pearl's friend Texas Guinan told reporters that Pearl had entered a Paris convent, but this was almost certainly a joke. There is no indication that Pearl had ever been within ten feet of a convent, and her behavior was never remotely nun-like. It's more likely that Pearl retreated from the United States for a physical and emotional rest cure.

Pearl White toward the end of her career, in 1920.

Pearl made one last film, the 1924 action feature *Terror*, released in the United States as *The Perils of Paris*. It was directed for the Epinay Film Company by Edward José, who ten years earlier had costarred with Theda Bara in *A Fool There Was*. This film is available on video today, but it is far more amateurish than her *Pauline* of a decade earlier. There are rumors of other French films made between 1923 and 1925, but none have surfaced. Pearl continued acting, headlining in a Montmartre revue called *Tu Perds la Boule* in 1925 and at a London music hall at an impressive $3,000 a week. When talkies became the rage, Pearl mused with reporters about becoming a character actress à la Marie Dressler, but she was probably having one of her little jokes.

She no longer needed to act; Pearl had other irons in the fire. She bought the Hotel de Paris in Biarritz, where she ran a successful gambling casino for several years, and ran a nightclub in Paris. She owned a remunerative stable of racing horses and wisely invested her earnings in trust funds. While the rest of the world was suffering from the financial Depression, Pearl White was a very wealthy woman. She owned a town house in Paris and a villa in Rambouillet; Pearl also found happiness with a handsome young Greek millionaire (as indeed, who wouldn't?). She and Theodore Cossika shared homes in France and Cairo and traveled all over the world: India, the Mid-East, the Orient, Russia. She returned to America three times, in 1924, 1927 and 1937, though reporters noted that she never once set foot in California.

On Pearl's last visit to the United States, fans were somewhat taken aback at her appearance. Fashionably dressed and wearing obviously expensive jewelry, Pearl was frankly overweight and looked far older than her forty-eight years. She told reporters that she thought acting in silent films had been more difficult: "We had to do much more expressive work with our hands and faces to convey the idea." She expressed admiration for Greta Garbo and added that "I'm just here for a short visit. It has nothing to do with the movies. I'm simply checking on my finances." Mentioning her weight, she turned down photo opportunities, snapping, "Why should I have my picture taken when I can get paid for it?"

By this time, Pearl was dying. Her old back injury was growing worse, requiring hospitalization in 1933, and Pearl turned to drugs and alcohol to relieve the chronic pain. This, in turn, caused liver failure. She entered the American Hospital in Paris in July 1938 and died there on August 4, after carefully reviewing her will and arranging her funeral. She was buried in the Passy Cemetery at a small, private service. Pearl left a small fortune: Most of it went to Cossika, as did much property and jewelry. Her father, nieces, and nephews were provided for, and $73,500 went to various charities.

Pearl White is one of the few silent stars whose names did not die with them. To this day, *The Perils of Pauline* and its star remain in the public consciousness, this despite Hollywood's efforts at memorializing her—the 1947 bio-pic *The Perils of Pauline*, starring a wildly miscast Betty Hutton, was an embarrassment. In 1967 a camp *Perils of Pauline* feature and TV series, starring "Dodge Rebellion" girl Pam Austin, also failed to ignite interest. But still, Pearl White is one of the handful of 1910s stars whose fame is sure to live into the twenty-first century.

Kathlyn Williams

Although Pearl White, with her *Perils of Pauline*, is generally thought of as the first serial queen, that title actually belongs to Kathlyn Williams. The serial is as old as the motion picture itself: There was *Miss Jerry* as early as 1894, *What Happened to Mary?* (1912), and no doubt others long lost to posterity. But the first widely popular serial was *The Adventures of Kathlyn*, the first segment of which premiered on December 29, 1913. There is disagreement as to whether it was a thirteen- or fifteen-part series, but its impact cannot be overstated. In its wake came successes like *The Million Dollar Mystery*, *Lucille Love*, *Patria,* and of course *The Perils of Pauline*, all starring modern, adventurous, and liberated women. Oddly, though, Kathlyn Williams never made another serial.

She was born in Butte, Montana, on May 31, in either 1884 or 1888, to a Norwegian father and a Welsh mother. "I had a fine voice ... and the chief desire of my mother's heart was that I should become a great singer," she recalled. "Nearly every girl has wanted to be a nun at one time and an actress at another, but I wanted to be both at the same time. It was a very real tragedy to me that I couldn't figure out some way in which the two could be reconciled." Kathlyn briefly attended college (Wesleyan University) before heading out to make a career for herself. Stagestruck from an early age, she started acting in local stock companies when a "patron" appeared in the person of local tycoon Senator W. A. Clark. It's not certain just what the relationship between Clark and the teenaged blonde actress was, but he financed her education at the Franklin Sergent Dramatic Academy in New York. While at school, she may have played bit parts in the Biograph films *A Politician's Love Story* and *Gold Is Not All* (both 1909).

It was back to stock companies after two years at Sergent's. "Then began the real hard work and real disappointments," she recalled in 1912, "...The horrors of one-night stands and catching early trains was enough to take the energy out of a less ambitious person." Kathlyn was acting in Chicago when yet another older man fell prey to her charms: forty-six-year-old producer "Colonel" William Selig signed her as leading lady for his Chicago-based Selig Polyscope Company, founded in 1896. Selig specialized in outdoor action films, setting up his own well-stocked zoo on the grounds of his studio. The year was 1910; Kathlyn was in her early twenties. A sturdy, athletic girl, she was perfect for Selig's films. Tall, slim, with golden hair, she had an imposing look about her. Indeed, Kathlyn's bone structure photographed as frankly middle-aged (though still attractive) from her earliest films. By the time she made her first film, she was already a divorcée: an early marriage to one Victor Kainer had failed, and Kathlyn was supporting a young son, Victor, Jr.

The film world was a revelation to the tired stage actress: "It is early to bed and early to rise, and we certainly are healthier, wealthier and wiser," she enthused. "The work is absolutely fascinating—there is change all the time; each picture is a new character and each character one creates oneself ... I could be in stock for years and never have the opportunity to play more than one line. In motion pictures one tries them all." Kathlyn made seven films for Selig in 1910, the first of which was *The Devil, the Servant and the Man* (remade in 1912). Eighteen films followed in 1911 (including *Dad's Girls*, *Back to the Primitive,* and *Captain Kate*, all with Tom Mix, and *The Two Orphans*, available today on video) and another twenty in 1912. One of these, *The Last Dance*, was written and directed by Kathlyn. "I believe there is a place for the woman director in the film business," she told a reporter at about this time. "They may not know about war and Wall Street, but what do men directors know about these 'big' things, save what they have read? Outside of my work I am just a peaceful Suffragette. I'm like the fellow who would fight to have peace. I absolutely demand it." She had little peace on the set, certainly not while filming *The Adventures of Kathlyn* in late 1913. This was only one of her twenty-nine films that year. She also acted in a series of films with matinee idol Harold Lockwood (who would perish in the 1918 Spanish flu epidemic), including *The Lipton Cup*, *A Welded Friendship*, *The Stolen Melody*, and *The Tide of Destiny*.

But it was *The Adventures* which made her an international star and trendsetter. Kathlyn starred as an unlikely African queen, menaced both by villainous Charles Clary and by Selig's cast of lions, elephants, and other assorted fauna. She was already too familiar with her four-legged costars by then, having encountered them in earlier films such as *Lost in the Jungle* (1911) and *A Wise Old Elephant* (1913). "I'll never forget my sensations as I walked among those three lions for the first time," Kathlyn told *Picture-Play Weekly* in 1915. "They tell me that I showed no fear, and that there was no danger, but if I didn't show fear, I certainly felt fear!" Soon, though, she was playing with her "pet kitties" and elaborated to *Motion Picture Classic* that "I have never had an animal turn upon me, no matter how treacherous its nature. Every one of the many accidents I have figured in was always due to some outside cause. If you can convince an animal that you are its friend, your problem is solved." She became especially fond of Caesar and Duke, two Selig lions, and Toddles, the "Wise Old Elephant," who followed her around the lot like an affectionate puppy. The leopards, she noted, "are doglike in their familiarity, and great pals."

The Adventures of Kathlyn played through early 1914, as well as being released as an eight-reel feature, and was serialized in *The Chicago Tribune*. It was an exhausting year for Kathlyn, who also endured another short-lived marriage, this one to actor Frank Robert Allen, some ten years her senior. Now a full-fledged star, she made another fifteen films in 1914. The best-remembered of these was *The Spoilers*, the first of umpteen screen versions of Rex Beach's western classic. Costarring with William Farnum and Tom Santschi, Kathlyn played an Alaskan gambling queen. She made another eighteen films at Selig in 1915 and 1916, as well as supplying screenplays for *The Strange Case of Talmai Lind* and *A Sultana of the Desert* (both 1915). She traveled to the Panama Canal, then under construction, to film Rex Beach's *The Ne'er-do-Well* (1916). On June 2nd of that year, she wed for the third and last time, to forty-two-year-old film executive Charles Eyton (the marriage lasted until 1931 and ended in an amicable divorce).

A youthful Kathlyn Williams (The Metaluna Collection).

Kathlyn's marriage also led to the end of her association with Selig. The "Colonel" retired from filmmaking in 1916 (his company folded in 1918, though its founder lived until 1948). Charles Eyton was working at Paramount, so it seemed only natural for Kathlyn to follow her new husband there. She signed in 1917 and made a total of twenty-six films there through 1926. By the time she switched studios, Kathlyn Williams was one of the country's most popular stars, specializing both in western adventures and society dramas. She lived in a huge movie star home in Hollywood, dressed to the nines, and was accosted by fans on a regular basis. "There is one thing in motion picture work to which I have not yet accustomed myself," she said. "That is the friendliness of strangers who have seen my pictures and who identify me as the heroine of some picture. The fact that someone has 'seen' you in Java or China, or someplace where you have never been, gives you a strangely uncanny feeling, almost as if your astral body had been engaged in enterprises that had not had the consent of your will." Those natives of Java and China might have actually known Kathlyn, however: She became a world traveler and particularly enjoyed the Orient (tragically, her sixteen-year-old son died of the flu on one of their jaunts to China, in 1922).

Not content with her animals and adventuring, Kathlyn had taken up aviation as early as 1913. "I really am fascinated with flying," she told *Photoplay*'s Richard Willis in 1914, "and one of these days I mean to fly regularly ... I believe I was the first woman ever to fly in a hydro-aeroplane," she added proudly. "Yes, the strange sensation of flying through space fascinates me."

Kathlyn's career continued strong through the early 1920s at Paramount, with an occasional loan-out. She was directed several times by her husband's good friend William Desmond Taylor, the last time in the drama *Morals* (1921). Both William and Cecil B. De Mille directed Kathlyn several times, Cecil in *The Whispering Chorus, We Can't Have Everything* (both 1918), and *Forbidden Fruit* (1921). Even matinee idol Lou Tellegen directed her, in *The Thing We Love* (1918). Her costars were also an impressive lot. She made three films with Paramount's star attraction, Wallace Reid. Their last together, the light comedy *Clarence* (1922), was filmed when Reid was in the last stages of the drug addiction that would kill him within months. She also costarred with a surprising number of female favorites, including Leatrice Joy (*Just a Wife*, 1920), Clara Kimball Young (*The Better Wife*, 1919), Barbara La Marr (*Souls for Sale*, 1923), and Pola Negri (*The Spanish Dancer*, 1923). Kathlyn costarred with May McAvoy five times in 1921 and 1922 alone, and she was also frequently seen onscreen with Agnes Ayres and Wanda Hawley.

By the mid–1920s, Kathlyn looked older than her age and was relegated to respectable supporting and character parts. She made fewer films, but she had saved her money and didn't need the work (indeed, after the death of her son she lost much interest in her career). *Wanderer of the Wasteland* (1924) was an early Technicolor effort, an outdoor tale costarring Jack Holt and Billie Dove. Kathlyn supported such up-and-coming young flappers as Esther Ralston (*The Best People*, 1925), Greta Nissen (*The Wanderer*, 1926), and Shirley Mason (*Sally in Our Alley*, 1927). One of her best latter-day roles was as the heartless social-climbing mother of Anita Page in *Our Dancing Daughters* (1928); the following year, she portrayed the equally unsympathetic mother of Greta Garbo in *The Single Standard*.

Talkies arrived, and Kathlyn lost what interest remained in her career. She made six in all: *Wedding Rings* (1929), *The Road to Yesterday* (with Loretta Young, 1930), the popular *Daddy Long Legs* (with Janet Gaynor and Warner Baxter, 1931), the *Madame Bovary* adaptation *Unholy Love* (1932), *Blood Money* (1933), and her swan song, the crime caper *Rendezvous at Midnight* (1935). By the time of her retirement, Kathlyn was very much alone, divorced and childless. Still very wealthy, she moved from her Hollywood mansion into a large apartment, luxuriously furnished and decorated with artwork from her many worldwide trips. Kathlyn didn't sit at home and pine for days gone by, however; she surrounded herself with a coterie of amiable female friends and became quite a social figure in her later years. Reading, travel, and regular bridge games occupied her time.

One of her social outings nearly took her life. On December 29, 1949, she was returning from a Las Vegas trip with two friends when their car went out of control and overturned somewhere between Baker and Death Valley. The driver was injured and a passenger killed, and Kathlyn was rushed unconscious to Lone Pine Hospital in critical condition, with badly fractured legs and a concussion. She lost one leg but was not, as her obituaries later stated, confined to a wheelchair for the rest of her life. "I wanted to die when I realized how bad off I was," she said, but she bounced back with great vitality—in fact, she gave a party in 1951 to inaugurate her new prosthetic leg, and she was soon making the social rounds, proud of her relearned dancing skills.

Kathlyn Williams during her character-actress period, in the 1920s.

She did maintain a wheelchair at home, and it was there, some reports stated, that friends found her dead of a heart attack on September 23, 1960 (though film historian Dewitt Bodeen stated that her maid found her on the floor). Kathlyn Williams was somewhere between seventy-two and seventy-six years old, though obituaries guessed her to be sixty-five (*Variety*) or sixty-six (*The New York Times*). She'd not made a film in twenty-five years, and her stardom was more than forty years past. Even so, the tiny obituaries were much less than she deserved.

Clara Kimball Young

Clara Kimball Young played the sort of roles in the 1910s that were taken over by Norma Talmadge in the 1920s. She starred in dozens of successful, weepy "women's pictures" featuring noble, mature characters coping with tragedy and heartbreak. The genre was later graced by the likes of Joan Crawford, Greer Garson, Susan Hayward, and Lana Turner. But Clara Kimball Young was there first, and her own life too often played out like one of her movies.

She was born of theatrical parents: Descended from Sara Siddons, Clara Kimball was the daughter of Edward Marshall Kimball and Pauline Maddern, successful stage performers. Clara was born in Chicago on September 6, probably in 1890. Her earliest childhood was spent on the stage; Clara's mother did not want to leave her at home, so she acted across the country until she was old enough for boarding school. She spent her teen years at St. Francis Xavier Academy in her hometown, then went right back onstage. While playing stock in Salt Lake City, she met actor/director James Young, and the two soon wed. In 1912, when Clara was in her early twenties, she and her husband signed with Vitagraph. She worked there for two years, getting her feet wet. "After the first strangeness had worn off," she reminisced in 1922, "I began to see the motion picture industry with new eyes and it dawned upon me that this was not a profession to use as a stop-gap until something on the legitimate stage loomed up, but was a tremendously important profession in itself."

Clara, while making some twenty Vitagraph films, learned to apply her own film makeup and design her own costumes for best effect. "I studied my clothes and soon learned to know the photographic values of materials, which in itself is an absorbing study—and discovered that while materials showed their values at times, it was lines that counted in the camera." She made both dramas and comedies at Vitagraph, often costarring with Maurice Costello and Earle Williams. But her dark, soulful looks (at twenty-five she appeared ten years older) suited her best for parlor dramas. A high point for Clara was the company's 1912 worldwide tour to make films on location. The little band traveled to Japan, China, India, Egypt, Italy, France, and England. Clara particularly loved Japan, where she explored Buddhist temples, and India, where she dined with the Nawah of Sachie.

Her biggest Vitagraph success was also her last film there: a Russian melodrama called *My Official Wife* (1914). Directed by her husband, it supposedly featured future Russian revolutionary Leon Trotsky. Though an extra resembling Trotsky is visible in stills from the film, Trotsky was actually not in the United States at the time *My Official Wife* was being made. Clara herself had harrowing memories of the film, especially one scene wherein she was lashed to a mast and thrown into icy waters. "For sheer strength, endurance, and yes—fright, this scene was the most difficult, physically, I ever experienced."

Lewis J. Selznick stole Clara from Vitagraph shortly thereafter, and she was to stay with him through her greatest successes in the late 1910s. She made twenty-four films for Selznick—mostly in California—her fame and popularity growing year by year. In 1914 at least one fan magazine poll named her the country's most popular actress. But in a plot not unlike that of *A Star Is Born*, Clara's success unnerved her husband, whose career was waning. The two quarreled, he fought with Selznick, and the Youngs divorced in 1919. Her career continued with one hit film after another. She played *Trilby* and *Camille* in 1915, and recreated dramatic Broadway hits such as *The Common Law* (1916, with Conway Tearle), *The Easiest Way* (1917), and *The Reason Why* (1918, again with Tearle, and Edmund Lowe). Her films' titles are delightfully evocative: *The Deep Purple* (1916), *The Price She Paid* (1917), and *Cheating Cheaters* (1919).

Clara Kimball Young when she *was* young, in the early 1910s.

Clara carefully melded into her roles, an early "method" actress. When playing Trilby, "I threw myself heart and soul into the character," the actress wrote. "I felt Trilby's every emotion, and approached the final climax forgetful of all else save the character herself." So forgetful was Clara, in fact, that she managed to overturn a candle and set her hair on fire. Luckily, an alert coworker threw a rug over her and she emerged safely, if slightly scorched. "I was the first star to finance my own production outfit," Clara proudly noted in later years. She wasn't quite the first (that was probably Helen Gardner), but she did indeed have her own company. In 1916, Selznick—to reward her for her great successes—formed The Clara Kimball Young Film Corporation within Selznick.

Then things—as they have a tendency to do—began falling apart. Clara married producer/director Harry Garson, who took control of her career at a dangerous point. The 1920s—the age of the flapper and jazz baby—was dawning, and Clara projected a rather matronly, old-fashioned image. She and Garson left Selznick and went out on their own. Things went all right for a year or two; she starred in the successful *Eyes of Youth* for Equity in 1919. Her leading man in this melodrama was Milton Sills, but supporting player Rudolph Valentino stole the film. Clara made a total of ten films for Equity, many directed by Garson and some of them quite successful: *Mid-Channel* (1920, costarring her father, Edward Kimball), *Straight from Paris* (1921), and *The Worldly Madonna* (1922).

But by 1922, Clara's passing vogue—and the unpopular Garson's mismanagement—were ruining her career. The two separated, and she freelanced at such studios as Samuel Zierler Photoplay (four films in 1922 and 1923), First National (*Wandering Daughters*, 1923, directed by her first husband, James Young), Metro (*A Wife's Romance*, 1923), and Ivan Films (*Lying Wives*, 1925). Her film career ebbing and with few offers, Clara took vaudeville offers and toured America and England with some success (everyone wanted to see a film favorite in person). From then on, it was just one damn thing after another for Clara Kimball Young. She was seriously injured in an auto accident in 1932, she declared bankruptcy the following year, having to sue an uncle for an unpaid debt of $5,900, and she even managed to lose $75,000 worth of jewelry in a taxicab. The one bright point in her life was Dr. Arthur Fauman, whom she wed in 1928 (they stayed married until Fauman's death in 1937).

Flat broke, Clara made her film comeback as a bit player in RKO's 1932 Joel McCrea film *Kept Husbands*, in which she played a flighty society matron. She was plump and middle-aged by now, but refreshingly unworried about it. "I just couldn't get myself down to a sliver," Clara told a reporter, "and I think it's bad for a person, too. I would like to make a picture once in a while, but not try to diet myself to death fifty-two weeks of the year." She did make a picture "once in a while," keeping body and soul together. Clara Kimball Young appeared in another sixteen films after *Kept Husbands*, for nearly as many studios. A few were for the majors: westerns *Three on the Trail* (1936), *Hills of Old Wyoming* (1937), and *The Frontiersman* (1938) for Paramount; *Romance in the Rain* (1934) and *His Night Out* (1935) for Universal; and *She Married Her Boss* (1935) and *The Mysterious Pilot* (1938) for Columbia. But the remainder were cut-rate films for Monogram, Chesterfield, Tiffany, and the like.

The newspapers played it up to the hilt: "Clara K. Young's Star Has Fallen," "She's Trying a Comeback," and other humiliating articles appeared regularly. What was remarkable was Clara's cheerful attitude about her plight. "Fame is fleeting," she said in 1934, "particularly so in the movies, and actresses must accept what Fate gives them. I had my share of glory." Her last film, *The Round-Up* (1941), was another low-budget western, in which fellow silent star Francis X. Bushman also made an appearance. Though out of the film industry,

Clara did not become a recluse. She appeared at film conventions and spoke to reporters, though she refused to become nostalgic. Claiming she threw out all her old photos and scrapbooks, Clara said in 1955 that "I'm living today, I'm in the rocket ship era. To hell with the past."

In 1956 she signed on as a "correspondent" with Johnny Carson's comedy variety show on CBS (before his *Tonight Show* fame). "I hope my reporting does more than entertain," Clara told reporter Vernon Scott. "Nobody has to be old at sixty, and I think senior citizens will get the idea when they see how full of pep I am. You have to keep your mind trained on the present and your eyes to the future if you want to stay young." Clara entered the Motion Picture Country Home after a bout with bronchial pneumonia in January 1960. When she died on October 15 of that year, she was broke and virtually forgotten. But she was also one of the happiest and most emotionally healthy actresses the film industry ever produced.

A more matronly Clara Kimball Young, in 1920.

Bibliography

Bankhead, Tallulah. *Tallulah*. New York: Harper & Brothers Publishers, 1952.

Bartelt, Chuck, and Barbara Bergeron, eds. *Variety Obituaries*. New York: Garland Publishing, 1989.

Blum, Daniel. *Great Stars of the American Stage*. New York: Greenberg Publisher, 1952.

_____. *A Pictorial History of the Silent Screen*. New York: Grosset & Dunlap Publishers, 1953.

_____. *A Pictorial History of the American Theatre*. New York: Crown Publishers, 1977.

Bordman, Gerald. *The Oxford Companion to American Theater*. New York: Oxford University Press, 1992.

Bowers, Q. David. *Muriel Ostriche, Princess of Silent Films*. Vestal, New York: The Vestal Press, 1987.

Castle, Irene. *My Husband*. New York: Charles Scribner's Sons, 1919.

_____. *Castles in the Air*. New York: Doubleday & Company, 1958.

Davies, Marion. *The Times We Had*. Indianapolis: Bobbs-Merrill, 1975.

Doherty, Edward. *The Rain Girl: The Tragic Story of Jeanne Eagels*. Philadelphia: MacCrae, Smith Company, 1930.

Doyle, Billy H. *The Ultimate Directory of the Silent Screen Performers*. Metuchen, New Jersey: The Scarecrow Press, 1995.

Eyman, Scott. *Ernst Lubitsch: Laughter in Paradise*. New York: Simon and Schuster, 1993.

Farnsworth, Marjorie. *The Ziegfeld Follies*. New York: Putman, 1956.

Fox, Charles Donald. *Famous Film Folk*. New York: George H. Doran Company, 1925.

Fox, Charles Donald, and Milton L. Silver. *Who's Who on the Screen*. New York: Ross Publishing Company, 1920.

Franklin, Joe. *Classics of the Silent Screen*. New York: The Citadel Press, 1959.

Gish, Lillian (with Ann Pinchot). *The Movies, Mr. Griffith and Me*. Englewood Cliffs, New Jersey: Prentice-Hall, 1969.

Guiles, Fred Lawrence. *Marion Davies*. New York: McGraw-Hill, 1972.

Joyce, Peggy Hopkins. *Men, Marriage and Me*. New York: The Macauley Company, 1930.

Katz, Ephraim. *The Film Encyclopedia*. New York: HarperCollins Publishers, 1994.

Keylin, Arleen. *Hollywood Album*. New York: Arno Press, 1977.

_____. *Hollywood Album 2*. New York: Arno Press, 1979.

Klepper, Robert K. *Silent Films on Video*. Jefferson, North Carolina: McFarland & Company, 1996.

Kreimer, Klaus. *The UFa Story*. New York: Hill and Wang, 1996.

Lahue, Kalton C. *Ladies in Distress*. New York: A.S. Barnes & Company, 1971.

Lambert, Gavin. *Nazimova, a Biography*. New York: Alfred A. Knopf, 1997.

Lamparski, Richard. *Whatever Became Of...?* Volumes 1–11. New York: Crown Publishers, 1967–89.

Lowrey, Carolyn. *The First One Hundred Noted Men and Women of the Screen*. New York: Moffat, Yard and Company, 1920.

Lyon, Ben. *Life with the Lyons*. London: Oldham's Press, 1953.

Maltin, Leonard. *TV Movies and Video Guide*. New York: Penguin Books USA, 1990.

Mann, William J. *Wisecracker: The Life and Times of William Haines, Hollywood's First Openly Gay Star*. New York: Viking, 1998.

Moore, Colleen. *Silent Star*. New York: Doubleday, 1968.

Morella, Joe, and Edward Z. Epstein. *The It Girl: The Incredible Story of Clara Bow*. New York: Delacorte, 1976.

Negri, Pola. *Memoirs of a Star*. New York: Doubleday, 1970.

Ralston, Esther. *Some Day We'll Laugh*. Metuchen, New Jersey: The Scarecrow Press, 1985.

Reid, Bertha Westbrook. *Wallace Reid, His Life Story*. New York: Sorg Publishing Company, 1923.

Ronnie, Art. Locklear: *The Man Who Walked on Wings*. New York: A. S. Barnes & Company, 1973.

Schessler, Ken. *This Is Hollywood*. LaVerne, California: Ken Schessler Publishing Company, 1989.

Shipman, David. *The Great Movie Stars, the Golden Years*. New York: Bonanza Books, 1970.

_____. *The Great Movie Stars, The International Years*. New York: St. Martin's Press, 1972.

Slide, Anthony. *Silent Portraits*. Vestal, New York: The Vestal Press, 1989.

Talmadge, Margaret L. *The Talmadge Sisters*. Philadelphia: J. B. Lippincott, 1924.

Ullman, S. George. *Valentino As I Knew Him*. New York: A. L. Burt Company, 1926.

Wagenknecht, Edward Charles, and Anthony Slide. *The Films of D. W. Griffith*. New York: Crown Publishers, 1975.

Walker, Alexander. *Rudolph Valentino*. New York: Stein & Day, 1976.

Watters, James. *Return Engagement*. New York: Clarkson N. Potter, 1984.

Zierold, Norman. *Sex Goddesses of the Silent Screen*. Chicago: Henry Regnery Company, 1973.

Videography

Hollywood. London: Photoplay Productions, 1979.

The Man in the Silk Hat. Paris: Films Max Linder, 1983.

INDEX